£2 99

CL00967821

CRICKET CALLING

Cricket Calling

ROWLAND RYDER

Foreword by
SIR COLIN COWDREY

faber and faber
LONDON · BOSTON

First published in 1995
by Faber and Faber Limited
3 Queen Square London WC1N 3AU

Photoset in Ehrhardt by Parker Typesetting Service, Leicester
Printed in England by Clays Ltd, St Ives plc

A CIP record for this book
is available from the British Library

ISBN 0-571-17475-2

2 4 6 8 10 9 7 5 3 1

For Eileen
and in memory of my father

Contents

Acknowledgements

For permission to publish copyright material, I gratefully acknowledge the following sources: C. R. ATTLEE, from *As It Happened* (Heinemann); JACK BAILEY, from *Conflicts in Cricket* (The Kingswood Press); JACK BANNISTER, from *The History of Warwickshire County Cricket Club* (Helm); MIKE BREARLEY, from *The Art of Captaincy* (Hodder and Stoughton); ALICE THOMAS ELLIS, from *The Sin Eater* (Penguin); GAVIN EWART, from *Collected Poems 1980–1990* (Hutchinson); JACK FINGLETON, from *Cricket Crisis* (Cassell); JOHN FORD, from *Cricket: A Social History* (David & Charles); DAVID FRITH, from *By His Own Hand* (Stanley Paul); ROBERT GRAVES, from *Goodbye to All That* (Penguin); GRAHAM GREENE, from *A Sort of Life* (Penguin); AUDREY LUCAS, from *E. V. Lucas: A Portrait* (Methuen); GAVIN LYALL, from *The Conduct of Major Maxim* (Pan); A. A. MAILEY, from *10 for 66 and All That* (J. M. Dent); RONALD MASON, from *Armstrong's Australians* (Epworth Press); ERIC MIDWINTER, from *W. G. Grace* (Allen & Unwin); IAN PEEBLES, from *Batter's Castle* (Souvenir Press); SIEGFRIED SASSOON, from *The Weald of Youth* (Faber and Faber); TOM STOPPARD, from *The Real Inspector Hound* (Faber and Faber); ALLEN SYNGE, from *Sins of Omission* (Pelham); H. A. VACHELL, from *The Hill* (John Murray); P. G. WODEHOUSE, from *Mike at Wrykin* (Penguin); GRAEME WRIGHT, from *Betrayal* (H. F. & G. Witherby); The chapters on The Pleasures of Reading *Wisden* and on G. L. Jessop have appeared in past issues of *Wisden Cricket Almanack*, and I would like to express my gratitude to Matthew Engel for permission to quote from various issues of *Wisden* in the course of the book.

While apologizing for accidental omissions I would like to thank for varied help: Colin Blakemore, Mike Brearley, Robert Brooke,

Terence Charman, David Clark, John Claughton, Ms Jacqueline Cox, Michael Davie, Mrs Norah Deakins, Mrs Jean Dollery, Robin Dyer, Gavin Ewart, John Field, Mrs Joan Gorle, Mrs Penelope Grierson, Jeff Hancock, A. D. K. Hawkyard, Canon Christopher Hewetson, Simon Hughes, Geoffrey Humpage, Thomas Keneally, James Lawson, Ian Lowe, Mrs P. J. Macrory, Dr John Maddicott, A. de la Mar, Vic Marks, Sir Brian McGrath, Dr Eric Midwinter, Hal Milner-Gulland, Charles Palmer, T. R. Piggott, Harold Pinter, Laurence Le Quesne, Alan Smith, Iain Sproat MP, Tom Stoppard, E. W. Swanton, Allen Synge, Colin Wolfe, Wilfred Wooller, Dr Blair Worden, Graeme Wright and Peter Wynne-Thomas.

I would like to thank the staff of the Warwickshire Country Cricket Club for their unfailing kindness and help, especially Dennis Amiss, Keith Cook, Mrs Anne Courbet, Stewart Edwards, Miss Janet Greenhill, Alan Oakman, Mrs Sue Smith, Peter Thompson and Bob Woolmer.

My warm thanks are due to Stephen Green and his assistants at the Lord's Cricket Museum; the staff of the International Cricket Council; the staff of the Birmingham Central Library; and to Miss Marie Lewis of the Eastbourne Central Library.

I am very grateful to Julian Loose and Charles Boyle, of Faber and Faber, for their help and encouragement, and to Trevor Horwood, for his work as copy editor; I would like to thank Mrs Hedda Heathcote, who typed the manuscript in its various stages. Finally, I would like to thank my wife for all her help during the three years that the work has been in progress.

Rowland Ryder
Edgbaston, January 1995

Foreword

The Game of Cricket is flourishing as never before.

Thanks largely to the miracle of television and its dramatic work, especially with regard to replays, cricket is spreading to new parts of the globe every year. I can say assuredly that the game is being watched, played by, listened to, viewed on television by more people across the world than ever before.

But cricket has always been dependent on the host of dedicated people who give of their own time, freely and in the most unselfish way, to support, encourage, coach, and write endlessly about it.

Such a person is Rowland Ryder, an inspirational devotee of the game. His father was secretary of Warwickshire County Cricket Club for forty-nine years – from 1895 to 1944. A most responsible post and a true labour of love. What a splendid successor was Leslie Deakins, at the helm until 1976; then Alan Smith, a great secretary as he had been a great captain; and the well-loved David Heath, whose death in 1994 at sixty-two was so untimely.

This is Warwickshire's year, well administrated under M. J. K. Smith and D. L. Amiss. Sue Smith is a major-domo lady-secretary, and Alan Oakman and Bob Woolmer are top-quality coaches, behind the scenes. They have a fine team, superbly led by Dermot Reeve, Brian Lara's arrival has had an electrifying impact and Edgbaston is one of the finest cricket grounds in the world, inbuilt with a friendly welcoming atmosphere.

What could be more appropriate than that one of Warwickshire's truest disciples, born within the sound of the umpire's bell on the Edgbaston ground, should produce this splendid book? His many and diverse writings on the game need no elaboration. Here is a book for the real cricket lover and I am delighted to commend it for its wide appeal.

Sir Colin Cowdrey
August 1994

Preface

Tantantara! Tantantara!
Trumpet call of Brian Lara!
with apologies to W. S. Gilbert and *Utopia Limited.*

The year 1994 was certainly Utopian for Warwickshire:

> Come cheer up my lads, 'tis to glory we steer,
> With our hearts of oak team through this wonderful year;
> We fought and we conquered on King Willow's swards
> And completed a hat trick of finals at Lord's.

We lost the NatWest final to Worcestershire: Tim Curtis, modest in victory, said that he didn't think any county would ever achieve the grand slam. Warwickshire came pretty near to it, winning three of the four assault courses: first, the Benson and Hedges competition; then the big one, the four-day Britannic Assurance county championship; and finally, against Gloucestershire – batting with masterly improvisation, bowling with ruthless accuracy, fielding superlatively even by Warwickshire standards, and with General Dermot Reeve combining the attributes of Wellington, Houdini and Grock – got the Axa and Equity Sunday League competition wrapped up shipshape and Bristol fashion.

How did it happen that in 1994, Warwickshire, completing a hundred years in first-class cricket, had become the best, the most attractive and the most talked-of side in the country, and in winning three titles had accomplished an unparalleled achievement?

The glorious NatWest triumph of 1993 did an enormous amount for the team's self-belief. And then came Lara.

Dennis Amiss called the side together.

'You've got one of the greatest batsmen in the world coming to play for you,' he said, and he gave them three pieces of advice:

'Don't stand in awe of him. Don't be jealous. Learn from him.'

They learnt.

When it came to a backup team, Warwickshire were batting on a good wicket. M. J. K. Smith, chairman, Dennis Amiss, chief executive, and Bob Woolmer, director of coaching, had between them 119 test match appearances to their credit. Bob Woolmer, capped for Kent by Colin Cowdrey in 1970, retired from first-class cricket in 1984: a piece by C. B. Fry motivated him to take up coaching; he came to Warwickshire in 1991 after several seasons with the deprived in South Africa. Warwickshire were very fortunate in having Woolmer, a communicator of exceptional qualities; his positive and innovative ideas tallied so well with those of Dermot Reeve, the captain; he had excellent rapport with Tim Munton, the vice-captain, and with the rest of the players in general.

What Bob Woolmer did demand of the players was positive thinking. He set out to help them achieve their potential. He encouraged them to increase their armoury of shots – anyone could employ the reverse sweep, provided he practised it. Without Alan Donald and with Reeve, Small and Paul Smith injury prone, Warwickshire needed to score more runs more quickly in order to get the other sides out. Lara himself was not only a prolific scorer, he lifted the side generally. Twose, Ostler, Penney and Piper in particular benefited from his presence and got runs during his brief lean period.

At the start of the season Lara saved us from imminent defeat against Leicestershire. On 99 in the second innings, he three times refused an inviting single in order to protect the tail. With June came Lara's 501, and by the end of the month people were noticing that Warwickshire hadn't been defeated in any of the four competitions. The first fortnight in July really quickened Warwickshire blood.

We beat Worcestershire in the final of the Benson and Hedges competition. Then came the turning point of the season, when we defeated Surrey in a four-day match – they had been going great guns at the top of the table. Warwickshire, 131 for 8 in the first innings, were saved by Graeme Welch and Dougie Brown, two of the side's newcomers, with a rousing century ninth-wicket stand. Surrey in their turn were 100 for 1 and scoring rapidly when Roger Twose was put on. He had made 277 at the start of the season; he now shone as a bowler, devastating Surrey with 6 for 28. Andy Moles, back from a broken arm and an appendix operation, made 203 in the second innings. Surrey had no answer to this; it was now Warwickshire that leapt to the top of the table. It was a place that they did not relinquish.

Warwickshire played with freedom and enjoyment. Steve Rouse gave them excellent fast pitches. They were a thrilling side to watch. The bowling was accurate, occasionally sensational; the batting exhilarating. As for the fielding, I've never seen anything like it. Piper, Warwickshire's splendid wicketkeeper, made the catch of the season when Graham Cowdrey in the NatWest semifinal snicked a fast rising ball from Paul Smith: jumping from a standing position, hands high above his head, he somehow managed to hold on. The quicksilver Penney is one of the best fielders in the world. Ostler made several fantastic catches; the whole side were wonderfully prehensile.

Unlike our championship teams of 1911, 1951 and 1972, this was an injury-ridden side. Dermot Reeve, nursing a groin injury, eventually confined himself to one-day matches, handing over county championship games to the equable Tim Munton, who, besides taking 81 wickets, skippered the side to eight victories in nine matches. Lara, Moles, Gladstone Small, Paul Smith and others all had their problems, none of which affected their cheerfulness and determination. It was a Warwickshire man who wrote that the labour we delight in physics pain.

Regular team meetings fostered genuine team spirit. From mid-July every match was crucial. Discussion, positive thinking and self-belief produced high achievement. Above all, Warwickshire played in the true spirit of the game, as they did in my childhood long ago.

CHAPTER I

Cricket Beguiles Me

As an eight-year-old I would tear down to the County Ground at Edgbaston for that first breathless sight of the scoreboard.

'You're left-handed,' said my sister Eleanor, when I was five.

'Which is my left hand?'

'The one nearest the wall.'

We were standing outside the attic in our house in Birmingham. I looked at the greenwashed wall, and memorized the way I was facing. After that, whenever in difficulty over right and left, I would think of myself as I stood by that wall, and it would be easy. When I was seven, my cousin Cecil Ryder, who for several years had opened the bowling for Wednesbury with the great Sydney Barnes, taught me to bowl overarm. I bowled left arm, but batted right-handed. I was no freak in this matter. According to the Oxford Dictionary, by 1892 to bowl left- and bat right-handed had become a common practice.

Cricket was in my blood. My father, R. V. Ryder, was the Warwickshire secretary. I assumed that cricket was everything. When people came to the door, more often than not, they were something to do with cricket. Once, a portly middle-aged gentleman rang the doorbell: I opened the door and he asked for Father. When he had gone, I asked who he played for. Father chuckled and said, 'I shouldn't think he's seen a cricket ball in his life.' He was a businessman.

Father had become Warwickshire secretary in 1895, the year that Warwickshire became a first-class county. His job became virtually to run the club. The committee expected him to select the team, to arrange trials for and to engage new players – or at least to recommend their engagement – and to attend to the thousand and one details of administration.

In 1902, when the first test match was played at Edgbaston, Father ran the administration without an assistant, without a telephone and without a typewriter. This was the match in which Rhodes and Hirst skittled Australia for 36, Rhodes taking 7 for 17 in 11 overs; Victor Trumper, playing one of the immortal innings of the game, scored 18. Father did have an assistant when play was over for the day, John Bates, the groundsman, who helped him add up the takings each night, until three or four in the morning.

At the end of the season Warwickshire were in the red – rain had stopped play rather too often. Father's reaction was to undertake a canvass in the city – a considerable proportion of which was residential – and in suburbs near the County Ground. His canvass of six thousand houses resulted in six hundred new members, and the club continued to enjoy precarious safety.

In those days English cricket was dominated by the Big Six – Yorkshire, Lancashire, Notts, Middlesex, Surrey and Kent. These were the counties with more victories than defeats to their credit, and it was always one of the Big Six that won the county championship.

In 1911 the captaincy of Warwickshire was accepted by a twenty-two-year-old all rounder named Frank Foster. At the end of June the side was at the bottom of the table, then Warwickshire won match after match, finishing with a victory over Northants that gave them the championship. The team returned in triumph, and Birmingham folk were proud of the side that played cricket at Edgbaston when the weather allowed them to do so.

In 1914 the war put an end to the golden age of cricket as it did to so many things. I saw a few minutes of county cricket in 1920 at the age of six, watched Warwick Armstrong's Australians playing in 1921, and by 1922, as an eight-year-old, I was really hooked. Whenever Warwickshire were playing at Edgbaston I would tear down to the County Ground from our house in nearby Oakfield Road. The first view of the scoreboard could be unbearably exciting. Breathless, heart pumping, eyes dilated, I had trained myself to the pitch of automatically taking in the essentials – total score and wickets down – at a glance. My heart was strong – it had to be – and I could take good news or bad; the main thing was to know the score, and of course occasionally you had to look to see which side was batting. The sudden impact of those figures – first on the eyes, then telegraphed to my one-track mind – gave me the news I sought, good or bad or enigmatic.

John Keats, who described the excitement of first looking into Chapman's *Homer*, would have known how I felt. He compares the astronomer's excitement when a new planet swims into his ken, or the wild surmise of Cortez' fellow adventurers, with his own feelings; to me there was nothing more dynamically thrilling than the sight of the white-on-black figures that recorded the Homeric struggle in progress at Edgbaston. These first flashes from the scoreboard could have much in common with the answers of the Delphic oracle (if Warwickshire were 88 for 0 it didn't mean that they wouldn't be 93 for 6) – or with Pandora's box, releasing horrors among which not even the pale shadow of hope was left.

The scoreboard obsessed me. Once, on a day when Warwickshire were not playing, I went with my sister Eleanor, she thirteen, myself eight, to the County Ground and we stole into the scorebox. There were no spectators watching when the scoreboard blazed the titanic legend:

NO. 1	TOTAL		NO. 2
555	999		444
		WICKETS	0

At least it spoke highly of the wicketkeeper.

It was not only in the realms of fantasy that the scoreboard did exciting things in 1922. I had been watching Warwickshire's promising batting disintegrate against Hampshire, a good start ending with them being all out for 223. Faced with the choice between watching Phil Mead batting or going home and having my tea, I had my tea. As I walked back to the ground three-quarters of an hour later, to my amazement I saw Eleanor dancing down the Edgbaston road towards me.

3

'They're all out,' she panted. 'They're all out!'

'I know they're all out.'

'I mean Hampshire are all out.'

I sighed despairingly. Even a girl should know which side was batting.

'It's Warwickshire that were batting,' I said.

It was Eleanor's turn to sigh.

'I know Warwickshire were batting, but Hampshire went in. And they are all out for 15.'

And so they were: dismissed in 53 balls. But Hampshire followed on, made 520, and won decisively.

I wanted to play cricket all the time, and if not play cricket, then read about it. MCC tours of Australia fascinated me. The eighteen-man team of Ballarat, the twenty-two of Bendigo, the twenty-two of Toowoomba.* I could hear the barracking, imagine the grounds with their rough-and-ready pavilions, sense the excitement.

When I went to bed, I counted cricketers, not sheep. I would try to count fifty England and fifty Australian cricketers. It wasn't so easy to think of fifty Australian cricketers in the days before Lillee and Tommo, before Lindwall and Miller – before Don Bradman even. I didn't realize it at the time, of course, but I was actually living in the days of a Bradmanless Australia. So I would snuggle in bed and start counting Australians. Armstrong, Collins, Macartney, Mailey – I could generally remember all fifteen of the 1921 team, and go adventurously back in time. Victor Trumper – never leave him out; W. L. Murdoch, the Bannermans, G. J. Bonnor – I read an account of a match in which he hit his first two balls for six, jumped out to the third, was clean bowled, and his one ejaculation was heard all round the ground; George Giffen, Noble, Darling, Duff, Kelly, Kelleway, Scott, Spofforth – never forget the Demon; Whitty, Ransford, Midwinter – the only cricketer to have played for England against Australia, and for Australia against England; Jones – a bumper through the beard; Hordern, Clem Hill, Blackham and

---

* Teams comprising more than eleven a side were common at the time.

– especially if I had already had a go at the England players – at this point I probably Trumbled into sleep.

At the age of ten I was playing in first game at my prep school, Stanley House. In those days they were not so fussy about age limits and there were half a dozen boys aged sixteen at Stanley House, two or three of whom were cricketers – games were not compulsory. Once I was sent in to open the innings with another boy of ten, against the bowling of two sixteen-year-old six-footers. They were not fast compared with Tate and Gilligan: they were fast enough for me.

However, I stayed in. The games master, a stern enough critic, became highly complimentary, then the cricket captain himself (he was fielding) came forward, said I was doing well, but should hold my bat like *that*, and made me use a grip that I found uncomfortable. I went back to my own grip, and continued with growing confidence.

Runs? You didn't think in terms of runs against two giants like these. Survival was everything. I did score a single, but after twenty minutes I was clean bowled, and went back to the pavilion to a standing ovation from the games master and the cricket captain; then I went home, walking tall. When I got back, Father was talking to George Stephens, an ex-Warwickshire captain, a forcing batsman who had scored several centuries for the county.

Seeing my flannels, George Stephens greeted me: 'Hullo, young feller-me-lad, and how did you get on?'

'I went in first,' I said, savouring my glorious twenty minutes.

'Went in first, did you? How many did you make?'

'I made 1,' I said, with the same quiet simplicity with which A. C. MacLaren would have said, 'I made 424.'

Father and George Stephens exploded with laughter, looked at me, looked at each other, and laughed convulsively again.

' "I made 1," ' guffawed George Stephens. ' "I made 1." Well, well, well.'

They talked for a further ten minutes about grown-up matters, such as gate money. At length George Stephens got up to go.

'Well, good-bye, Roy,' he chuckled, 'and try to make more than 1 next time you bat.'

*

5

A little later I commanded success as a bowler, taking 5 for 5, playing for the under-11s. I walked home prepared to give my father a ball-by-ball account of the day of my success.

This was how the conversation went.

'How did you get on?'

'We won. I took 5 for 5.'

'How many overs did you bowl?'

'Six.'

'Did you bowl them straight off, or in two spells?'

'I bowled six overs in one spell. I wasn't taken off.'

'You should never bowl more than three overs in one spell at your age.'

Single-wicket games with friends were fun: you were always in the game, batting or bowling. Another form of cricket was to fling a tennis ball against a brick wall ten yards away from the position of wicketkeeper so that the ball would arrive first bounce at your opponent, stationed in front of you, who used a stump as the bat, and hit runs either awarded or taken. You couldn't be bowled out like this, but snicks could be plentiful, and it was good catching practice.

In the school holidays the baker's roundsman would bowl to me in the back garden, and during seaside holidays at Cromer there were glorious games of beach cricket. I chiefly liked it when Father was bowling, Eleanor (who was invariably Sutcliffe) was batting, and I was wicketkeeping, waiting for snicks. We had a sixpenny-ha'penny cricket bat, and a couple of wooden spades served as the wicket.

I loved playing outside the house at Oakfield Road. There weren't many cars about in the early 1920s, and I would stand in the middle of the road and fling a tennis ball hard against the wall outside the front garden. This wall, like many in the suburbs, was made of rugged grey oblong stone blocks, so the ball would bounce back at varying angles. The only way the phantom batsman would be out was caught. You could devise your own scoring system.

My family were regular churchgoers. I often listened to the

sermons, and I enjoyed the hymns, but I wasn't particularly interested in what P. G. Wodehouse described as the song hits from the psalms, so here I introduced cricket, playing a match between the letters 'a' and 'b', while reading the psalm of the day. It was quite simple. If the a's were batting, you counted a run for every letter except for the letter a, which counted as a wicket. The same method applied to the b's who of course always won easily, but it was interesting to see if the a's could score 200, or, if it was a short psalm, could hold out for a draw.

About this time Warwickshire had an amateur fast bowler named Andy Speed. If we were in a tricky position after Saturday's play, I would join in fervently at Matins when the Vicar intoned 'O Lord make speed to save us.'

In 1927 I went to King Edward's, playing cricket with enthusiasm and some success. In 1929 I was ill and in bed for a fortnight, with something akin to pneumonia. The illness stood me in good stead, because Bartle Logie, a distant relative in more senses than one, who was a housemaster at Parktown High, Johannesburg, wrote to ask if I would like to spend the winter of 1929–30 in South Africa, where I could convalesce and also go to school.

It seemed too good to be true. On Friday, 13 September, I set out for Cape Town on the *Balmoral Castle*. It so happened that the 1929 South Africans were returning on the *Balmoral Castle*, though without Herbie Taylor and Nummy Deane, the captain. However, Nummy Deane came on to the boat to see the team off. When Father told him I was going to Parktown High, Nummy said that he knew the Cochrane family well – Jack Cochrane was captain of the school. He picked up a refreshment tariff, and on the blank space wrote:

Dear Jack,
Look after young Ryder for me, as his father is a great friend of mine.
Nummy Deane.

I never showed Jack Cochrane the note, but kept it for years, before eventually giving it away to an autograph hunter.

This seventeen-day voyage was wonderful beyond my wildest dreams, but, like Alice, I quickly adapted myself to the rules and routines of Wonderland, discovering that the inhabitants were first, second and third class. I travelled full fare, second class, £32 return. This worked out at about eighteen shillings and six pence (92.5p) a day for four meals a day, plus accommodation and travel.

First-class passengers dressed for dinner; third-class food and accommodation were relatively basic, but sheer luxury compared with what Other Ranks were to enjoy on troopships a dozen years later.

The classes – upper, middle and lower – did mix from time to time. There were dances, fancy dress balls, and concerts in which first and second class mixed; occasionally second and third, never first and third – possibly for geographical reasons.

My father had asked George Beet, ex-Derbyshire wicketkeeper and first-class umpire, to keep an eye on me: he was going as a coach to a South African school. Other professionals going on similar duties included Bill Ashdown (Kent), Tommy Cook (Sussex), Sam Cadman (Derbyshire), Walker Wainwright (Yorkshire) and 'Triggy' Tregear (Minor Counties). 'Farmer' Burton (Hertfordshire) was going as coach to Parktown, but was travelling third class, as was Louis Duffus, the distinguished South African cricket journalist.

During these seventeen days I saw a good deal of Tommy Cook and Bill Ashdown; they were nearer to my own age and treated me as a younger brother. Always immaculately dressed in their county blazers and flannels, they were reaching the height of their careers as cricketers.

Tommy Cook, who went in No. 4 for Sussex – he had played football for Brighton as centre forward – chatted to me, asked me about my cricket, even about my lessons. Like Ashdown, he must have been on the verge of the England side. I loved chatting to him or trying to get him to play deck tennis with me, and teased him about his Sussex blazer emblazoned with the six heraldic ducks.

There weren't many teenagers on the boat, most of the

passengers were in their forties or even older. There was one girl of my own age; her name was Doris Varney. She was demure, fair and always with her parents. I was paired with her in the mixed doubles competition at deck tennis, in which we did battle against an elderly couple in their late twenties. Youth will have its fling, but we didn't fling successfully enough, and went down 4–6. In the singles I was drawn against Tommy Cook and although I made some of the best catches in my fifteen years of life I lost 5–6, Tommy Cook saying I had given him a real fright; with the benefit of hindsight I realize that he was extremely skilful in making his own dropped catches look accidental.

My greatest triumph on the *Balmoral Castle* was against Bill Ashdown.

I had been given a cricket bat (it cost £1) for my fifteenth birthday, which had been signed by the South African touring team when they were at Edgbaston. I took the bat with me to Johannesburg. Once, when I was on the deck, with the bat in one hand and a tennis ball in the other, Ashdown appeared and asked to have a look at the bat. I handed it to him. He appraised it keenly and made two or three imaginary strokes, then, standing against the rails, said, 'Come on Roy, bowl me a ball and I'll try the bat out.'

With all the modesty of my fifteen years I said, 'Yes, but what happens if you miss it?'

Ashdown was scoring about 3,000 runs a season in those days: he looked at me incredulously. 'If I do *what*?'

His tone of voice in no way allayed my anxiety.

'If you miss it the ball will go into the sea.'

With marked restraint he answered, 'If I miss it I will get you another ball from the shop.'

'Oh, all right then.'

The deck in that part of the boat was about ten yards wide. I bowled him a slow, left-handed lob. I used to spin the ball automatically, and the tennis ball, bowled underhand, turned about forty-five degrees. Ashdown played forward and was 'bowled' comprehensively through the gate, the ball going soundlessly into the sea. I stared at him in mute reproach.

He turned scarlet and said, 'I'll go and buy you another ball.'
There were no tennis balls in the shop.

It seemed to me at the time that Cook and Ashdown had much in common. Perhaps on the whole the former was more introspective and the latter more extrovert. Ashdown, a fine attacking batsman, beautiful drives and square cuts among his repertoire, was opening batsman for Kent from 1920 to 1937. He scored forty centuries; his highest innings, 332 against Essex, was scored in six and a quarter hours. He was a fine, fast medium bowler. Playing days over, he became a first-class umpire, coach at Rugby School, coach and then scorer for Leicestershire, and died in 1979, at the age of eighty. His dry sense of humour was mixed with sound common sense. When Kent were on the way to scoring 219 to win in seventy minutes, he walked up to his partner and said, 'I suppose you know you're wasting time with all those 6's.'

Tommy Cook was an outstandingly talented and patriotic man, whose life came to a tragic end. Born in Cuckfield, Sussex, on 5 February 1901, he had lied about his age during the First World War in order to join the Royal Navy, and won a gallantry medal after diving over the side in Archangel harbour to rescue a shipmate. Between the wars he scored over 20,000 runs for Sussex, was near to attaining test match honours, and won an England cap at football.

At the outbreak of the Second World War he was coaching in Cape Town, and joined the South African Air Force. While on a training flight the aeroplane returned to the airfield because of engine trouble and crashed on the runway, all aboard perishing in the flames, except Cook, who was thrown clear and was to spend months in hospital. The screams of his comrades haunted him in continual nightmares. His condition grew worse with chronic bronchitis. 'On January 15, 1950,' wrote David Frith, 'he went to the local hospital in the hope of lessening his pain and misery, only to be told that he should see his doctor instead. He went back home and took a fatal overdose of tablets.'*

* David Frith, *By His Own Hand* (Stanley Paul).

Arthur Ochse (pronounced Oosh), the South African fast bowler, was one of a number of first-class passengers who would come down to the second-class deck and sun himself in the afternoons. A kindly, honest man, strong as an ox, he asked me a lot about myself. Did I learn boxing at school? I didn't.

'You should take up boxing, man. Do you read your Bible?'

Yes, I did. I didn't know much about the Old Testament. The New Testament I found exciting and disturbing, but I answered cautiously in a monosyllable.

'You should read your Bible, man,' said Arthur Ochse in his kindly, thick Afrikaans accent. 'Read your Bible and take up boxing, and you'll be all right.' He chatted to me several times during the voyage, and on each occasion he gave me this advice.

During the last week of the voyage I came across a rudimentary, sparsely furnished bar – a kind of Wild West saloon – in the second-class quarters. Here Vincent and Catterall, of the South African team, and hardly anybody else, were regular customers, talking cricket nineteen to the dozen. I told them that I was going to Parktown for a couple of terms and of my Edgbaston connexions. They both liked Edgbaston. Vincent, a dashing, sandy-haired all-rounder, was a hero of mine, and I was able to tell Catterall that I had seen his century in the first test in 1924. This was the test in which Hobbs and Sutcliffe opened the England batting together for the first time and Tate and Gilligan made their debut as England opening bowlers, skittling South Africa for 30 in their first innings. I was fortunate enough, as a ten-year-old, to have been behind the bowler's arm on that occasion.

I didn't butt into the conversation of the two South Africans, but just listened, and they occasionally addressed pleasant inclusive remarks to me. The surroundings, the cricketing talk, the lilting South African accents and the gentle chug of the ship's turbines were unforgettable. At fifteen I was always making up limericks, and composed one about each of them, which with modest exhibitionism I handed to them during one of the rare lulls in their conversation. They enjoyed, or said they enjoyed, my offerings, and afterwards greeted me jovially, 'Any more limericks, Ryder?'

My last memory of C. L. Vincent was in 1935 at Edgbaston. He hit a drive like a bullet shot towards cover, where Tom Collin, of Warwickshire, half stopped the ball, which flew from his hands over his head; Collin caught the ball brilliantly behind his back. Vincent, in mid-run, put his bat down, and joined in the applause before walking back to the pavilion. Catterall I last heard quite unexpectedly in 1956: he was on one of the South African grounds, giving a test match commentary.

My stay in South Africa lasted from the beginning of October 1929 to the end of March 1930. Kaleidoscopic sunsets; the nightly orchestra of frogs and crickets; lines of jacaranda trees; the green purple enthralling veld; isolated dorps with stores straight from *Prester John*; garish petrol pumps; spruits and rondavels; sudden screaming echelons of outlandish, bright-plumaged birds; a bathe in the Vaal; six o'clock breakfast on the main road midway between Johannesburg and Pretoria; a hailstorm that rattled like musketry – I picked up a dozen hailstones each bigger than any hen's egg: these are memories.

Captain of cricket at Parktown was Eric (Bill) Newson, a fast bowler of nineteen, already playing for the Transvaal. A year later he was playing for South Africa against England. Unfortunately, the experts started improving his run-up, and he only played in three tests, the last in the timeless test of 1939 that went on for ten days and was called off as a draw to enable the English team to catch the boat.

At Parktown High, playing for my house second eleven, I had my first experience of matting wickets. Going in to bat for the first time in South Africa, I cut the first ball wide of first slip and was amazed to see it scud in no time over the hard red sand and rattle against the boundary fence. The same stroke in England would normally yield me a single. I got another 4 with the same stroke next ball, and then tried it once too often.

One of the masters, named Pilkington, an England expatriate, was a keen cricketer and did a lot of umpiring. He had a goatee beard and couldn't stand the expressions – frequently used in South

Africa – 'backstop' and 'over up'; the bravest of the brave among the fielders had been known to call out, 'Sir, the backstop says it's over up.'

Bartle Logie took me to see a Currie Cup Match, Transvaal *v* Western Province, on the Wanderers Ground in Johannesburg. I remember Owen-Smith's superlative fielding in the covers, the matting wicket and dark red outfield of South Africa's premier cricket ground.

The voyage home was on the *Arundel Castle*. Fellow travellers were Laurie Eastman and Norman Kilner. Eastman, the Essex all-rounder, was a great humorist. However, he suffered from recurrent malaria, and I remember him suddenly grey and sweating profusely for a couple of days before reclaiming his customary élan. Norman Kilner, as Yorkshire as they make them, was a fine opening bat who had qualified for Warwickshire. He was full of richly pointed, sardonic anecdotes about the game, and he had the Yorkshireman's devastating gift of understatement.

I had evidently grown too fast in South Africa and developed curvature of the spine; when I was seventeen a specialist barred me from cricket for a season. At least I could watch the game and tear into the County Ground to see what joys or horrors the Delphic scoreboard had to offer, and to watch the batting of Norman Kilner and R. E. S. Wyatt and the bowling of Danny Mayer and George Paine.

About this time I fell victim to alphabet cricket, which was ravaging King Edward's. This was quite a complicated game, far superior to dab cricket, from which you could get a complete scoreboard, including bowling analyses.

This, if I remember correctly, is the code that we used:

a – dot	n – 1
b – 4	o – dot
c – 1	p – bowled
d – 1	q – stumped
e – dot	r – dot
f – extra	s – dot
g – 2	t – dot
h – dot	u – 4
i – dot	v – 3
j – lbw	w – dot
k – caught	x – run out
l – 2	y – 2
m – dot	z – 6

With an average work of fiction, if there is such a thing, you get a run rate of a little more than 3 an over and an average total of round about 250.

The greatest temptation lay in the choice of pages. It was easy to decide on, say, page 67 of some novel, and find that the name Pippa occurred twice in a couple of lines: six batsmen clean bowled in next to no time. One was inclined to take another page, and the practice was liable to become habit forming.

Half a dozen in my form alone worked hard at alphabet cricket, especially when the text books we were supposed to be reading provided suitable material. One or two of the more frivolous souls made up sides consisting of their own friends, pitting them against teams ranging from the school staff to historical characters such as Julius Caesar, though not the one in *Wisden*. However, the majority of us were traditionalists who considered such matches unrealistic, and stuck purposefully to the county championship.

My friend Jack Fleming, a mathematician, devised a game using two letters of the alphabet to represent one delivery – thus, FR – IE – ND would represent three deliveries, not six. Employing this 26 × 26 method he had a code of 676 options, and was thus able to include bad light, rain stopped play, retired hurt and all the other ingredients of the summer game. Jack Fleming eventually became a meteorological expert, organizing the weather for NATO.

When I was allowed to play cricket again I made up to some extent for lost time, doing the hat trick in a house match and winning my second eleven colours. At Exeter College, Oxford, faced with the choice of taking cricket seriously or simply enjoying it, I elected to play for the Exeter Busters, and also, having friends at Oriel, for the Oriel Outcasts. The cricket was good fun, relaxed, pleasant and of a competent standard.

There were two less serious games. I had started a Gilbert and Sullivan society at Exeter, and we challenged the D'Oyly Carte Opera Company to a game, which we played on the Exeter ground in the Parks. Set 90-odd to win, we were getting along quite nicely when a dozen or more members of the company, who had been rehearsing, came to watch. A couple of them, wearing ordinary civvies, asked if they could field. Others joined them. When I went in to bat at No. 11, we had already got the runs, which was just as well, as I counted no fewer than twenty-four fielders, so I was well pleased at hitting two 4's and a 3 during my five-minute stay at the wicket.

Later in the term I was invited to play for the Paralytics in their annual match against the college servants. The Paralytics team was selected by the president of the JCR, an ability at the game being considered a liability rather than an asset when it came to team selection. It was a tradition in this match that a barrel of beer was brought on to the field, just inside the boundary: anyone on either side hitting a 4 or taking a wicket had to drink a pint on the spot.

L. R. (Jim) McIntyre, the captain (and president of the JCR), was an Australian Rhodes Scholar. A great cross-country runner, he was later to chair the Security Council of the United Nations at the time of the 1973 war in the Middle East.

When he put me on to bowl I immediately did the hat trick. At the end of the over, in which I had duly drunk a pint at the fall of each wicket, McIntyre, with a typical Aussie chuckle, said, 'I think you had better come off.' I was inclined to agree with him, but these were the best bowling figures I have ever returned:

O	M	R	W
1	1	0	3

During my late teens and early twenties I stayed at Oldcastle Farm, Colwall, during the first fortnight of September, often with school friends. We played a sort of padless, primordial cricket with village teenagers on the rough, cantankerous pitch at Colwall Green.

It was whilst staying at Colwall that I played the most enjoyable game of cricket I have ever played in my life. One Friday evening I called in at the village pub in Bushley, near Tewkesbury, and found out that the village team had a home match the next day. Were they short of a player? In those days every village team was short of a player.

'You turn up at 1.30 tomorrow then, and we'll give you a game.'

The next day, I walked from Oldcastle Farm, up the Herefordshire Beacon, along the earthworks, down into Castlemorton Common and along the Tewkesbury road to Bushley. There I found my team mates in the pub, we piled into a car and went half a mile to the ground.

The loveliness of the tree-fringed cricket field was almost beyond belief. There was a general sense of varied and entrancing greenness, a drowsy farmyard, several black-beamed cottages, an intoxicating smell from a late hay crop.

Our opponents batted first. I fielded cover point, I didn't have a ball to field, nor was I put on to bowl. Our opponents made about 80. When I went in, No. 7, the first ball that I faced pitched just short of a length. Unfortunately, there was a spot – in fact a cowpat – just short of a length, and I was clean bowled. We were all out for 30-odd. Seven of us got into an Austin 7 and we went back to the pub. On the way we discovered that all seven of us had made precisely the same score.

I drank a couple of sociable pints of scrumpy – it had reached the extortionate price of fivepence a pint – and walked back along the Tewkesbury road, through the gentle wilderness of Castlemorton Common, over the hills and down to Oldcastle

Farm. I hadn't bowled, hadn't had anything to field and was out first ball, yet the whole day had been marvellous.

After Oxford there was occasional club cricket, and there was bowling in the nets at Edgbaston. At this time the county players would often appear at the nets, and I enjoyed watching the slow bowlers like Hollies and Fantham from close at hand. When I was in the Army I played a few games at Bovington in 1941, and some months later a few games in Egypt – fifteen-over matches of eight-ball overs, on matting wickets again. After the war, my playing gradually merged into coaching, and especially coaching prep school teams, which I found was as rewarding as actually playing.

CHAPTER 2

The Essence of Cricket

Cricket is not so much a game as an extension of being English: a gallimaufry of paradoxes, contradictions, frightening logic and sheer impossibilities, of gentle courtesy and rough violence. The greatest exponents of this essentially English game have included Australasians, West Indians, Pakistanis, Hindus and Dutch South Africans; for a quarter of a century there were Americans from Philadelphia, one or two of whom attained world class. The first missionary to encounter the Papuans was eaten, the next one taught them to play cricket, and Papua competed in the first World Cup. Those who would not see eye to eye with the first statement in this paragraph would no doubt include Sir Donald Bradman, Kepler Wessels, Viv Richards, Sir Richard Hadlee, Kapil Dev and Imran Khan, together with millions more for whom English is not even their first language. Cricket, like time and television, can be a great healer, though not necessarily. The argument of one historian that if the French aristocrats had played cricket with their peasants there would have been no French Revolution was rejected by I. A. R. Peebles, of Cambridge University, Middlesex and England, with the assertion that, from what he knew of the Gallic temperament, the Revolution would simply have been accelerated.

Turning from the possible influence of cricket on the French to the probable influence of the English on cricket, it has been contended that if some giant force of nature were to destroy everything in England except the Laws of Cricket, historians would be able to unravel the English way of life that had existed before the disaster: when in doubt, let the present state of things continue.

My father used to claim that the first recorded reference to cricket was in the Old Testament, when Rebekah came out with a full pitcher. So far as cricket in England is concerned, a more serious claim refers to the wardrobe accounts of the royal household, in 1300, to the effect that 100 shillings was paid out for the Prince (son of Edward I) to play at CREAG and other sports. The Oxford English Dictionary dates cricket to 1598, bowling to 1755 and batting to 1773: it must have been paradisal to have been a bowler during those eighteen intervening years.

Cricket would have developed in the years immediately following the Civil War, when royalist squires, thinking it wise to remain on their paternal acres, played with their servants: the diarist Thomas Creevey refers to an analogous episode in 1827, when he visited Viscount Milton, the future fifth Earl Fitzwilliam: 'On our arrival here on Saturday, we found Milton and his eldest son without their coats playing at cricket with their servants.'

Cricket holds up a mirror to the times: in violent times it could become a violent game. In 1715 William Waterfall, from Derbyshire, was found guilty of manslaughter for killing an opponent in a village cricket match. He was burnt on the hand and imprisoned for nine months. In 1726 an Essex justice of the peace became obsessed with the idea that such games as cricket were only pretences to collect a crowd of disaffected people in order to raise a rebellion. If this JP saw Jacobites under the bed, cricket had a fatal attraction for Frederick, Prince of Wales, who died as the result of a blow from a cricket ball in 1751. In 1776 a match between Kent and Essex was abandoned, Essex refusing to take part in the game as Kent were trying to play a man who was not qualified for the county: at least three people were killed in the ensuing riot. Quarrels were not unusual in single-wicket matches. Ensign A. Mahon killed Assistant Surgeon Louis O'Hara in a duel after a dispute in a game at Malden in 1809. Dissent is not a new factor. Drinking and gambling were other concomitants of the game in Hanoverian times – 'Beef and beer are the things to play cricket on' – as William Caffyn was to say.

There were gentler facets: growing professionalism, patronage, clubs, foreign travel. Young gentlemen on the foreign tour arranged cricket matches among themselves in Brussels, Paris, Rome. The first overseas cricket tour, in which the Duke of Dorset was to have taken a team to France, was cancelled owing to the outbreak of the French Revolution. British officers arranged an impromptu game in Brussels a day or two before their away match against Napoleon in 1815.

Cricket provides a convenient peg for all sorts and conditions of men on which to hang their sociability. Old boys from the public schools kept up their acquaintance by playing cricket, the servants from the big houses would be excused work for the evening to play against the village side, barristers would arrange matches, as would captains of the Italian and Turkey trade. There were village matches on the village green, and there were matches of Married *v* Bachelors, Smokers *v* Non-smokers, Over 30s *v* Under 30s, and so forth. The aesthetic appeal and complexities of the game were as well appreciated by the farm labourer as by the public schoolboy, the majority of the population still lived in villages or small market towns.

'Note that your good cricketer is commonly the most industrious man in the parish,' wrote Mary Russell Mitford in 1823, 'the habits that make him such are precisely those which make a good workman – steadiness, sobriety and activity.' Perhaps this still applies; however, a hundred and fifty years later, Leslie Deakins, Warwickshire secretary, said to me, 'The trouble is that all the best cricketers are blasé,' – an indication of cricket's contradictory nature.

In 1859 the first English cricket tour – of twelve professionals – took place in the form of a visit to America. The 1860s celebrated the birth of *Wisden's Cricketers' Almanack*; 'overhand' bowling was authorized; the first cricket tour of England – by Australian aboriginals – took place; the county championship started: the three-day county game which formed the backbone of English cricket until the end of the 1992 season.

With the Victorian era came the days of muscular Christianity, and the Oxford English Dictionary cited the word 'cricket' as denoting fair play; dating from 1902, 'it isn't cricket' became analogous to '*it isn't fair*'. We couldn't get away with that today. Make an obscene gesture at the spectators, fling your aluminium bat on the ground, swear at the batsman who has been in too long – that's news, and people will tell you that they don't like cricket because of the way cricketers behave.

Dog bites man isn't news, man bites dog is news, consequently the thousand minor courtesies of the game, evident throughout the summer on every first-class cricket ground, not to mention the humbler ones, go unrecorded. The batsman scores 50, and the fielding side clap him; he scores 100 and they clap him again, though he will have been doing a good deal of no good to their bowling averages and their prospects in the county championship. It's not uncommon for the bowler to applaud a batsman who hits him for 6. Thirty or forty times a day you will probably see a batsman who has blocked a ball that trickles a couple of yards from the bat, pick the ball up and throw it back to the bowler or to the nearest fielder. This action is always recognized as a gesture of goodwill; literally thousands of such incidents occur during the course of a cricket season. To an appeal for handled the ball the umpire could only give one answer, yet season after season goes by without anyone demanding his pound of flesh. The reason? Cricketers are pleasant people who play cricket as a game to be enjoyed. Most of them play in this manner all the time; some of them most of the time. In a recent test match between England and New Zealand, Sir Richard Hadlee was no-balled by the umpire; Hadlee's response was to put his arm round him. Then Gladstone Small hit Hadlee for 4; Hadlee patted Small on the back. Watch the players walking back to the pavilion at the end of a game: batsmen shake hands with fieldsmen; batsmen and fieldsmen shake hands with umpires; the fielders clap the batsmen, especially if the batting side has won.

Of course there is ill temper and dissent in cricket. There are batsmen who make their dissent obvious if they think they have been given out unfairly; others contain themselves until they get back into the dressing room, and then relieve their feelings; many simply shrug it off. Bowlers can get mad if they are no-balled or denied a wicket: 'Cricket is a warm-blooded game,' said Ted

Dexter, referring to an incident when a player stepped out of line. 'You are a cold fish if you don't get emotional about it.' Even so, the majority of players contain their feelings. Sledging (deliberate abuse of a batsman to put him off his stroke) is a pernicious tactic, but the sledgers of recent years were no more offputting to batsmen than George Macaulay and the Yorkshire slip fielders of seventy years ago.

And what about ball tampering? Could it be that in 1992, one or two of us were complaining because the Pakistanis proved the better team? Ball tampering has gone on in cricket since the game began. Silver Billy Beldham, the mildest of men, annoyed by Lord Frederic Beauclerc's cantankerous behaviour, applied a mixture of mud and sawdust to the ball, and clean bowled him. This was in 1806 or thereabouts. Nigel Haig made no secret of the things he did to the seam with a penny, until he was stopped, when he would have to be more covert. After the 1992 hoo-ha about the Pakistanis, Surrey and, later on, the Transvaal, were fined for tampering.

But why shouldn't bowlers use their initiative in this manner? I. A. R. Peebles made a strong case for the bowler to use his own implement to advantage, as the batsman does with his. The batsman can have a rubber handle on his bat, why shouldn't the bowler take wickets literally with the sweat of his brow, or by using ingenious and innocuous products of modern technology? Perhaps one of these days Law 42 will be changed: such things have happened.

In general there is far more courtesy, friendship and laughter in the game than there is sledging and cheating; cricket has altered very little in this respect over the years. What is being lost to the game is the occasional custom of letting a young batsman, playing in his first match, get off the mark with a single. Joe Manton, playing his first and only game for Warwickshire, was greeted by Tom Richardson with the words 'Full toss on the leg side, sir.' County captains used to make similar arrangements: 'Hit the ball to me and run,' said John Daniell of Somerset to a young batsman making his Worcestershire debut; the batsman did so, and Daniell fumbled the ball. David Sheppard (now Bishop of Liverpool), going to the wicket to play his first innings for Sussex, was intercepted by Les

Berry, the Leicestershire captain, 'There'll be a run for you on the on side if you want it.' The on-side fielders moved back, and Sheppard got the first of his thousands of runs for his county.

The same sort of courtesy used to be offered to batsmen who were a run or two short of their century. Not always. Tommy Cook, the great Sussex batsman of the Gilligan era, once told me how, when he had made 96 not out against Essex, J. W. H. T. Douglas said to him 'I'll toss you one up.' Cook's concentration changed to anticipation, but, instead of a bland half-volley to hit for 4, Douglas sent down a veritable fizzer which bowled him. Tommy Cook had mistaken *realpolitik* for chivalry.

In 1924 I saw a game given away by the Sussex captain, A. E. R. Gilligan, with the support and connivance of the rest of his team. Sussex, all out 94 in their second innings of a rain-ridden match at Edgbaston, left Warwickshire 14 to win with nearly an hour left for play. It had been drizzling for some time, but as soon as the Sussex innings finished the drizzle turned to heavy rain; it seemed obvious that the match would be abandoned, and most of the spectators made for home. However, the few of us that remained saw Gilligan lead his team out as though the sun was shining. Warwickshire, he felt, deserved to win, and, rain or no rain, he would give them the chance. The runs were knocked off, and Sussex came off the field with their heads high. 'It's just the sort of thing Mr Gilligan would do,' said Ted Bowley, who had played in the match, thirty years later.

Michael Davie felt that for Edmund Blunden 'cricket provided some sort of escape from his ever present and haunting memories of the trenches in the First World War' and agreed that his love of cricket might well have helped to keep him sane. Davie, however, did feel that Blunden had too roseate a view of the game: he had on his mantelpiece 'a torn out newspaper photograph of Bradman shaking hands with Hutton at the Oval in 1938 when Hutton passed Bradman's highest individual test innings. Blunden regarded the photograph as proof that chivalry had survived.'*

* This was the famous test match when England declared with their score at 903 for 7.

23

In September 1987, Norman Gifford, the Warwickshire captain, was playing his last game of first-class cricket. Warwickshire, nine wickets down in the second innings, were facing defeat against Somerset. Gifford survived what in any case was the last over of the match against his opposing captain and fellow spinner, Vic Marks. The last ball fended away, Marks ran up to Gifford, shook hands and walked back to the pavilion with him in animated and joyous conversation, while the rest of the Somerset team clapped Gifford off the field. An Edgbaston memory of 1991: Paul Smith bowling to Adrian Dale of Gamorgan, who had got stuck on 99. A raucous appeal for lbw, Dale was given out, Paul Smith gave an exuberant leap, then, remembering the batsman's disaster, ran up to Dale and put his arm round him in consolation.

Such inter-team spirit is international: not even a state of war between India and Pakistan could stop the test match series between the two countries going ahead in 1988.

Cricket is a paradoxical game: that the English of all people should have invented this summer sport in so rain-bedizened a land! – a sideways game; a fast game – six 6's in succession for Sobers; Ambrose and his orchestra of slips; a slow game, with anonymous batsmen blocking for a draw; a tranquil game, that can give sessions of sweet silent thought to the spectator. Above all, there is the agony of cricket, reflected in the dying minutes of mighty dramas that participants, temporarily uninvolved, dare not look upon, of cardiac arrests among the spectators, of umbrellas discarded, their handles gnawed away. Early test matches prompted Masefield to write '85 to Win' and Neville Cardus to record the ordeal of the luckless Fred Tate. Never shall I forget listening to the wireless in a remote Norfolk cottage, the wind outside soughing in the trees, the hysterical baying clamour of the spectators carried over the soundwaves from the Caribbean, while Jones and Alan Knott, England's last men in, met in the middle of the pitch, to boost each other's morale before the predatory Lance Gibbs bowled the last over of the test match, that he intended would bring a West Indian victory. As each ball was sent down the screaming over the airwaves rose higher. But England survived. What did they talk about, before that fatal last over, the two lonely men in the middle of the pitch? Alan Knott remembered: the noise was so terrific that they couldn't hear themselves speak, so they sang, at the top of their voices, 'We'll Keep a Welcome in the Hillside'. There was. Such games, the climax agonizing and almost unendurable, are the very stuff of cricket.

John Claughton, of Oxford University and Warwickshire, who now runs the cricket at Eton, believes that cricket goes further than the mere paradoxical, and should in fact never have been invented:

> Cricket . . . takes too long, the earth needs to be too flat and the grass too short, the equipment is too complicated and at any one time twenty or twenty-two players could do their jobs sitting in deck chairs. If cricket is under threat in the state system, it may just be that common sense has broken out there and it is independent schools who are mad to persist.
>
> But cricket is not only a stupid school game, it is a stupid game. No one seems to be happy about it; batsmen lament that they have only one chance, bowlers that they, the batsmen, have too many, whilst they, the bowlers, labour interminably without profit and honour.
>
> Why does anyone bother?*

Cricket is an uncertain game. I think whoever it was that first referred to the glorious uncertainty of cricket was parodying Field Marshal French, who spoke of the glorious uncertainty of war. Look at the things in cricket that can turn triumph into disaster, yawning defeat into joyous victory – a brilliant catch, an inspired bowling change, a cunningly casual remark (see Chapter 11); beware the sudden hat trick, the sudden shower of rain, and although a last-wicket partnership of over 300 is unlikely, it *can* happen. Remember Kippax and Hooker, who put on 307 for the tenth wicket for New South Wales against Victoria in the 1928–29 season.

Cricket is a game of many crafts. Some say that it is as difficult to

* Wellington College Cricket Club, *Hong Kong & Australia Tour 1989–90*.

become a good batsman as it is to become a good violinist. A young Indian described a day's cricket as a day's meditation: not, presumably, when Ambrose is around. Cricket not only provides great aesthetic enjoyment, it can also demand great physical courage. It is a game for princes and prime ministers, poets and publicans, rajahs and ragamuffins.

Cricket is a game so various, so full of diversity. There is the story of the young Englishman who was asked by an American girl to explain the game to her. Excited by her interest, the Englishman let himself go, and for the next two hours expounded on such facets of cricket as hooks, pulls, cuts, glides, swing, drift, swerve, looping, bodyline, bouncers, beamers, bosies, long hops, leg-glances, seamers, silly points, sosteneuters, nets, sawdust, declarations, the Carmody field, the umbrella field, jaffas, perfumed balls, sticky dogs, bunsen burners, sledging, wicket maidens, half volleys, googlies, sawn-off batters, wild shots, asterisk merchants, average mongers and a dangerous Chinaman. The American girl, startled and amazed, acknowledged his exposition, exclaiming, 'Well, my, isn't that dandy? And to think that you do all that on horseback!'

One of the reasons why cricket is so different from other games – I am not writing of one-day matches – is because county, inter-state and test matches last anything from three (now four) to five days, involving intervals for luncheon, tea and alfresco drinks. And in 1939, remember, there was the timeless test in South Africa already referred to, played with the intention of achieving a definite result, but abandoned after ten days to allow the England team to catch their boat.

Once a young married couple from Dortmund were questioning me closely about cricket. They were worried that people should play for so long – as they thought – without getting anything to eat or drink. I explained that they did have lunch and tea.

'What, in the middle of a game?'

'Yes. Forty minutes for lunch.'

'And five o'clock tea?'

'Not necessarily at five o'clock.'

'What time, then?'

'It would depend on how many wickets had fallen and how many overs had been bowled.'

They gave up.

The game is so fashioned that comments and conversations on the field of play, including conversation with the enemy, can be a matter of routine. Peter Roebuck, in *It Never Rains*, gives a pleasant example of an affable chat he had with a batsman, while fielding at silly mid-on. Before Roebuck's time, Bertie Buse of Somerset went in to face Eric Hollies, the Warwickshire leg-spinner. He took a long time with the preliminaries, taking guard, looking round the field, prodding the pitch, and so on. When he started looking round the field again, Eric Hollies called out 'Bertie, you take longer to get ready than my missus!' A tail-end batsman, facing Macaulay of Yorkshire, managed to survive an over, each ball more precariously than before. At the end of the over, George Wood, the Yorkshire wicketkeeper, gazed at him earnestly, and enquired 'Have you ever tried walking on the water?'

Batsmen hold conferences between overs, generally concerning tactics for the immediate future. Three slips can be together the bulk of the time for a whole day, certainly for a two-hour session. A whole range of topics can be discussed as the bowlers walk back to their marks. Peter Roebuck mentions a conversation about the best way of cooking an egg for breakfast. Sometimes more serious matters crop up. Mike Brearley when captain and wicketkeeper of Cambridge University would have fascinating discussions with his first slip, E. J. Craig, now lecturing in philosophy at Cambridge:

> It is true that I would, as WK, ask him many questions about free will or knowledge of other minds, etc. and he would answer (or we'd discuss). There weren't many edges off our bowling!

To play cricket well, you not only need courage, co-ordination and good eyesight: it is also an advantage to be intelligent. There must be at least twenty or thirty in the county circuit who could have easily taken an honours degree but who preferred to sign contracts as professional cricketers. Mike Brearley, a distinguished England captain, is also a distinguished academic; Peter Roebuck did not let his cricket for Cambridge University prevent his getting a first in law, then deciding on the life of a cricketer rather than a lucrative career in the legal profession.

'Cricket ain't fun,' said Wilfred Rhodes; none the less, there are people who would go to any lengths for the chance of a game. Simon Hughes gives an interesting cameo of cricket in the Australian outback:

> It is rough out there and unforgiving, but immensely rewarding. Some players regularly travel 500 kilometres just for a game. One, from the depths of NSW, does so on a moped, avoiding stone and snakebite, riding home again that night. A farmer's son drives 1,000 kilometres through Friday night to open the bowling on Saturday morning. The farm needs him back again on Sunday. They arrive at grounds where the changing room is the back of a truck, the drinks means a queue for the tap; the shower afterwards is a local swimming pool.*

For some there are no half measures: 'If I knew I was going to die today,' said an enthusiast (G. H. Hardy), 'I should still want to hear the cricket scores.'

Denis Hills, who had been in his youth a lusty games player, was sentenced to death in Uganda in 1975, for describing Idi Amin as a village tyrant. The death sentence concentrated his mind, among other things, on cricket. With no books to read, from time to time he would try to recall the names of the 187 cricketers who played regularly for the seventeen first-class counties. When James Callaghan, then foreign secretary, was able to bring Hills back from Uganda, the minister had memorized the cricket scores, which he related to Hills on the aircraft over a steak and a glass of champagne.

It is perhaps fitting to conclude this chapter with a story told by Field Marshal Alexander to Lieutenant General Sir Oliver Leese: they were both to become presidents of the MCC. Alexander, who

---

* Wellington College Cricket Club, *Hong Kong & Australia Tour 1989–90.*

had taken over from Lord Gort command of the BEF at Dunkirk, reported to the War Office on his return at the end of the evacuation, where he saw Walter Monckton (Viscount Monckton of Benchley), then a junior minister. They both played for Harrow in Fowler's Match (1910) when Eton won by 9 runs in a sensational finish. No sooner had they met than Alexander, who had been Harrow's fast bowler, chipped Walter Monckton, the wicketkeeper on that occasion, about dropping a vital catch. They discussed the matter with so much animation that Churchill's arrival passed unnoticed, until the prime minister, whose displeasure had been mounting steadily, upbraided them: 'Gentlemen, please talk about serious matters.'

'We are, sir,' said Monckton. 'We're talking about cricket.'

CHAPTER 3

Armstrong's Australians

Warwick Armstrong's Australians have always beguiled me. It was in 1921 that I awakened to cricket, and the visits of the Aussies to Edgbaston – they came twice in that year – generated great excitement in Birmingham, and violent emotion in my sister Eleanor and her friend Violet Pickard. They were both twelve at the time, and I was seven; their excitement infected me as they whirled up and down the stairs, calling out to the world at large 'I got Andrews' autograph!' and suchlike. Even my father, who seldom said more than 'I didn't see half a dozen balls bowled the whole day', came back from the ground and spoke animatedly over the cold beef.

The historian who wrote that there has never been a successful invasion of England since 1066 was presumably writing before the arrival of Warwick Armstrong's Australians in 1921. William of Normandy showed astute captaincy, his half-brother, Odo, Bishop of Bayeux, with his two-headed mace, had the ability of an aggressive opening batsman, but the devastation of the 1921 Australians was condign. Their very names should freeze the blood of Englishmen:

W. W. Armstrong (captain), H. L. Collins (vice-captain), J. Ryder, E. R. Mayne, E. A. McDonald, C. E. Pellew, W. Bardsley, T. J. E. Andrews, C. G. Macartney, J. M. Gregory, A. A. Mailey, J. M. Taylor, H. L. Hendry, H. Carter, W. A. Oldfield.

In a tour beginning on 30 April and ending half-way through September, they played thirty-eight matches, of which they won twenty-two, drew fourteen and lost two – these last were festival matches at the end of the season. They won three of the five test matches and drew two. What was remarkable was the manner in which they won. There was no answer to the vast and imposing presence of Armstrong, a batting line-up that virtually went down to No. 11, the frightening speed of Gregory and the lethal pace of McDonald.

Sydney Pardon's words, as editor of *Wisden's** for 1922, stand out today as vehemently as they did when they were written:

> I am sure that some of our batsmen, knowing they would have to face Gregory, were out before they went in. Since Knox bowled his fastest in 1906 I have never seen batsmen as obviously intimidated. McDonald struck one as being really the finer bowler of the two, but Gregory was by far the more alarming. Gregory was apt when he pitched at all short to get up dangerously high, but old cricketers were inclined to be sarcastic when they saw batsmen frightened by long hops. They perhaps remembered Mr R. D. Walker's dictum some years ago that the batsman who could not look after himself should not play cricket.

R. D. Walker, incidentally, was certainly a batsman who knew how to look after himself. The youngest of the seven Walker brothers of Southgate, he played for Middlesex in the 1890s, when there were some pretty fast bowlers around, never wore pads or batting gloves and never received any serious injury.

Armstrong's Australians didn't just defeat England, they overwhelmed us. The first two test matches were virtually lost in the first half hour, the third was lost by 219 runs. Having won all five of the 1920–21 series, the Australians had now won eight tests in a row. England did better in the last two tests, which were drawn, but by then it was too late.

Warwick Armstrong, the Australian captain, was in every sense one of the giants of the game. Like Alfred Mynn and W. G. Grace, he would top the scales at around 20 stone, and was probably the heaviest of the three.

I saw Warwick Armstrong when as a seven-year-old I was sent with a message from home to my father at the County Ground, Edgbaston. Father was upstairs in the committee room, talking to

* The *'s* was dropped from *Wisden's* in 1938.

an alarming, gigantic cricketer, immaculate in green blazer and flannels.

Father performed the introduction. I goggled.

Warwick Armstrong picked me up from under my shoulders and lifted me above his head so that I was nearly touching the ceiling. At this point I thought that he was going to eat me; however, he only gave me a kiss, set me down, and I was able to escape with my life.

Despite the absence of television and radio in those days, Armstrong certainly left his mark on the year 1921. He was now forty-two, and had been playing test match cricket for nearly twenty years. You had to get up very early in the morning to outwit him. At the Oval in August 1909, when trial balls were still allowed, England were trying to level the test series against Australia. Woolley went in to bat, and had to stand at the wicket for nineteen minutes while Armstrong bowled trial balls before starting his bowling proper, and Australia were nineteen minutes nearer to safety.* Brian Close could have taken his correspondence course. Not surprisingly, the law about trial balls was altered in 1910.

Armstrong was good at getting his own way, and tact was not his strong point; as a result, this basically amiable man was not given as good a press as he deserved. Often his so-called awkwardness arose because he wanted to protect his team from playing too long hours, and above all to allow them reasonable travelling time in the immense programme that had been planned for them. The Australians played thirty-eight matches in 1921: none of the first-class counties played more than twenty-eight; Middlesex, the county champions, played twenty.

Armstrong was a strict disciplinarian with his own side. There were daily boot inspections in which he checked the laces and studs of the team. Fielders were expected to throw the ball in first bounce from the boundary. Once, when Armstrong was bowling, a fielder threw the ball in along the ground to Armstrong, who stopped the ball with his foot: the wrongdoer had to run up to the wicket, pick the ball up, hand it to his captain and then trot back to his position on the boundary.

* This incident is reported by E. H. D. Sewell in *Cricket Under Fire* (Stanley Paul).

To my mind, the most glorious of the Armstrong stories concerns the occasion when the fifth test match at the Oval was petering out into the dullest of drawn games. Armstrong, fielding in the deep, picked up a piece of newspaper that was being blown across the field and glanced at it for a matter of half a minute before getting rid of it. When asked why he had done this, he replied 'To find out what team we were playing.'

H. L. (Horseshoe) Collins, the vice-captain, was quite a different kettle of fish. Like most Australian sportsmen, he was a devotee of the racecourse: he would bet on anything except cricket. He had skippered the Australian Imperial Forces – 'the little corporal'. Arthur Mailey knew him well. This is how he described him in his autobiography *Ten for Sixty-Six and All That*:

> At heart Collins was a gambler. His hunting grounds were the race course, the dog track, Monte Carlo, 'The Den of Thieves' (near the Strand in 1921–6), a baccarat joint at King's Cross, a two-up school in the Flanders trenches in WW1 and anywhere where a quiet game of poker was in operation.

He was also one of the best opening batsmen Australia has ever had.

Second only to Armstrong as an eye-catching personality was J. M. Gregory, who, like Collins, Johnny Taylor, Oldfield and Pellew, had been a member of the Australian Imperial Forces side. Tall and broad-shouldered, with an exuberant tearaway run-up to the crease, he was also a fine attacking batsman. In the AIF he often opened the innings, but on this tour he was a middle-order batsman. Jack Gregory was a member of a great Australian cricketing family: he had dallied with the idea of taking up farming immediately after the war, and it was unfortunate for England that he changed his mind. As a slip fielder he was breathtaking: Arthur Mailey wrote of him that he could catch anything from a cold to a train.

McDonald, less charismatic, was perhaps technically more proficient as a bowler. He didn't like being pulled. He played regularly for Lancashire in the 1920s, and was killed in a car crash in 1937.

Arthur Mailey, the googly bowler, was of Irish extraction; he had been a manual worker before he made his name as a cricketer. The twists and loops and dips and drifts and swerves that could be imparted to a cricket ball exercised his mind consciously and sub-consciously every day of the year. Simultaneously with his progress as a bowler ran his progress as cartoonist and as a cricket writer. In the fourth test match at Melbourne in 1921, Mailey had taken 9 for 121 in England's second innings, out of a total of 315. Against Gloucestershire at Cheltenham, August 1921, he took all ten wickets – an achievement, which years later, occasioned the title for his autobiography mentioned above.

This is how he describes the ball that took the wicket of his first great victim – Victor Trumper:

> Again fortune was on my side as I bowled the ball that I had often dreamed of bowling. As with the leg-break, it had sufficient spin to curve in the air and break considerably after making contact with the pitch. If anything it might have had a little more top-spin, which would cause it to drop rather suddenly. The sensitivity of a spinning ball against a breeze is governed by the amount of spin imparted, and if a ball bowled at a certain pace drops on a certain spot, one bowled with identical pace but with more top-spin should drop eighteen inches or two feet shorter.

And so to the dénouement:

> Vic's bat came through like a flash, but the ball passed between his bat and legs, missed the leg stump by a fraction, and the bails were whipped off with the great batsman at least two yards out of his ground.

C. G. Macartney, 'the Governor General', diminutive and with wrists of steel, could score at phenomenal pace. Against Notts in one day he scored 345: when A. W. Carr put himself on for one over so that his main bowlers could change ends, Macartney hit him for six 4's. Perhaps second only to Bradman of Australia's great batsmen, he was more attractive to watch. 'He existed at the crease,' wrote Ronald Mason, 'in a kind of supercharged fret of snorting rapacity.'*

Horace Carter, born in Yorkshire, was at forty-three the oldest of the party. His career as a wicketkeeper was drawing to a close: he would then be able to devote more time to his career as an undertaker. His successor, Bert Oldfield, was lucky to have survived the war, having been buried alive at Polygon Wood when serving with the Australian forces. Genial, liked and respected by friend and foe, he became one of the greatest wicketkeepers of the century.

Warren Bardsley, a versatile left-handed opening batsman, scored nine of the Australians' thirty-seven centuries during the tour. A companionable man, according to Arthur Mailey he was always cutting long stories short. Tommy Andrews and Johnny Taylor were two highly competent batsmen, 'Nip' Pellew was a brave batsman and scintillating in the field. Neither Jack Ryder nor the avuncular Edgar Mayne were selected for any of the five tests, despite the former's thousand runs at an average of forty.

Last survivor of Warwick Armstrong's Australians was H. L. ('Stork') Hendry, all-rounder and prehensile slip fielder, who died in 1988.

The MCC went about the appointment of test selectors in a pretty amateurish manner, picking H. K. Foster, John Daniell and Reggie Spooner for the task. They didn't pick A. C. MacLaren.

H. K. Foster, eldest of the seven Worcestershire Fosters, a brother of 'Tip' Foster who had made 287 in his test match debut against Australia, was a bluff all-round games player: a county cricketer, he was not in test match class. John Daniell was captain of Somerset. He was a 'character', educated at Clifton and Cambridge, he had played for England at rugby football. He had an outlandish taste in headgear, and got away with using blue language at MCC meetings at Lord's. Owing to his Somerset commitments he would have little chance to see matches in which his county was not engaged. He did in fact miss three of the five tests. Reggie

* Ronald Mason, *Warwick Armstrong's Australians* (Epworth).

Spooner, of Lancashire, another rugby international, had played for England in ten test matches. We cannot hold the selectors entirely responsible for the results they obtained, or failed to obtain. England had suffered even more grievously than Australia in the 1914–1918 war, whilst injury and illness virtually deprived us of the services of Jack Hobbs and Jack Hearne; however, the selectors' tendency to vary between insouciance and panic was more than a little puzzling.

It would be an understatement to say that the advent of Warwick Armstrong and his merry men caused quite a problem. They were travelling to Tilbury on the same boat as the English touring side they had so heavily defeated. New players would have to be given a chance, and, if possible, a new captain. J. W. H. T. Douglas had done wonders as Warner's replacement in 1911–12, but had been on the wrong end of a whitewash in the tour just completed. P. G. H. Fender, the Surrey captain, would very possibly have been the man for the job, but it was said that Lord Harris, who seemed at times to have had more say than the test selectors, disapproved of him. Amazingly, C. B. Fry, who twenty years before had scored six centuries in succession, was asked to captain England. Fry, like Macbeth, was not without ambition, but he had the common sense to realize that, in his fiftieth year, he was unlikely to be able to cope with the flyers of Gregory and McDonald: he sent a temporizing answer. Spooner, a selector, and a mere forty, became a possibility; in the end, Douglas was given another chance.

The Australians came down like wolves on the fold. Their first match was against Leicestershire, and with the first ball of the tour, Gregory had Whitehead caught at the wicket; the Australians won devastatingly by an innings and 154 runs.

Their second game, against Lionel Robinson's XI, on a club pitch at Attleborough, Norfolk, was something of a sensation. Perhaps the tourists were affected by a change to cold wet weather; in the event Robinson's XI had much the better of a drawn game. The match was marred by a disaster, so far as English hopes for the series were concerned: J. B. Hobbs, England's premier batsman, 85 not out and batting superbly, strained his thigh so badly that he played no more until the end of June – and then he developed appendicitis! The Australians played six further matches in the next three weeks – four victories and two draws – before the first test match, at Trent Bridge, where H. K. Foster remarked engagingly to a member of the Notts committee that he had never seen George Gunn bat. Gunn, who had not been selected, was arguably the best English batsman available at the time.

The first test match was over by the second afternoon. J. W. H. T. Douglas won the toss and elected to bat. Within half an hour the game was as good as lost, Knight, Tyldesley and Hendren falling to Gregory. Three wickets were down for 18. *Wisden's* makes the surprising statement that England had a piece of bad luck when Woolley was out to 'a marvellous catch by Hendry at second slip'. Was it unusual for Australia to have excellent slip fielders? Gregory took 6 for 58 and England were out for 112. Australia replied with 232. England did little better in their second innings, and were all out for 147. D. J. Knight made 38 and Woolley batted an hour and a half for 34; he was evidently mesmerized by the accurate spin bowling of Armstrong, who took 0 for 33 in 27 overs. Sydney Pardon (*Wisden's* 1922) wrote that hitters like A. N. Hornby or C. I. Thornton, rather than be pinned down by Armstrong, would have hit him off his length or have perished in the attempt. However, Woolley, going in at No. 6, when four wickets had fallen cheaply, could hardly be blamed for his caution. McDonald, with 5 for 32, was the chief destroyer. When England were all out, Bardsley and Macartney knocked off the necessary runs in twenty minutes, Australia winning by 10 wickets.

Whether panic ensued or the selectors couldn't remember whom they had chosen for the first test, it is difficult to say. At any rate, six changes were made for the second test. Among those who were dropped were Rhodes, who, apart from his considerable powers as a batsman, was probably the best slow bowler in the world, and Holmes, who was always an excellent slip fielder, and who had made a highly competent and perky 34 in England's first innings. Dipper, who replaced him, had claims as a batsman, but even in county cricket had to be hidden in the field. Holmes went on to score fifteen hundred runs during the season for an average of forty, besides snapping up some splendid catches. Rhodes, like Holmes, was not chosen again during the series. He had taken 2 for 33 (Pellew and Andrews) in 13 overs during the first innings. Wilfred Rhodes's test appearances for England, incidentally, spanned thirty years. He had taken 7 for 17 against the Australians in the Edgbaston test of 1902. In the final test in 1926 he was to play no small part in England's regaining the Ashes.

Of the replacements, the two most surprising were C. B. Fry and A. J. Evans. Fry was now nearly fifty. He played half a dozen matches for Hampshire in 1921 with an average of 27: he cried off from the test match at the last moment as he was not satisfied with his form. A. J. Evans was a Wykehamist with a fine war record. He wrote an excellent book, *The Escaping Club*, in connexion with his adventures. He had played county cricket before the war; in 1921 he had two games for Kent and scored a hundred against Northants. A fortnight before the first test he played for the MCC against the tourists and scored 69; it was presumably on the strength of this that he was chosen to play against Gregory and McDonald at their fastest.

Also chosen for this test was Nigel Haig, a versatile all-rounder who could do felicitous things to the seam of a cricket ball with the aid of a penny as he walked back to his bowling mark. The fact that he was a nephew of Lord Harris would have been no disadvantage. George Gunn was again omitted, as he was throughout the series.

England won the toss in the second test, again Douglas elected to bat, and again the match was lost in the first half-hour; Knight, Dipper and Hendren were out for 7, 11 and 0 respectively. Woolley and Douglas did their best to repair the damage, and England scored 187. Woolley scored 95 and 93 in this match: those who saw his two innings were fortunate indeed. Australia made 342, and England, in the second innings, 283. Gregory was off form in the first innings, but Arthur Mailey had come in for H. L. Collins, who had broken a thumb, and took 4 for 55. Tennyson made an ebullient 74 not out in the second innings and Dipper a painstaking 40; the 130 Australia required to win was achieved at rather more than four an over for the loss of a couple of wickets. Evans scored 4 in the first innings, and batted courageously for 14 in the second. Spectators who had seen this match, and had seen Cambridge against the Australians a few days before, were in no doubt that the university team were far better than England as a fielding side.

So to the third test: both sides batted for exactly the same number of overs (93.1) in the first innings, but Australia scored 407 and England 259. Australia this time won by 219 runs. In doing so they had retained the Ashes and won eight consecutive test matches.

England had cruel luck. Hobbs's stomach illness was at last diagnosed, none too early, as appendicitis, and Tennyson, who had taken over the captaincy from Douglas – the latter was still in the side – split the webbing of his hand in trying to stop a snorting drive from Macartney and scored 36 and 63, hitting bravely and virtually one-handed.

In the fourth test, at Old Trafford, England's fortunes began to improve. The first day was lost to rain. On the second day, England scored 341 for 4, when Tennyson declared, forty minutes before the close of play.

What ensued was pure farce. Armstrong, primed by Carter, pointed out to Tennyson that he couldn't declare. What the English captain had forgotten – if, indeed, it had ever occurred to him – was that, as the first day's play had been cancelled, the match had become a two-day match, and that therefore any declaration should have taken place at least an hour and forty minutes before the close of play.

Lionel Tennyson was grandson of a poet laureate, a valiant cavalier of cricketers, an Old Etonian and a distinguished anti-teetotaller; he was just the man to captain England when the going was tricky. To expect him to have read the laws of cricket as well was never really on.

After twenty minutes of chaos and confusion, profuse apologies were offered to Armstrong, and Australia took the field again, with Tyldesley and Fender the not out batsmen. The crowd, deciding that Armstrong was the cause of all the delay, greeted him with jeers and boos. Armstrong replied by sitting down on the pitch, a not infrequent response for cricketers to take following unruly crowd behaviour. Tennyson and one of the umpires then went out and explained to the crowd what had happened, and the game proceeded. This time it was Armstrong who broke one of the laws of cricket; he bowled the next over, and not until it was completed did anyone realize that he had bowled two overs in succession. The umpires, Street and Moss, had permitted an eccentricity that would not have been tolerated in the most rustic of village games.

Tennyson declared on the Tuesday morning, with England 362 for 4. Collins played a skilful defensive innings of 40 in four hours and fifty minutes, removing all danger of defeat, and Australia were all out for 175 in 116.4 overs. Parkin took 5 for 38; Charlie Parker, who took 2 for 32 in 28 overs, never played for England again. England played out time in the final forty minutes.

England further recovered self-respect in the fifth test, declaring at 403 for 8 in a match ruined by rain on the Saturday. Perhaps if Woolley had held on to that red-hot snick from Macartney – but cricket is a game of ifs. As it was, Mead made a massive 182 not out and Tennyson a jovial half century. Australia scored 389 at nearly four an over – Andrews 94, Taylor 75, Macartney 61. This left half a day's pointless play, England scoring 244 for 2, largely against Australia's picnic bowlers.

With the fifth test match over midway through August, it seemed certain that the Australians would be the first touring side to go through a season undefeated. At the tail end of August the sensation of the season took place.

All through the summer of 1921 A. C. MacLaren had been saying that it would be possible to find a team to beat the Australians. It had been arranged before the season began that he himself, now nearly fifty, would captain an England XI against the visitors. This was the team: G. N. Foster, G. A. Faulkner, Gilbert Ashton, Hubert Ashton, A. P. F. Chapman, Claude Ashton, Michael Falcon, G. E. C. Wood, C. H. Gibson, W. Brearley, and himself. They were all amateurs. MacLaren had captained England v Australia in three series at the turn of the century, Walter Brearley had played in four test matches for England, the last in 1912; G. A. Faulkner, one of the greatest South African all-rounders, had played in twenty-five test matches. Of the others, five were in the current Cambridge University side, Michael Falcon was a player of test match calibre who played for his native Norfolk, G. E. C. Wood and G. N. Foster played a bit for Kent, but none of the side was playing regular first-class county cricket.

The match against MacLaren's team was played on 27, 29 and 30 August in fine weather. MacLaren won the toss and elected to bat. His England XI were all out in 20 overs for 43. The young A. P. F. Chapman – he was not yet twenty-one – was the only batsman to offer any resistance, showing considerable verve in a cameo innings of 16. The Australians, who, apart from Ryder for Taylor, had their full test side, played perhaps a little carelessly against excellent bowlers that they hadn't come up against before, Michael Falcon taking 6 for 67 and Aubrey Faulkner 4 for 50, in a score of 174. However, with a lead of 131, they shouldn't have worried, and probably didn't – at least, not at first. MacLaren's side had scored 60 for 4 in their second innings when Faulkner and Hubert Ashton came together. Had either of them been out within the next ten minutes, MacLaren's men would almost certainly have been decisively defeated and the match quickly forgotten. In the event, they stayed together for two and a half hours, and the match became one of the immortal games of cricket.

Aubrey Faulkner, nearly forty, thicker set than in his halcyon days, and rather out of practice, recaptured magically the aggressive stroke play of his early years. Hubert Ashton was twenty-two. He had made a name for himself at Winchester as a batsman, had served in the Royal Artillery in 1917–18, winning the Military Cross. Demobilized in 1919, he had gone to Cambridge, getting into the eleven as a freshman in 1920, and had been top of the batting averages. Next year he was to captain Cambridge in succession to his brother Gilbert.

The partnership between Faulkner and Hubert Ashton produced 154 runs before Ashton's beautifully fluent innings came to an end. Faulkner continued, with majestic fury, until he eventually mistimed Armstrong, and was out for 153, the innings closing for 326, with the Australians needing 196 to win. In the last three-quarters of an hour of the second day the Australians scored 21 for 1, Collins being caught in the slips.

Next morning, Armstrong looked on with equanimity as Bardsley and Carter, the night watchman, saw the fifty up very quickly. Walter Brearley, demon bowler of pre-war days, had ricked a muscle, and was unable to bowl. Then Gibson came into his own. He had been hit about in the first innings and couldn't find a length at the start of the second. He was now to produce the best bowling feat of his life.

> He was a tall loose-shouldered youth with the whippy nagging swing and length . . . and he had occasional command of a brute of a ball which swung in to the leg stump and came back sharply to hit the off – a kind of Barnes special that if rightly pitched could bowl any batsman in the world, in or out of form.*

He bowled one of these at Bardsley, and then Carter was caught in the slips off a rising ball from Falcon.

Then came the ball that decided the issue of the match; it was Falcon who bowled it. Macartney, frustrated at the restrictions resulting from MacLaren's astutely placed field – A. P. F. Chapman and the three Ashton brothers, with the advantage of youth and obsessive fielding practice, were much better fielders than the majority of the thirty players who had represented England in the five test matches – tried one of his unorthodox aggressive slashes at a straight ball, hitting deliberately across, but he did not allow for it keeping low: he was bowled, and the score was 73 for 4.

At lunch the Australians were 106 for 5. Ryder and Andrews took the score along comfortably after lunch until Gibson deceived Ryder into mistiming a drive, to be caught at extra cover by Gilbert, one of the ubiquitous Ashton trio, and – as Ronald Mason would say – the world was only a few minutes older when Gregory was out lbw. Andrews was next to go, bowled by a spinning, whirling,

---

* Ronald Mason, *Warwick Armstrong's Australians*.

malevolent ball from Faulkner. Armstrong, at the other end, must have realized that the end was near. He himself was lbw to Faulkner; Mailey joined McDonald with 42 runs still wanted. Thirteen of these had been scored when Gibson bowled Mailey, the Australians were all out for 167, and MacLaren's XI had won by 28 runs. Armstrong showed up to great advantage at the end of the game when he addressed the excited Eastbourne crowd and, although confessing himself a disappointed man, paid generous tribute to MacLaren and his eleven. After this famous victory the Australians' defeat by 33 runs at the hand of C. I. Thornton's XI was almost an anti-climax.

It has been said that Armstrong chose the England teams, by letting players do well in other games and then making mincemeat of them in test matches. That is rather a doubtful assertion. What there is no doubt about is the vacillation of the selectors, who didn't give much in the way of second chances, even to some of the greatest players. These were the teams in the five test matches together with the number of test matches they played in the series:

1st TEST	2nd TEST	3rd TEST
D. J. Knight (2)	D. J. Knight	H. T. W. Hardinge (1)
P. Holmes (1)	A. C. Dipper (1)	F. E. Woolley
E. Tyldesley (3)	F. E. Woolley	J. W. Hearne (1)
E. Hendren (2)	E. Hendren	A. Ducat (1)
J. W. H. T. Douglas (5)	J. W. H. T. Douglas	J. W. H. T. Douglas
F. E. Woolley (5)	A. J. Evans (1)	V. W. C. Jupp
V. W. C. Jupp (2)	L. H. Tennyson (4)	G. Brown (3)
W. Rhodes (1)	N. Haig (1)	J. C. White (1)
H. Strudwick (2)	C. H. Parkin (4)	L. H. Tennyson
H. Howell (1)	H. Strudwick	C. H. Parkin
L. Richmond (1)	F. J. Durston (1)	J. B. Hobbs (1)

4th TEST	5th TEST
A. C. Russell (2)	A. C. Russell
G. Brown	G. Brown
F. E. Woolley	E. Tyldesley
C. P. Mead (2)	F. E. Woolley
E. Tyldesley	C. P. Mead
P. G. H. Fender (2)	A. Sandham (1)
C. Hallows (1)	L. H. Tennyson
C. H. Parkin	P. G. H. Fender
C. W. Parker (1)	J. W. Hitch (1)
L. H. Tennyson	J. W. H. T. Douglas
J. W. H. T. Douglas	C. H. Parkin

With thirty-eight matches to play, and long journeys to be made by London, Midland and Scottish and Great Western Railways, the Australians didn't have much time for socializing. If they finished a game early they would be packed off to some stately home or other where the lady of the manor would show them her rose garden. Once, at the end of a match against Warwickshire, they were taken to Stratford-upon-Avon to meet Marie Corelli, the fashionable and controversial lady novelist, who was also a cricket fan.

Away from the serious business of first-class cricket, the day they enjoyed most was probably the carefree Sunday, 21 August, midway through the Gloucestershire match at Cheltenham, when they were driven over to Stanway, where J. M. Barrie had rented the delightful house that belonged to his secretary, Cynthia Asquith.

It is an understatement to say that the diminutive J. M. Barrie was a cricket enthusiast: he was mad on the game, and was himself a good spin bowler. He loved cricket whether on the village green or in the test match arena. Once, when asked if he had ever tossed up flats or rounds at cricket, he replied 'Is there any other way?'

Having arrived betimes at Stanway, the Australians gave a dazzling display on the village cricket ground for the benefit of a string of excited children, then Mailey bowled googlies to Cynthia Asquith's small son, Gregory keeping wicket. After that they sat down to a Homeric lunch; E. V. Lucas, a member of the house party, whose knowledge of cricket and cricketers was encyclopaedic, arranged the seating.

'Barrie,' wrote Cynthia Asquith, ' "tremendously wee", sat beside the huge, amiable, invincible Armstrong; I, to the dazzled envy of my small son, between Collins and Gregory, each of whom profanely told me that he preferred lawn tennis to cricket!'*

Barrie always got on very well with the Australians. In a speech of welcome to them in 1926, he said that Gregory, Hendry and Mailey in the slips with their arms extended looked as if they were simultaneously proposing to the same lady.

Armstrong's men were, I believe, the greatest Australian touring side ever to visit this country. Everywhere they went the crowds flocked to see them. As Lionel Tennyson's grandfather wrote of earlier and less fortunate combatants: 'When shall their glory fade?' Let A. C. MacLaren have the last word:

> No cleaner cricketing side ever played anywhere . . . a nicer lot of men never came over, and we are heartily sorry to say good-bye.

* Cynthia Asquith, *Portrait of Barrie* (Barrie).

CHAPTER 4

Bodyline

The MCC tour of Australia in 1932–33 was the famous or infamous 'bodyline' tour, when Jardine's tactics won the Ashes, and nearly lost a dominion. It had at one time seemed likely, in connexion with letters written to him by Lord Hawke and Lord Harris, that my father would go as manager of the MCC team. This did not eventuate, but it has been challenging to wonder whether, had he gone, the course of cricket might have run a little more smoothly during that tour.

The story of the MCC 'bodyline' tour of Australia is one of high drama, not only because of the matches that took place, but also because of the way it affected the destiny of several of those who had taken part in the tour. The scores are set down in *Wisden's Cricketers' Almanack* for 1934; what we know of the aftermath of these conflicts evokes thoughts of Somerset Maugham at his most imaginative.

It was von Clausewitz who said 'War is an extension of politics by other means.' Douglas Jardine, England's captain during this series, had more than a little of von Clausewitz in his nature. His employment of what became known as bodyline bowling was a complete success – or a complete disaster, according to which way you look at it.

Warwick Armstrong's Australians had demolished England. In 1924–25 Arthur Gilligan's men fought bravely, but lost the series. In 1926 England won the Ashes for the first time for fifteen years, and retained them in 1928–29. However, it was in this series that a self-taught genius from Bowral astounded the cricketing world. His name was Donald Bradman. In 1930 he came over to England, scored runs galore, was nicknamed 'The Unbowlable', and

Australia regained the Ashes. How to contain Bradman was the problem that would face England's captain in the 1932–33 tour of Australia. The choice of captain was not an easy one. A. P. F. Chapman would have been favourite if his form had been better. R. E. S. Wyatt was a possibility. In the event the prize went to D. R. Jardine.

There were people at Lord's who felt misgivings at his appointment; the MCC touring captain was expected to act as ambassador as well as cricketer. In previous tours Gilligan and Chapman had filled the bill admirably; Jardine was already known in some quarters for his hatred of Australians – they had roughed him up verbally in 1928–29. They disliked his Harlequin cap and his general abrasiveness, several of his acquaintance feared the worst.

Jardine had had little experience of captaincy when he was chosen in 1931 to skipper England in the first test against New Zealand at Lord's. He did reasonably well and the invitation was extended to the other two tests. In 1932 he was chosen to captain England in the only test against India at Lord's. In this match he ordered Voce and Bowes to bowl full tosses from the pavilion end, where at that time there was no sightscreen. In this match also he had shown himself unquestionably as one of England's best batsmen, when he stemmed a collapse with a confident 79.

His abrasive manner, the full tosses at Lord's, his regard for the Australians as the working class who had escaped, caused the more old-fashioned among those in authority at Lord's to have grave doubts as to his suitability for the captaincy in Australia. It was 'Plum' Warner who pushed the decision through. 'Plum' Warner, Oxford, Middlesex and England, knew how to pull the strings, and in mid-July 1932 it was announced that Jardine would captain the MCC touring team.

When the full side was announced some weeks later P. F. Warner had been chosen as tour manager, largely to take care of the social side, and R. C. N. Palairet was selected as his assistant. The men chosen to tour Australia were:

47

D. R. Jardine (Surrey)
(captain)
R. E. S. Wyatt
(Warwickshire) (vice-
captain)
G. O. Allen (Middlesex)
F. R. Brown (Surrey)
The Nawab of Pataudi
(Worcestershire)
W. R. Hammond
(Gloucestershire)
H. Sutcliffe (Yorkshire)

M. Leyland (Yorkshire)
H. Verity (Yorkshire)
E. Paynter (Lancashire)
G. Duckworth (Lancashire)
L. E. G. Ames (Kent)
T. B. Mitchell (Derbyshire)
H. Larwood
(Nottinghamshire)
W. Voce (Nottinghamshire)
M. W. Tate (Sussex)
W. E. Bowes (Yorkshire)

Bowes was selected five days before the ship sailed.

Jardine could not be accused of indecisiveness on being appointed captain. According to his daughter, watching a film of Bradman batting in a test match, stepping away to make his stroke, evoked from Jardine the triumphant shout 'He's yellow!' Therefore, presumably, attack him with intimidatory bowling. But is it surprising that Bradman, at that time the greatest batsman in the world, should step away from a fast ball, the better to drive it through the covers?

It is typical of Jardine's meticulousness that he instructed all the touring side to have their teeth checked thoroughly before leaving England: Larwood, in particular, needed considerable attention from his dentist, as a result of which, according to E. H. D. Sewell among others, he became faster than he had ever been before.

In the late summer of 1932 Jardine made several visits to the London flat of F. R. Foster, whose brief but glittering cricket career lasted from 1908 to 1914, and included devastating bowling against the Australians in 1911–12. Foster bowled left-hand, fast-medium to a legside field, but he didn't use intimidatory tactics: Jardine's main interest in visiting him was to discuss leg theory and field placing.

The *Orontes* set sail and Jardine was soon holding informal discussions with his amateurs. The forthcoming test series, so far as Jardine was concerned, could be summarized under the title

48

'Operation Hatred', and he explained that the side would act accordingly. None of the other amateurs to whom he explained his ideas had ever thought of playing cricket like that. To them cricket was a game, even at international level. G. O. Allen, an Old Etonian who was born in Australia, said that he didn't see the tour in terms of hatred and wasn't going to play that way. Wyatt, as vice-captain, was in a difficult position. He liked Jardine very much as a person, but referring to the tour many years later he emphasized the point that in cricket you are playing the game not only against but also with your opponents. Pataudi and Freddie Brown were much too charismatic to entertain the hatred motive. Pataudi made his attitude more than clear in the second test, and, despite having made a century in the first, was not selected for the next three. Brown didn't play in any of the tests.

When the tourists landed at Fremantle 'Plum' Warner, who excelled at making speeches about the spirit of the game, did so at the first opportunity. 'The very word "cricket",' he said in his first interview with the Australian press, 'has become a synonym for all that is true and honest. To say "that is not cricket" implies something not in keeping with the best ideals.'

For the next five months he was to see the steady development of bodyline bowling.

Perhaps more than the intimidatory bowling – under instructions – of Harold Larwood, the cause of Australia's reaction was the actual personality of Jardine. In this attitude of non-fraternization with the enemy he was a dozen years ahead of Montgomery. He regarded and treated Australians with icy contempt. He either could not or would not accept their ribald comments in good part. Barracking, at first good-natured, and then unfriendly, he simply ignored.

The spectators called him Sardine, and when he was out called out gleefully 'Now you can get back into your tin'; but their hostility towards him increased almost daily. He brought it on himself. If you were prepared to be friendly, there was no problem. Pataudi, in the long field, was chipped by the spectators, 'Do we have to call you Your Highness?'

'Just Pat to you boys,' came the instant reply. That was good enough. Leyland in the outfield was another who gave as good as he got; his laconic Yorkshire humour went down well. But friendly repartee on any level was not for Jardine.

In the first six matches of the tour, largely against state sides, Jardine assiduously nursed Larwood, who only played in three of the matches, bowling a total of 29 eight-ball overs.

So to the first test match at Sydney. Bradman did not play, being unfit. Australia batted first and made 360 in their first innings. Larwood, who was 5 feet 7 and weighed 10 stone, took 5 for 96 in 31 eight-ball overs. McCabe made 187 not out, scoring off Larwood's bowling with great enterprise and daring. England replied with 524, Sutcliffe making 194, Hammond and Pataudi also scored centuries, but the England batting was painfully slow. Australia made a weak response in their second innings, Larwood taking 5 for 28 this time, and England won by 10 wickets.

Three more games, including two against Tasmania, followed before the second test started at Melbourne on 30 December. Bradman, recovered, was able to play. Humiliatingly out first ball in the first innings, he had much to do with Australia's eventual victory. A crowd of 70,000 saw him make 103 not out in Australia's second innings of 191. England, set 251 to win, lost by 111 runs, Bill O'Reilly bowling superbly.

Fingleton had batted with great courage and patience for four hours during Australia's first innings. He records an interesting incident that took place while he was at the non-striker's end. When a ball from Larwood hit Woodfull over the heart, Jardine's reaction was to call to Pataudi to go from the off to the on-side. Pataudi ignored the call.

'I see that His Highness is a conscientious objector,' observed Jardine. 'You go across, then, Hedley,' he said to Verity. That was Pataudi's last test of the tour.

And what about P. F. Warner?

'The truth was,' wrote Jack Fingleton, 'that Warner did not know which way to turn in Australia. His cricket ideals and his standing crumbled and thrashed around his unhappy ears. As well as any man in Australia he knew what effect the English tactics were having on the game and the individuals playing it, and he knew also that the repercussions would be prolonged and intensely bitter.'*

Warner probably made a few placatory attempts to get Jardine to tone down his tactics; whatever advice he did give was ignored.

It was in the third test match, the most unpleasant test match in the history of the game, that affairs reached boiling point. 'The Battle of Adelaide', as it became known in Australia, took place on 13, 14, 16, 17, 18 and 19 January 1933, and resulted in a win for England by 338 runs.

It is indicative of Jardine's mounting unpopularity that, in the primly Victorian city of Adelaide of all places, he was jeered at when the team were at the nets the day before the match, and insisted that people be excluded from the ground while the English side were practising.

Jardine won the toss and England batted first, Jardine himself opening the innings with Sutcliffe this time. To the spectators' delight he was clean bowled by Wall for 3. Worse was to follow for England: Sutcliffe, Hammond and Ames were soon out and 4 wickets were down for 30. Then came the stand that turned the game, Leyland and Wyatt adding 156, and England were eventually all out for 344.

Australia went in to bat on the Saturday afternoon, Larwood bowling at a tremendous pace, but to an orthodox off-side field with three slips. Woodfull, misjudging the bounce, ducked, and was hit over the heart by the last ball of Larwood's second over. There was a noisy demonstration from the Adelaide crowd while Woodfull was recovering. Jardine's reaction to the incident, for whatever reason, was to say 'Well bowled, Harold.'

Allen bowled an over at the other end, and Larwood embarked on his third over. It was then that Jardine set the series well and truly alight. As Larwood started on his run up to the wicket Jardine stopped him and, to Larwood's surprise, altered the field, removing the three slips and packing a close on-side field. This, when

* Jack Fingleton, *Cricket Crisis* (Cassell).

Woodfull was still shaken from the last ball of Larwood's previous over. The crowd's fury now reached boiling point; both of the umpires and several of the fieldsmen thought that at any moment the crowd would come over the fence. Fortunately for Jardine's wellbeing, they didn't.

Shortly afterwards, Woodfull was out, off Allen's bowling; Warner and Palairet didn't improve matters when they went into the Australians' dressing-room to offer their sympathy. William Maldon Woodfull was lying on a massage table. A Master of Arts of Melbourne University, gentle, quiet and dignified, he was a man of few words. Those that he spoke to P. F. Warner on this occasion will be remembered as long as cricket is played:

'There are two teams out there on the oval,' said Woodfull. 'One is playing cricket, the other is not. This game is too good to be spoilt. It is time some people got out of it.' Fingleton recorded that words failed the usually ready Warner, and with Palairet, he strode embarrassed from the room.

At the close of the second day's play, Australia had scored 52 for 4; Larwood had claimed the important scalps of Bradman and McCabe. On the third day Ponsford, wearing a towel round his chest, played Larwood's bowling in splendid style; he and Richardson put on 80 runs for the fifth wicket; Oldfield stayed in for two hours, but his innings was cut short when he was hit on the head by a ball from Larwood. Like Woodfull, he had misjudged what he took to be a rising ball and, typically, he blamed himself for the injury. But the crowd was already angry and when Oldfield had to be assisted off the field pandemonium reigned.

So far as the record is concerned, England won on the sixth day (19 January) by 338 runs.

It was on 18 January that the battle of the cables began, and the Australian Board of Control put the cat among the pigeons with the following broadside at the MCC:

> Body-line bowling has assumed such proportions as to menace the best interests of the game, making protection of the body by the batsmen the main consideration.

This is causing intensely bitter feeling between the players as well as injury. In our opinion it is unsportsmanlike. Unless stopped at once, it is likely to upset the friendly relations existing between Australia and England.

This was an explosive cable. For a few days there was an awful and ominous silence. On 23 January the MCC replied:

We, Marylebone Cricket Club, deplore your cable. We deprecate your opinion that there has been unsportsmanlike play. We have fullest confidence in captain, team and managers and are convinced that they would do nothing to infringe the Laws of Cricket or the spirit of the game. We have no evidence that our confidence has been misplaced. Much as we regret accidents to Woodfull and Oldfield, we understand that in neither case was the bowler to blame. If the Australian Board of Control wish to propose a new Law or Rule, it shall have our careful consideration in due course.

We hope that the situation is not now as serious as your cable would seem to indicate, but if it is such as to jeopardize the good relations between English and Australian cricketers and you consider it desirable to cancel remainder of programme we would consent but with great reluctance.

In tennis terms this was a good return of service that would put the ball in Australia's court. The MCC had a valid point in saying that with regard to the accidents to Woodfull and Oldfield, in neither case was the bowler to blame. They made no reference to the fact that several good judges of the game had said that if this type of bowling was allowed to continue, someone would be killed. But Jack Fingleton felt that it was the conditional offer to call off the series that sent the Australian Board scurrying to its foxholes: the series was making good money. The second Australian cable was conciliatory and the third, sent just before the fourth test, stated that the sportsmanship of the English team was not in question – a complete reversal of what was asserted in their first cable.

The series went ahead to its miserable end. There was little

fraternization. English close-in fieldsmen no longer showed con-
cern when an Australian batsman was hit, realizing that in the
circumstances such behaviour would be sheer hypocrisy. Of course,
it didn't make them feel any better. The Australian Board of
Control were not the only people who felt that Jardine's tactics were
spoiling the game of cricket.

Gubby Allen, Australian born, who had lived most of his life in
England, expressed his feelings during the tour in letters to his
parents: 'Douglas changes his mind every five minutes ... he is
difficult and whines away if he doesn't get everything he wants ...
someone will have the very hell of a row with him ... sometimes I
feel I should like to kill him.'

Of bodyline bowling he wrote 'I just hate it and will not do it', and
he had a low opinion of Larwood and Voce for their compliance
with their captain's wishes.

Australia (without Oldfield) started off well enough in the fourth
test match, at Brisbane, scoring 340 in their first innings. England
managed a lead of 16. Australia could only score 175 in their
second innings, and England, set 160 to win, were 107 for 2 at the
end of the fifth day – these were the days of timeless tests. Jardine,
again opening the innings with Sutcliffe, was taking no chances. He
made 24 in two hours and ten minutes, at one time playing eighty-
two deliveries without adding to his score.

On the last day, 16 February, flags all round the ground were set
at half mast, owing to the death of the brilliant Australian batsman,
Archie Jackson, at the age of twenty-three. Four years earlier, he
had made 164 on his test match debut at Adelaide against England.
While lying in hospital, not long before his death, he was married.

The necessary runs were scored for the loss of two more wickets,
and England had won the Ashes. It was typical of Woodfull that he
was the first person to go into the England dressing-room and
congratulate Jardine.

The final test started a week later at Sydney. Jardine still
employed bodyline tactics. 'We've got the bastards down there, and
we'll keep them there,' was his comment. Australia made 435 in
their first innings, England 454. Larwood, sent in No. 4 as a

nightwatchman, made 98 in two and a quarter hours, actually outshining Hammond when the two were together. When he was out he received a tremendous ovation from the crowd. It was also noticed that when Oldfield – now fit to play – batted, Larwood always bowled a full length to him. It was not generally known that when Oldfield was injured in the third test, Jardine had sent a telegram of sympathy to the Australian's wife.

Larwood damaged his foot when bowling in the final test – probably a cumulative effect: his body pivoted on his left leg when pounded down into the ground. As a result of this injury he took no part in the remaining five matches of the tour (in New Zealand), and was never really the same again as a bowler.

It was a famous victory. After Adelaide, rather than after Blenheim, what good came of it at last? Jardine had succeeded in his quest; but at what a cost.* Bodyline developed because of Jardine's obsession about containing Bradman at all costs. But Bradman missed the first test through illness, in the second he scored a century against bodyline bowling; he finished the series top of the Australian batting averages and with a higher average than Sutcliffe, Hammond, Wyatt, Pataudi and Leyland, who didn't have Larwood to contend with.

Were Jardine's tactics necessary, even from his own point of view? Warwick Armstrong and E. H. D. Sewell, who both knew a thing or two about cricket, considered that England were the better team anyway and would have won just as easily if Larwood had bowled to an orthodox field with three slips.

The series was full of contradictions. When, in the third test, Woodfull was hit over the heart and Oldfield on the head, in neither case were the balls bodyline deliveries. What provoked the crowd's full fury was Jardine's setting an on-side field when Woodfull was already shaken by the blow. An interesting postscript to the whole

---

* Jardine was not as insouciant as he pretended. After the bodyline tour he stayed in New Zealand with relatives of A. P. F. Chapman, 'and evinced symptoms of acute paranoia – i.e. fear of assassination, insisting the back door be kept open for a quick get away, and a phobia about Australian flies' (Allen Synge, letter to the author, 23 October 1992).

story is that Larwood did not bowl bodyline to the Australian tail-enders: no one below No. 7 had to cope with it.

The tourists back in England, W. M. Findlay, the MCC secretary, offered his sympathy to Gubby Allen on the difficult time he had endured. Allen then explained to Findlay something of what the bodyline tour had been like, and Warner gave his own evidence to an MCC subcommittee. Warner, who had found himself unable to control the Frankenstein's Monster which he had created, was now hoping that it would be destroyed, and that he would be able to return to his position of pre-eminence in the cricket world without having to face any further disturbing behaviour from anyone whose personality was stronger than his own.

Repercussions continued. The county captains made a gentleman's agreement not to employ bodyline tactics during the new season, Jardine, Jupp and Carr including themselves out.

Jardine wrote a book – Warner had pleaded with him not to – *The Quest for the Ashes*, 'marked by hatred of Australians of every description, and read like the report of a battle commander, or even an officer of the Black and Tans'.* Larwood, who only bowled 10 overs in 1933 and was presumably short of cash, was soon persuaded to give his name – foreword by D. R. Jardine – to a ghosted account of the Australian tour, and his statement that Bradman was frightened was promptly and understandably denied by the Australians.

The West Indies were touring England in 1933; the MCC, having endorsed Jardine's methods in Australia, could not now drop the pilot. In the second of the three test matches, at Old Trafford, the spectators had the opportunity to see what bodyline bowling – or what *Wisden's* preferred to call fast leg theory – was like. Jardine himself batted superbly against the flyers of Martindale and Constantine, scoring 127 in five hours, thus possibly proving himself the world's best batsman against a bodyline attack.

But English spectators had now had a good look at this kind of bowling, and even when euphemistically called fast leg theory, the

---

* Allen Synge, *Sins of Omission* (Pelham Books).

smell was no sweeter. It may have been just within the laws, but it definitely was not nice. This test match presaged the end of bodyline bowling as such, but there is little doubt that what is fair and what is not fair about fast bowling will be a problem for cricket legislators as long as the game is played.

The MCC toured India in 1933–34, and Jardine rode again – for the last time as an England test captain. He didn't have Larwood, Voce or Bowes with him, but he did have 'Nobby' Clark of Northants, and again he employed bodyline tactics. Jack Fingleton recounts that in the Calcutta test, Frank Tarrant (Australia and Middlesex) was umpiring. When Clark hit Dilawar Hussain, Tarrant told Jardine he would stop Clark from bowling. 'I will stop you from umpiring' was Jardine's retort, according to Tarrant; and he did!

In 1934 came the eighteenth Australian team to tour England. Woodfull again was to captain the Australians. Who was to skipper England? Jardine, who had stayed on in India, simplified the situation by announcing in an *Evening Standard* exclusive 'I have neither the intention or the desire to play cricket against Australia this summer.'

That simplified matters. R. E. S. Wyatt, Jardine's loyal lieutenant, was appointed captain. In the event, C. F. Walters captained the side in the first test, as Wyatt was injured. Larwood was also injured and England's speed attack devolved upon the twenty-three-year-old Cambridge blue, Kenneth Farnes. He took 10 wickets in the match, but this did not prevent Australia winning by 238 runs. It seemed likely that Larwood and probably Voce would be chosen for the second test at Lord's. However, in between the two tests Notts played Lancashire at Trent Bridge; Larwood and Voce under their rogue elephant captain A. W. Carr – he had been deprived of the England captaincy for the final test in 1926 – let rip, and injured several Lancashire batsmen, including George Duckworth, the England reserve wicketkeeper during the bodyline tour. T. A. Higson, Lancashire chairman, and also a test selector, protested vigorously to the MCC; this caused Larwood to bowl his ultimate bumper, saying, supported by Voce, that he had made up his mind not to play in any further tests against Australia, and saying of the MCC, 'They never admitted that my bowling is directed at the body . . . If I was right in Australia I must be right now.'

Wyatt had a thankless task as captain. It was not surprising after all the arguments, bad blood and eruptions during the season that England, although by no means disgraced, had to surrender the Ashes.

In 1936, the MCC tacitly admitted the folly of their ways in 1932 by choosing 'Gubby' Allen as captain of the 1936–37 MCC team to tour Australia. That he was Australian by birth of course told in his favour; added to this, his outgoing and friendly personality helped him possibly to excel even Gilligan and Chapman as an ambassador for English cricket. Allen and his opposing captain Bradman in fact played so much golf together that one feels it surprising that they had time to fit in any test matches. Socializing among members of the two teams became the rule rather than the exception, and a fascinating series ended in Australia coming from behind, after being two down, to retain the Ashes.

In the years following, relationships between the two sides have been, to say the least, good. To give a few random examples: Bradman was the first to shake hands with Hutton when the latter broke Bradman's individual test match record of 334; Grout refused to run out Compton in a test match when Compton had slipped and fallen; Cowdrey and Lawry read the lessons in a 1960s sportsman's service at St Ambrose Church, Edgbaston, midway through a test match. English cricketers, playing regularly for Australian states; Australian cricketers, including Border, a captain, playing for English counties – these factors have contributed to cementing many Anglo-Australian friendships.

Let us return to the main characters of the drama. 'Plum' Warner, who pressed for the selection of Jardine, and who explained so evocatively to the Australian press the meaning of fair play, withdrew, shattered, from the selection scene, but only for a couple of years. Frankenstein's Monster had spoilt his tour of Australia and the friendship was ended. However, he returned as chairman of the selectors from 1935 to 1938, during which time he was given a knighthood for services to cricket.

When Jardine died in 1958, P. F. Warner gave the impression of having switched back to his original assessment of the man he had once considered would make the ideal England captain; having evidently forgotten that he had once written to his wife 'DRJ is half mad. He must not captain England again. He is most ungracious, rude and suspects all.' In the issue for 1959, *Wisden* quotes Warner thus:

> A very fine captain, both on and off the field, and in the committee room he was also extremely good. If there ever was a cricket match between England and the rest of the world, and the fate of England depended upon the result, I would pick Jardine as England's captain every time.

De mortuis nil nisi bonum. P. F. Warner died in 1963.

The last years of Harold Larwood's cricket career showed bitterness and frustration. He gave his name to a belligerent account of the 1932–33 tour. In 1934 he said he had no wish to play against Australia again: was Jardine, a persuasive letter writer, encouraging him in this decision?

His bowling in the third test in 1933 marked not only the zenith of his career but also the beginning of his deterioration as a fast bowler. True, in 1936 he was top of the national averages, but in 1937 he was seeing bowlers with half his ability getting twice his own tally of victims. He himself took 68 wickets at 24 runs apiece, whilst Nichols, 'Lofty' Herman, Jim Smith, Wellard, Gover and Perks all took well over a hundred wickets at a cheaper rate. His frustration evidently showed in his behaviour; he was left out of the side in the last two matches 'owing to a breach of discipline'.

After the war, his cricketing days over, Larwood was running a general stores in Blackpool. What the future had in store for him almost passes the bounds of credibility. At one time the second most hated man in Australia, Larwood was to find his future in that country, thanks to the efforts, compassion and friendship of one of his opponents in the bodyline series, Jack Fingleton, and also John Arlott.

In the late 1940s, Fingleton, now not only a cricket writer but also a political journalist in Canberra, suggested that Australia should invite Larwood to revisit Australia. On 27 April 1950, this time travelling tourist class on the *Orontes* with his wife and five daughters, he sailed to Australia again.

Fingleton had persuaded the Australian prime minister, Ben Chifley, to have a word with Larwood. After a few minutes, as Michael Parkinson reports, Chifley came out of the room, shaking his head.

'Be blowed if I can understand a word he's saying,' said Chifley.

Fingleton then spent the next hour as interpreter, translating the Nottingham dialect into Australian, and vice versa. The upshot of all this was that Larwood settled in Australia with his family. He met Bradman rarely, but he and Bert Oldfield became great friends, and until the latter's death in 1984 the two often watched test matches together.

Larwood has made visits to see cricket in England. Leslie Deakins, former Warwickshire secretary, received Christmas cards from him regularly: these Christmas greetings would generally arrive in August.

'You are still the fastest of them all,' wrote Deakins.

After his marriage in 1934 Jardine played little cricket. There were a few broadcasts, a little part-time journalism. A qualified solicitor – he had read law at Oxford – he worked in the City as director of the Scottish Australian Company. During the Second World War he served with the Royal Berkshire Regiment in France, Belgium and India.

A writer to the *Observer* recalls that during the Second World War several people were billeted at his father's house. These included Jardine, who instructed his batman to go to the bathroom each morning to 'bag' the room and lock the door until Jardine himself arrived, with bath towel and shaving gear. This simplified the queueing system. Protests were disregarded. The correspondent once asked the great man to sign his autograph book; a request that was at first refused, but eventually granted: there were even instances of affability.

While on holiday in Southern Rhodesia in 1957 Jardine was taken ill with tick fever. He never really recovered, and died in Switzerland on 18 June 1958.

Sir Lawrence Jones wrote of him in an appreciation (*The Times*, 24 June 1958):

It is always a little disconcerting to the friends of great players of games to read obituary notices which confine themselves to the field of play. Jardine himself always regarded cricket as 'only a game'. He never wanted to talk about it. His main preoccupation in the years when I knew him both in a City office and in my own house, was Hindu philosophy. He had a speculative mind, intent on ethical and religious problems. Kindly and high-minded, he had in those years an antipathy to Christianity, to which he always referred as 'Rewards and Fairies', equal to Gibbon's. Nor, in his manner and bearing was there the faintest trace of the stern, aloof, decisive cricket captain., He was gentle and diffident in all his ways; slow and hesitant in speech, and, as it seemed to us, in thought; he chewed things over, and came to cautious and tentative conclusions, except when attacking 'Rewards and Fairies'. Then he could be trenchant, and we realized how this mild-mannered philosopher could have been the instigator of 'bodyline' bowling.

It must be seldom that a great cricketer can have played the game so seriously and yet, on retirement from it, have put cricket so firmly in its proper place.

I had seen Jardine batting in the 1920s on several occasions: he had rescued Surrey at Edgbaston in 1926 with a score of 167. His Harlequin cap fascinated me – there was a good deal of colour in amateur headgear in those days – but the last time I saw him on the cricket field was more or less by chance, at Amersham in 1956 on discovering that a team of mainly ex-England cricketers was playing against Amersham as part of the club's centenary celebrations. First I noticed the familiar figure of R. E. S. Wyatt, spotting him immediately by his run up to the wicket. Who was the umpire at the bowler's end? He was a man in his middle fifties, wearing, not a

Harlequin cap, but a trilby hat; he was contentedly smoking a pipe. I have seldom seen a man looking so completely at peace with the world. It was, of course, D. R. Jardine.

Harold Larwood has spent half of his life in Australia. In 1983, fifty years after the bodyline series, a strongly angled TV film was shown in Australia which put him on the receiving end of abusive telephone calls. He told an interviewer that there wasn't the ill feeling on the field that the film claimed; that he himself was good friends with most of the Australians, especially Fingleton, Oldfield, McCabe and O'Reilly.

Sixty years on he was awarded the MBE. Chuckling over the airwaves, his Nottingham accent unimpaired, he told the world that it was all a long time ago.

CHAPTER 5

Bradman's Last Tour

The 1948 Australian tour was in some ways a corollary of that of 1921. It took place three years after a world war with all its disasters, one of the least of which was that talented cricketers of both sides had passed their peak. Australia was perhaps the less affected and had assembled an immensely powerful team. Australia again was under the captaincy of a great cricketer who had been on the test match scene for twenty years. Once again, in an exciting though one-sided series, the Australians had the best of the argument, and this time they went through the season without defeat.

Bradman's Australians played thirty-four matches – compared with Armstrong's thirty-eight – of which they won twenty-five (seventeen by an innings) and drew nine; Bradman's men won four tests and drew one; Armstrong's won three and drew two. Bradman had the advantage of having seventeen men to call on; Armstrong, with four more matches to cope with, had only fifteen. These were the tourists of 1948:

D. G. Bradman (captain)	R. R. Lindwall
A. L. Hassett (vice-captain)	S. J. Loxton
D. Tallon	D. Ring
I. W. Johnson	A. R. Morris
C. L. McCool	W. A. Johnston
K. R. Miller	E. R. H. Toshack
S. G. Barnes	R. Saggers
R. N. Harvey	R. Hamence
W. A. Brown	

The Australians of 1948 will be remembered chiefly for the dominance of Bradman, and the devastating bowling of Lindwall and Miller. Bradman scored eleven centuries during the season, two of them in test matches – a splendid conclusion to an illustrious career. Lindwall had something of the technical perfection of E. A. McDonald, he was a protégé of W. J. O'Reilly, and there was more than a little of Larwood about him; the cavalier Miller, known to his team mates as Nugget, because of his gold tooth, could change the balance of a game, as bowler, batsman or fielder, in anything from a split second to a few brief minutes. Nor should we forget the fielding of Barnes, never more than a few feet from the bat in those unprotected days, at silly mid-on, as one of the factors that won the Ashes.

The Australian tour went off to an excellent start, thanks to the fluency of Bradman, on this occasion as an after-dinner speaker. The twenty-six-year-old Duke of Edinburgh, not long married to Princess Elizabeth, was president designate of the MCC, and attended a dinner in honour of the visitors. Bradman, replying for the Australians, declared that they didn't wish to appear ungenerous towards their hosts in not drawing attention to cricket talent that the English selectors might have overlooked, and said that he would like to bring the Duke of Edinburgh's talents as a cricketer to the notice of the selectors – to the obvious amusement and delight of Prince Philip. This was not an easy joke to bring off, but Bradman got it exactly right and his speech was greatly enjoyed.

The Australians opened their tour, against Worcestershire, in cheerless, cold and sometimes showery weather, on 28 April. Bradman scored his traditional century in the opening match, and they won by an innings, as they did in their second game, against Leicestershire, when Keith Miller, the *enfant terrible* of the tourists, scored a double century.

In their third match, against Yorkshire at Bradford, the Australians came nearer to defeat than in any other match of the tour, including tests. Wet weather, followed by sunshine, ensured a spinner's wicket, and 35 wickets fell in the game for 324 runs, in just over six hours of actual play. Yorkshire batted first, and were all out for 71 in 54.3 overs, Miller, bowling medium-pace off-breaks, taking 6 wickets for 42. The Australians, in their turn, were all out for 101 in 31 overs, Miller's 34 turned out to be the highest score of the match. Yorkshire were then all out for 89, Johnston, bowling slow-medium left arm, taking 6 for 18. The Australians now needed 60 to win: 6 wickets fell for 31, and Loxton, who was injured, could not bat. At this stage the nineteen-year-old Neil Harvey hit a chance to short leg. Had that catch been taken the score would effectively have been 31 for 8, with Tallon not out and only Lindwall and Johnston to go in. As it was, Harvey settled down, and won the match by hitting Smailes with a huge off-drive for 6.

Surrey came next. Bradman won the toss; the Australians went in and scored 632 at an average of four runs an over. Barnes, Bradman and Hassett all scored centuries; Bradman, driving magnificently, making 146 in two and three-quarter hours. This was another game that the Australians won easily by an innings, as they did their following match against Cambridge University.

Determined perhaps to stamp out memories of their nearness to defeat against Yorkshire, they then set about Essex at Southend, scoring 721 in a six-hour day. Brown, Bradman, Loxton and Saggers scored centuries. Bradman's 187 was made in two hours and five minutes; Loxton and Saggers put on 166 for the sixth wicket in sixty-five minutes. The Australians scraped home by an innings and 451 runs. Oxford University, their next victims, did a little better, losing by just an innings and 90 runs.

The tourists now took on an MCC eleven. This was the strongest opposition they had yet encountered, the side including Len Hutton, W. J. Edrich, Denis Compton, M. P. Donnelly, Norman Yardley, J. C. Laker and J. A. Young. Bradman's men made 552. Miller's 163 included three 6's and twenty 4's. Bradman failed, with a mere 98. Only Hutton, who made 52 and 64, could cope with the bowling of Toshack and Miller in the first innings, and McCool's leg-breaks and Johnston's off-spinners in the second, the Australians winning by an innings and 158 runs.

In the game against Lancashire, which was drawn owing to rain, a nineteen-year-old named Malcolm Hilton, playing in his third match for the county, captured Bradman's wicket – comprehensively – twice. In the first innings he had Bradman tickle a leg-break on to his stumps. Within a few hours he had become a national figure, pressmen thronged about him, wanting the story of his life. In the second innings he did better still. This is how W. J. O'Reilly described the incident:

> When the Australian captain walked to the wicket it seemed to be written all over him that he intended to make the boy pay dearly for his first innings' presumptuousness. His method of dealing with Hilton left nothing to doubt about this course. Bradman made a crude agricultural swipe of the rusty gate variety at a leg break which eluded the bat, hit his pads and was fielded in the slips; it missed his bat and his stumps by the proverbial coat of varnish. The breath-taking show finished with Bradman flat on his back, legs pointing towards heaven and arms in knots with the keeper quietly removing the bails.*

Bradman did not always find slow bowlers to his liking.

Next came a match against a Nottinghamshire side that fought bravely and avoided defeat. Notts made 179 in their first innings, Lindwall taking 6 for 14 in 15 overs. The Australians replied with 400; Notts, in their second innings, finished with 299 for 8, Hardstaff scored 107, the first century against the Australians.

Hampshire now proved to be the second county to give the tourists a fright. Hampshire, put in to bat on a drying pitch, did well to make 195, Johnston, bowling left-arm medium, taking 6 for 74. The Australians, 54 for 2 at the close of play, lost their remaining 8 wickets for 63 runs, and were 78 behind on first innings; C. J. Knott, an off-spinner, took 5 for 57, and J. Bailey, left-arm slow, 4 for 27: only Miller, who hit three successive 6's off Knott, showed any resistance. Hampshire were all out for 101 in their second innings, Miller and again Johnston doing the damage. The Australians needed 182 to win in a little less than three hours. Barnes was out without a run scored. However, Ian Johnson, sent in five minutes before lunch as a stop-gap, scored 74 (three 6's) very quickly, and the Australians triumphed by 8 wickets.

* W. J. O' Reilly, *Cricket Conquest* (Werner Laurie).

In their last match before the first test the Australians made mincemeat of Sussex, who were all out for 86 and 138, the visitors making 549 for 5, Morris, Bradman and Harvey scoring centuries. Lindwall, who took 6 for 34 and 5 for 25, worked up a tremendous pace.

The first test match, which commenced at Trent Bridge on 10 June, was the thirteenth game of the tour, but it was England that were the unlucky side. There was doubt to the last moment as to the composition of the England team, chiefly because the spinner D. V. P. Wright had lumbago. In the event he didn't play, the spinners chosen being J. A. Young, of Middlesex, and J. C. Laker, a York-shireman playing for Surrey who had just entered the test match scene. The England team, in batting order, was Hutton, Wash-brook, W. J. Edrich, Compton, Hardstaff, Barnett, Yardley, Evans, Laker, A. V. Bedser, Young. This was the Australian team: Barnes, Morris, Bradman, Miller, Brown, Hassett, I. W. Johnson, Tallon, Lindwall, W. A. Johnston, Toshack.

Yardley won the toss and chose to bat. There was only twenty minutes' play before lunch, but this was time enough for Miller to clean bowl Hutton for 3. As in the days of Gregory and McDonald in 1921, so, in 1948, two or three England wickets were liable to fall in the opening overs of the Australian speed attack.

A downpour during the interval made the ball skid through, and the light was never good. At tea England were 74 for 8, and the game, it seemed, already as good as lost, although midway through the innings Lindwall pulled a groin muscle, and, as it turned out, could not bowl again during the match. Thanks to a ninth-wicket stand of 89 by Laker and Bedser, England recovered after tea to the extent of making 165.

When Australia went in England opened with a wide by Edrich, and bowled much of the time to a defensive field: Young, for instance, bowling leg-breaks just outside the leg stump, took 1 for 79 in 60 overs, at one period sending down eleven maiden overs in succession. Even Bradman was subdued, his 138 taking four and three-quarter hours. Hassett took five hours and fifty minutes to score 137, none the less he hit a 6 and twenty 4's. The innings closed at 509, Yardley's defensive tactics keeping Australia's scoring rate down to two an over.

In England's second innings Australia again made a fine start, Miller getting Washbrook caught behind in his second over. Edrich was out at 39, and then on the Saturday evening Hutton and Compton scored fluently; this made Miller change from medium-paced off-breaks to really fast hostile bowling. Hubert Preston (editor of *Wisden* 1944–51) wrote of Miller's bowling when the latter had got his dander up: 'His habit of wheeling round, flying into an abnormally fast start and tossing back his head before releasing the ball gave an impression that petulance more than cricket tactics dictated his methods at such times.'

Miller changed from medium to fast after he had gone for 14 in one over, including two successive 4's by Hutton. Sections of the crowd showed noisy disapproval when he bowled five bumpers to Hutton in his last eight balls.

On the following Monday, before play began, Mr H. A. Brown, for many years the popular secretary of Nottinghamshire, broadcast an appeal to the crowd to leave the conduct of the game to the umpires, emphasizing that he deplored the barracking of Miller on the Saturday.

Play was resumed in appalling light. Miller bowled Hutton with a fast breakback. There were a couple of interruptions for bad light and rain, but Compton, Hardstaff and Godfrey Evans batted splendidly in dreadful conditions. Compton played one of the greatest innings of his life, scoring 184 before losing his balance while trying to hook Miller, and tumbling into his wicket.

Compton's dismissal meant the end of whatever hopes England had; they were all out for 441. Miller took 4 for 125, and Johnston, who had much extra work to do owing to Lindwall's absence, took 4 for 147 in 59 overs with his left-arm medium-pace bowling. Australia got the required 98 runs for 2 wickets, one of which was Bradman's, out for a duck.

In their next game, against Northants, the Australians gained their ninth innings victory. This was followed by a drawn game against Yorkshire; then came the second test, at Lord's.

England replaced Barnett, Hardstaff and Young with Dollery, Coxon and Wright. Lindwall was able to bowl in this test, and very efficiently he did so; this time it was Miller who was unable to bowl; however, Australia made no change from the side that played at Nottingham. They didn't need to.

Australia batted first, and Coxon got Barnes caught at short fine leg in his second over of test cricket – the only test match in which he played. Bradman got 38 and Miller 4; they were both victims of Alec Bedser, who took 4 wickets for 100. Morris made 105 before becoming Coxon's second victim of the match, and Australia totalled 350.

England's batting was unimpressive. Lindwall had Washbrook caught behind in his first over, and then bowled Edrich and Dollery, beating them by sheer pace: Hutton was bowled by Johnson, and England were 46 for 4.

Wisden (1949) said of Lindwall: 'Not only did he combine controlled pace and accuracy, which allowed batsmen few moments of respite, but he helped bowlers the other end to their triumphs because, worried by Lindwall, batsmen often took undue risks to score from his colleagues.'

Compton and Yardley added 87 in a hundred minutes, before Lindwall bowled Yardley with the new ball, and Compton was out next over. England were all out for 215.

Australia declared at 460 for 7 in their second innings. When the score was 296 for 1, Yardley bowled an inspired over: he had Barnes caught out on the boundary (for 141), with the next ball he clean bowled Hassett, and, if Miller hadn't jabbed his bat down just in time, Yardley would have done the hat trick. England, set 596 to win, were never in the hunt, the innings folded for 186. Australia, superior in every department of the game, had won by 409 runs, leaving the England selectors to think furiously.

The Australians next played Surrey. Another Bradman century. Surrey batted bravely in their second innings, scoring 289 and setting the tourists 122 to win: Harvey and Loxton got the runs in under an hour. Gloucestershire were the victims by an innings and 365 runs. The Australians declared at 774 for 7, Morris 290,

Harvey 95, Loxton 159 not out. Bradman? He wasn't even playing.

The England selectors made four changes for the third test match. Hutton, surprisingly, was dropped in favour of the Gloucestershire batsman, Emmett. Wright, Coxon and Laker were replaced by Young, Pollard and Crapp.

The third Test at Old Trafford was one that England might easily have won. At the end of the third day England were 322 ahead in their second innings with 7 wickets in hand. It was Jupiter Pluvius, rather than Bradman, who prevented an England victory.

Yardley won the toss and elected to bat. England made a dreadful start, losing Washbrook and Emmett for 28. Compton attempted a big hit off a no-ball bouncer from Lindwall, the ball flew off the edge of his bat on to his forehead, and he had to be helped off the field. Edrich and Crapp then played extremely cautiously – meanwhile Compton was able to rest; Edrich scored 32 in three hours. Compton returned to bat with the score 119 for 5. He received excellent support from Godfrey Evans and Alec Bedser, and faced with great courage the lightning deliveries of Lindwall, hitting the Australian bowling all over the field, with sixteen 4's in his 145 not out. Towards the end of the England innings, Barnes, fielding close in at short leg, was hit in the ribs from a full-blooded pull by Pollard. He was taken to hospital but discharged after a short time. England were all out for 363.

Fortune favoured England at the start of Australia's innings. Ian Johnson, opening with Morris in place of Barnes, was soon out to Bedser, and at 13 Bradman was lbw to Pollard. Barnes went in at the fall of Miller's wicket, but he was obviously in great pain, and after half an hour had to retire. He was again taken to hospital, where he was kept under observation for ten days. Australia were all out for 221, Bedser 4 for 81, Pollard 3 for 53, and England, by the close of play on Saturday, had scored 174 for 3, Washbrook 85 not out.

Then the rains came. No play on Monday. Two and a half hours play on Tuesday. The prospect of an exciting England victory was turned into the reality of the dullest of drawn games. Yardley, of course, declared, but Australia, 92 for 1, had no problems on a sodden, lifeless pitch. There being only two test matches remaining, Australia could not lose the series and had thus retained the Ashes, which they had regained in 1934.

Australia beat Middlesex by 10 wickets, and the fourth test started on 22 July, nine days after the third had finished.

By scoring 404 for 3 to win by 7 wickets on the fifth day, Australia achieved one of the most amazing victories in the history of cricket.

The England selectors did Australia great service by leaving out Young, the slow left-arm bowler, who had actually been invited to Leeds as one of the original party. For that matter they might have chosen Eric Hollies, the Warwickshire leg-spinner who, though more expensive than Young, was considerably more penetrative. As it was, Yardley had to make do with Laker, who was off form, and Compton, who was not in the first flight of spinners.

Australia were without Barnes, and without his irritating attention at short leg England perhaps batted with more than usual freedom. Hutton and Washbrook put on 168 for the first wicket, Washbrook and Edrich 100 for the second. When Washbrook was out for 143 in the last over of the day Bedser was sent in as night watchman. He lasted until the afternoon of the second day. At one stage the England score stood at 423 for 2, when Bedser, on 79, gave a return catch to Johnson. Edrich was out for 111 and after that wickets fell rapidly, England being all out for 496.

Australia made a poor start, losing Morris, Hassett and Bradman for 68. However, there was spectacular hitting from the middle order, Miller making 78, Harvey 112, Loxton 95 (five 6's), Lindwall 77, and Australia made 458. The pitch was still playing well when England went in again, Hutton, Washbrook, Edrich, Compton all scoring half-centuries and Evans 47 not out.

When Yardley declared at 365 for 8 after two overs on the last day, the pitch was taking spin and the ball was lifting. Australia needed 404 to win in five and three-quarter hours. A lovely pitch for Young or for Hollies or for Laker; Young and Hollies, however, weren't playing and Laker, who was, did not bowl well. Godfrey Evans, the wicketkeeper, usually excellent, did not have a good day, and the England fielding in general was not up to standard.

Compton held a return catch from Hassett at 57, then Morris and Bradman took command of the situation, putting on 64 in the thirty minutes before lunch. None the less, Bradman was puzzled more than once by Compton's slow left-arm deliveries; he was dropped twice, and once Evans missed a palpable stumping chance. Laker dropped Morris at square leg – nothing went right for England. Not until the score was 358 was Morris out, caught Pollard, bowled Yardley, 182. Miller was soon out, but by then it was too late. Australia won with fifteen minutes to spare, Bradman (twenty-nine 4's) 173 not out. There might have been a different tale to tell if the selectors had chosen more wisely, and if England had held their catches. If ifs and ands were pots and pans . . .

After a match against Glamorgan at Swansea, which was ruined by torrential rain, the Australians travelled to Edgbaston for their match against Warwickshire. Bradman put Warwickshire in on a wet pitch, the home team managing to score 138 against some very awkward bowling. When the Australians went in, Hollies flighted the ball cunningly with his leg-breaks and occasional googlies, keeping the ball well up to the batsmen, making them play so defensively that both Brown and Morris, the opening batsmen, were out 'hit wicket', playing back. He clean bowled Bradman, had Hassett lbw and bowled Neil Harvey for a duck; taking 8 for 107 in 43.5 overs – the Australians making 254, and subsequently winning by 9 wickets. Hollies had bowled so well that even the selectors noticed, and he was chosen for the final test.

Leslie Deakins, at that time the Warwickshire secretary, told me that Keith Miller, who was not playing in the match, on the third day entered the secretary's office and asked to use the telephone. Miller, having made the call, was just going out when Bradman came in:

Bradman: 'You should have been here three days ago.'

Miller: 'I was here three years ago. In a uniform.'

Miller was making the point that he had served in the war and that Bradman hadn't. (Bradman, who had had severe fibrositis, had been unfit.) This passage of arms had presumably escaped the knowledge of the Australian manager, who stated at the end of the tour that there had been no discordant note in the party.

The Warwickshire match was followed by a drawn game against Lancashire, in which Washbrook injured his thumb and had to withdraw from the fifth test. A crowd of 17,000 saw a rain-soaked game against Durham, and the Australians travelled south for the final test at the Oval.

For this match the selectors picked both Young and Hollies – better late than never. The injured Washbrook was replaced by J. G. Dewes, the Cambridge blue, and Cranston by Alan Watkins, of Glamorgan. For Australia Barnes, now fit again, replaced Johnson, and Tallon replaced Saggers as wicketkeeper.

Yardley won the toss. As with the first test, it was not a good toss to win, the conditions being so unsettled; he probably did the best thing in the circumstances by deciding to bat. It was difficult for both batsmen and bowlers to secure a foothold, none the less Lindwall, Miller and Johnston bowled superbly. England gave a lamentable batting display, being all out for 52 in 42.1 overs, Lindwall taking 6 for 20, Miller and Johnston two wickets each. Hutton alone offered any resistance, he was last out, having made 30; there were 6 byes, Yardley made 7 and the other nine batsmen made 9 runs between them.

Australia opened with a century partnership, but at 117 Barnes was caught at the wicket off Hollies, and Bradman went in for his last test innings. On his arrival at the crease Yardley shook him by the hand and called for three cheers for Bradman. It was no doubt an emotional moment for the Australian captain, and John Arlott, who was commentating at the time, seemed to think that this was the reason for his dismissal, and a good many cricket journalists have since concurred. Well, Bradman was not exactly an inexperienced cricketer – and Hollies was a great bowler. Only a week previously, when no dramatic incidents had taken place, Hollies had also bowled Bradman in quick time.

Before he left Birmingham Hollies had had a chat with Tom Dollery, and said that he didn't think Bradman had spotted his googly, and if he had to bowl to Bradman he would bowl it second ball. As it happened Bradman came in to bat in the middle of an over by Hollies.

This is what Leslie Duckworth wrote about Bradman's dismissal:

The first ball Hollies bowled to him was a leg-break which Bradman played defensively down the pitch. The second was a good-length googly to which Bradman had to play forward. Hollies says he moved three parts of the way forward to it, but not far enough to smother the spin, which he seemed to anticipate would come from leg, but the ball broke in and hit the off and middle stumps, though in fact Hollies did not see it do so – the wicket was hidden by Bradman's legs.*

Bradman himself said it was a perfect ball – but he never admitted it was a googly – or a bosie, as the Australians call it, after B. J. T. Bosanquet, who invented the delivery. Australia went on to make 389, Morris being run out for 196. Of the England bowlers, Hollies was easily the most successful, taking 5 wickets for 131 in 56 overs – his victims were Barnes, Bradman, Miller, Harvey and Tallon. Young took 2 for 118, Bedser and Edrich had one wicket each.

England's second innings was brightened only – if brightened is the word – by Hutton's 64, made in four and a quarter hours. England, at one stage 125 for 2, were all out for 188, much of the innings was played in deepening gloom, the last 3 wickets falling for 10 runs on the Wednesday morning, 18 August, Australia winning by an innings and 149 runs. A crowd of about 5,000 turned up to see the last rites.

The test matches over, the visitors continued on their trail of destruction. They put out Kent at Canterbury for 51 in eighty-five minutes, and for 124 in their second innings, though Pawson and Godfrey Evans put on 71 in half an hour: the Australians won by an innings and 186 runs.

In his last game at Lord's against the Gentlemen, Bradman made an exhilarating 150, and threw away his wicket, Hassett made 200 not out, Brown 120, in a total of 610 for 5 declared; the Gentlemen losing by an innings and 81 runs. Against a total of 560 for 5 declared – centuries by Hassett, Harvey and Johnson, 99 by Hamence –

* Leslie Duckworth, *The Story of Warwickshire Cricket* (Stanley Paul).

Somerset scored 115 and 71, losing by an innings and 374 runs. Bradman, Hassett and Harvey next scored centuries against the South of England in a total of 522 for 7 declared. The match was drawn owing to rain. So too was the next game against H. D. G. Leveson Gower's XI, at Scarborough, which Bradman described as his final first-class cricket match. Leveson Gower's XI made 177 and 75 for 2, the Australians scored 489 for 8 declared. Barnes made 151; Bradman, having reached 153, again threw his wicket away, skying the ball to cover point, and he bowled the final over of the match.

The tour finished with two matches against Scotland. In the first of these, at Edinburgh, the Australians were, amazingly, all out for 236, W. K. Laidlaw, bowling third change, taking 5 for 51. The tourists, standing no nonsense, then dismissed Scotland for 85 and 111. The final game of the tour, at Aberdeen, resulted in the tourists' seventeenth victory by an innings. Bradman, playing in his last innings in Britain, scored 123 not out, delighting the crowd with his breathtaking fluency.

Where do they stand, the Australians of 1948? Bradman himself said that the side bore comparison with any of its predecessors. They certainly did. The only challengers, Armstrong's side, lost two festival matches, but won the first test in a day and a half, and virtually won the second in the first half-hour. Bradman had seventeen men for a tour of thirty-four games, Armstrong fifteen for thirty-eight.

As to the greatest side ever to tour England, a strong case can be made for the West Indies of 1984 and of 1988 under Clive Lloyd and Viv Richards respectively, but what team under the sun could successfully have taken on an Australian side of 1921 that included such figures as Armstrong, Bardsley, Collins, Gregory, Mailey, Macartney, McDonald and Oldfield? However, the 1948 Australians were the first side to tour England undefeated. Barnes, Neil Harvey, Lindwall and Miller were players of world class, Morris and Hassett very little below the first flight.

Bradman, metaphorically at least, was more of a Colossus than

Warwick Armstrong. Bradman was a nonesuch, as Tom Emmett said of W. G. Grace. R. C. Robertson-Glasgow summed it up when he wrote of Bradman 'he did not mean to be one of the stars, but the sun itself', and claimed that no other batsman has ever been able to score so fast while at the same time avoiding risk.

Critics of course he has had, that is the lot of anyone who achieves greatness. He has been accused of being a loner, of not being a team man, of being self-orientated. Great achievers have often been self-taught and self-secure. A cricketer, and especially a captain, with a touch of remoteness is just as likely to succeed as is 'the life and soul of the party' type. Bradman may not have won universal popularity: he never sought it. What he did win was respect.

Bradman never made a song and dance about his innate kindness. Lady Margaret Leese, wife of General Sir Oliver Leese, wrote in her diary (1946) about the joy that he gave with his impromptu, unobtrusive and informal coaching of some Indian youngsters, contrasting his attitude with that of the memsahibs, whose arrogance, she felt, had lost us an empire.

One last detail about Sir Donald Bradman: in first-class cricket his batting average was 95.

CHAPTER 6

The Pleasures of Reading *Wisden*

As my father was secretary of the Warwickshire County Cricket Club from 1895 to 1944, it is not altogether surprising that the game was a frequent topic of conversation at the family meal table: cricket was our bread and butter.

Reaching double figures in the early 1920s, I naturally heard a good deal about the achievements of Hobbs and Sutcliffe and, in the cricketless winters, learnt from my father, and from the yellow-backed pages of *Wisden's*, about Grace and Spofforth; 'Ranji' and Fry and Jessop; Blackham and Lilley; and, of course, 'My Hornby and my Barlow long ago.' I knew about the cricketing giants of the past before I had learnt about Gladstone and Disraeli; looking back on those days of enchantment, and with all respect to those eminent statesmen, I have no regrets.

We had in our living-room a formidable Victorian bookcase, its shelves protected by glass shutters. In one of these shelves, over-spilling into a second, were editions of *Wisden's*, in strict chrono-logical order – and woe betide anyone who took out a copy and put it back in the wrong place: a bad school report might on some rare occasion be forgiven, but to cause havoc in the thin yellow line – that was another matter.

It was always a red-letter day for me when our stock was increased by a new volume, Father announcing 'I've got the new *Wisden's*!' with the same quiet pride that Disraeli – whom I eventu-ally did get to hear about – would have announced that he had secured shares in the Suez Canal. My excited request to peruse the magic pages was always countered by my father with dark allusions to homework; but the reply deceived neither of us, for we both knew that he wanted to read *Wisden's* first.

We all have our foibles about the Almanack. For each, of course, his own county. We study our own side's home matches times without number, paying scant attention to the achievements of the other counties. Sir Arthur Conan Doyle, who played for the MCC and for Sussex, who had 'WG' as one of his victims, and who wrote 'The Missing Three-Quarter', might well have written a cricket detective story, entitled, say, 'The Missing Mid-On':

'Did you not observe, my dear Watson, that in the library were thirty-seven editions of *Wisden's*?'

This makes Watson forget the Afghan campaign. 'By heavens, Holmes, then the man was possibly interested in cricket?'

'More than that, my dear Watson. I noticed that in all these editions the home matches of Loamshire were heavily thumbed. This put me on the scent of the miscreant . . .'

Sherlock Holmes, in any case, is not unconnected with *Wisden*. In the Births and Deaths section of earlier editions will be found the names of Shacklock, F. (Derbyshire, Notts and Otago) and Mycroft, Thomas (Derbyshire), who inspired Conan Doyle to use the names Sherlock and Mycroft Holmes for his detective stories. Perhaps Sir Arthur played against them: certainly the line 'Doyle, Sir A. C. (MCC) b. May 22, 1859' appeared for many years in *Wisden's*. A shame that space could not be found for the famous though fictitious Raffles in the Births and Deaths. He would enjoy being on the same page as Ranjitsinhji.

For each, too, his favourite editions of *Wisden*. If I were permitted to take eight editions of the Almanack with me to some remote island, I would find the task of selection an extremely difficult one. To choose the first half-dozen, recording the most absorbing of the England *v* Australia test match series, would be a tricky enough problem in all conscience.

What of the final pair? The first of all the *Wisdens*? – the current issue? – the copies recounting Warwickshire's championship triumphs of 1911 and 1951? – the 1915 edition, in which batsmen were laconically recorded as 'absent' during the fateful first week in August? – how does one choose two from these?

But if on my desert island I could have one *Wisden* and one only, then there would be not the faintest tremor of hesitation: I would plump for the issue of 1903, recording that superb vintage year (1902) when the Australians came over with Darling, Trumper, Noble, Clem Hill and Warwick Armstrong, and when, during the course of the series, the English selectors could actually leave out G. L. Jessop, C. B. Fry and Ranjitsinhji.

This, the fortieth edition, informs us of marquees to be bought for £10, tents for £5, lawn tennis nets for five shillings, Lord Harris eulogizes Bartlett's 'repercussive' cricket bats, on sale at prices varying from nine and six to a guinea. Cricket balls on sale for tenpence, leg guards for three and six. Peru House Private Hotel, Russell Square (for convenience, quietude, comfort and economy) offers Bedroom and Meat Breakfast for four and six.

The real feast, of course, is provided in the test match accounts. Of the first test match, played at Edgbaston, on Thursday, Friday and Saturday, 29, 30 and 31 May, the *Wisden's* chronicler writes most evocatively, and many authorities have since considered that the England team in this game was the greatest ever to represent the Mother Country – A. C. MacLaren, C. B. Fry, K. S. Ranjitsinhji, E. S. Jackson, J. T. Tyldesley, A. A. Lilley, G. H. Hirst, G. L. Jessop, L. C. Braund, W. H. Lockwood, W. Rhodes. *Wisden's* reports that

A beautiful wicket had been prepared, and when MacLaren beat Darling in the toss for innings, it was almost taken for granted that England would make a big score. In the end expectation was realized, but success came only after a deplorable start, and after the Australians had discounted their chances by two or three palpable blunders in the field. Fry was caught by the wicketkeeper standing back in the third over; a misunderstanding, for which Ranjitsinhji considered himself somewhat unjustly blamed, led to MacLaren being run out, and then Ranjitsinhji himself, quite upset by what had happened, was clean bowled, three of the best English wickets being thus down for 35 runs.

England recovered and finished the day with 351 for 9, Tyldesley scoring 138 and Jackson 53. Owing to rain the game did not commence until three o'clock on the second day:

Some people expected that MacLaren would at once declare the English innings closed, but acting, it was understood, on Lilley's advice, he decided to let his own side go on batting for a time, so that his bowlers might not have to start work on a slippery foothold. He declared when the score had been raised to 376 and then followed one of the chief sensations of the cricket season of 1902, the Australians being got rid of in less than an hour and a half for 36, Trumper, who played fine cricket for seventy minutes, alone making a stand.

Trumper made 18. Wilfred Rhodes returned the extraordinary figures:

O	M	R	W
11	3	17	7

In 1961, when Australia were batting against England once again at Edgbaston, I had the privilege of meeting Wilfred Rhodes, sole survivor of the twenty-two players in that struggle of 1902, and observed that we sorely needed his 7 for 17.

'Ah, yes,' said Rhodes reflectively, 'you know how we got them out, don't you? We changed over!' Len Braund, who made an immortal slip catch to dismiss Clem Hill, had bowled one over to allow Hirst (3 for 15) and Rhodes to change ends. Following on, the Australians had scored 8 for no wicket at close of play.

Writing in *Wisden's*, 1936 ('Trials of a County Secretary') my father has this to say about the third day:

Torrents of rain fell overnight, and at 9 a.m. the ground was a complete lake. Not a square yard of turf was visible and play was, of course, out of the question that day. The head groundsman agreed; I paid off half my gatemen and dispensed with the services of half the police. It proved to be a 'penny wise pound foolish' action. The umpires arrived; the players arrived – the captains were there. I have never known any men more patient, more hopeful than those umpires and captains. They just sat still and said nothing most effectively. At two o'clock the sun came out and a great crowd assembled outside the ground. What I

80

hadn't thought of was that two umpires and two captains would sit and wait so long without making a decision. The crowd broke in, and to save our skins we started play at 5.20 on a swamp. The game ended as a draw with Australia 46 for 2.

The second test match, says *Wisden's*, was 'utterly ruined by rain', the third 'a severe disaster for England' who lost by 143 runs. Of the last agonizing over in the fourth test, when England had 9 wickets down and needed 8 to win, *Wisden's* relates: 'Tate got a four on the leg-side from the first ball he received from Saunders, but the fourth, which came a little with the bowler's arm and kept low, hit the wicket and the match was over.'

For the fifth test match Ranjitsinhji was left out. England, set 263 to win, were saved by G. L. Jessop with possibly the best innings of his life. 'He scored', says *Wisden's*, 'in just over an hour and a quarter, 104 runs out of 139, his hits being a five in the slips, seventeen 4's, two 3's, four 2's and seventeen singles.' Hirst and Rhodes, the last pair, scored the necessary fifteen runs to win. It was of this occasion that the apocryphal story 'We'll get them in singles, Wilfred!' is told. *Wisden's*, preferring accuracy to romance, records 'Rhodes sent a ball from Trumble between the bowler and mid-on, and England won the match by one wicket.'

Yorkshire's victory over the Australians, who were dismissed for 23 in their second innings, is described as 'a big performance'; an Australian victory over Gloucestershire is chronicled in a burst of Edwardian prose – 'the Colonials had no great difficulty in beating the western county in a single innings'; and of a match against Surrey we are told 'Trumper and Duff hit up 142 in an hour and a quarter' – this against Richardson and Lockwood. The historian is chatty and informative about the match with Cambridge University. 'So greatly were the Australians weakened by illness that they had to complete their side by playing Dr R. J. Pope, a cricketer, who it will be remembered, appeared several times for H. J. H. Scott's eleven in 1886. Dr Pope came over from Australia for a holiday mainly to see the cricket, and was a sort of general medical adviser to the eleven.' Anyway, he made 2 not out.

The 1923 edition contains the saga of the Warwickshire *v* Hampshire match at Edgbaston; surely the most extraordinary game of county cricket ever played. Warwickshire, batting first, were out for a mediocre 223 on a good wicket. They then proceeded to dismiss their opponents in 53 balls for 15. The analyses of Howell and Calthorpe speak for themselves:

	O	M	R	W
HOWELL	4.5	2	7	6
CALTHORPE	4	3	4	4

Hampshire followed on, and lost 6 wickets for 186. However, as *Wisden's* observes, 'Brown batted splendidly for four hours and three-quarters and Livsey made his first hundred without a mistake.' Brown made 172, and Livsey 110 not out; Hampshire made 521, bowled Warwickshire out for 158 and won by 155 runs. 'The victory, taken as a whole,' says *Wisden's*, 'must surely be without precedent in first-class cricket.' And has there been anything like it since?

Not long ago I had the good fortune to discuss the match with the late George Brown in his house at Winchester where, appropriately enough, a framed scorecard of the conflict hung in the hall. He contended that Hampshire should have been out for 7 in their first innings, explaining that 'Tiger' Smith, while unsighted, had let a ball go for 4 byes, and that Lionel Tennyson was missed at mid-on, the ball then travelling to the boundary.

The chief joy of reading *Wisden* is also the chief snare – once you have picked up a copy you cannot put it down. How many wives have become grass-widowed on account of the limp-covered, yellow-backed magician it is impossible to say. If a teasing problem crops up – when was WG's birthday? Who captained the Australians in 1909? Who won the championship in 1961? – then 'I won't be a minute,' says the cricket enthusiast, 'I'll just look it up in *Wisden*', and he disappears in search of his treasures. And, of course, he isn't a minute: he may be away for an hour or for the rest of the day. He may even never return.

There is one thing that you can be quite certain of in 'looking it up in *Wisden*'and that is that you will pick up a whole miscellany of information before you find the thing you have been looking for.

Suppose, for instance, that you want to look up the match between Kent and Derbyshire at Folkestone in 1963. You pick up your *Wisden* for 1964, open it at random, believing firmly that the problem will be solved in a matter of seconds, and you find yourself confronted with a Lancashire–Yorkshire match at Old Trafford.

The result is a draw. Forgetting now altogether about Kent and Derbyshire at Folkestone, you next turn up the Table of Main Contents to see if you can find out how Yorkshire and Lancashire have fared over the years in their Roses battles. On skimming down the Table of Contents, however, you come across a heading about Test Cricketers (1877–1963). This immediately starts you off on a new track, and you turn to the appropriate section to find how many cricketers have played for their country. The names Clay, Close, Coldwell, Compton, Cook, Copson leap up at you from the printed page: memories of past test matches dance in bright kaleidoscopic colours before you. *Wisden*, you feel, is as exciting as a Buchan thriller. The word 'Buchan' leads logically enough to Midwinter.

Midwinter – of course! – now, didn't he play for England *v* Australia, and also for Australia *v* England? Research confirms that such was indeed the case. You look him up in Births and Deaths; but this entails searching an earlier edition. At random you select the issue for 1910; and sailing purposefully past an offer on page 3 of a free sample of Oatine (for Men after Shaving) you find that Midwinter, W. E. was also a regular player for Gloucestershire and for Victoria. Meanwhile, you have hit upon another test match series.

In the first of this series of tests England were trying out a twenty-six-year-old opening batsman named Hobbs (Cambridgeshire and Surrey). He made a duck in his first innings, but did better in the second. 'England wanted 105 to win, and as it happened, Hobbs and Fry hit off the runs in an hour and a half without being separated.'

There are now two tracks that lie ahead. You can follow the Australians on their tour, to find that they won the Ashes but came close to defeat against Sussex and Somerset, and also played some unusual sides – Western Union (Scotland), South Wales, two rain-ridden draws against combined Yorkshire and Lancashire elevens, and, towards the end of the tour, Mr Bamford's eleven at Uttoxeter. The other track, of course, is the golden trail of the Master's 197 centuries.

Wisden's attractions are endless. A county cricketer of former days recently told me how much he enjoyed browsing over the Public School averages 'so that I can see how my friends' sons are getting on.'

Even the briefer obituaries are always interesting to read and, when occasion demands, amusing – as surely obituaries should be. To return again to the 1903 edition, we read of the Reverend Walter Fellows, described in Scores and Biographies as 'a tremendous fast round-armed bowler'. For Westminster against Rugby (1852) he took a wicket in the first innings and 6 in the second. However, in the course of so doing he bowled 30 wides, 'thereby giving away as many runs as Westminster made in their two innings combined'. In 1856 he hit a ball 175 yards 'from hit to pitch . . . In 1863 he emigrated to Australia, and joined the Melbourne Club the following year. He was interested in the game to the last. Height 5ft 11in, and playing weight as much as 16st 4lbs.'

And again, in the 1961 edition there is the superb obituary of Alec Skelding. Of the many selected tales *Wisden* recounts of him, perhaps this is the loveliest: 'In a game in 1948 he turned down a strong appeal by the Australian touring team. A little later a dog ran on to the field, and one of the Australians captured it, carried it to Skelding and said: "Here you are. All you want now is a white stick." '

Wisden is indeed better than rubies. Wisden is an inexhaustible goldmine in which lies embedded the golden glory of a century of cricketing summers. In the 1964 edition (page 1024) we read the brief statement '*Wisden* for cricket.' I think that sums it up.

CHAPTER 7

Gilbert Jessop – the Most Exciting Cricketer of Them All

> At one end stocky Jessop stands,
> The human catapult,
> Who wrecks the roofs of distant towns,
> When set in his assault.

So wrote an American rhymester after Jessop had invaded the United States to play against the Gentlemen of Philadelphia.

'There will never be another Jessop,' said H. W. Bainbridge. 'He spreadeagled any bowler in ten minutes, however good, unless the stars were against him,' wrote C. B. Fry. 'It was a great treat to me,' said George Hirst of Jessop's immortal century against Australia at the Oval, 'watching their bowlers' faces change with wonder and consternation in their efforts to try and block his shots by changing the field.' Gerald Brodribb, the Croucher's biographer, wrote recently, 'It is strange and sad to think that if a new English batsman came to light and scored innings at even half the pace of Jessop, he would soon be hailed as an outstanding player.'

'Jessop?' said Leslie Deakins of Warwickshire. 'The greatest box office attraction the game has ever known. There's never been anyone like him.' The statisticians' comment is perhaps the most breathtaking of all, for they tell us that Jessop got his runs at eighty an hour, whereas Hobbs, Hammond and Bradman were well under the fifty mark.

Jessop was an astonishing cricketer. His fast scoring figures only tell part of the story. The good batsman will generally play the right stroke to the good length ball; Jessop had an assortment of strokes to deal with anything the bowler could send down. A fast ball on the off might be swept to the fine-leg boundary; a nagging delivery on the leg stump cut savagely through the slips; a length ball on the middle stump could be cut, pulled or lofted over the bowler's head, according to the placing of the field or the incalculable whim of the moment.

He was a very fast bowler and a brilliant field at cover point. In the fourth test match at Sydney in 1902, Hugh Trumble, Victor Trumper, Clem Hill and Syd Gregory fell to him for 23 runs in the course of a forty-minute spell before lunch. His throwing out of batsmen was lethal, as the Australians found out to their cost. A. C. MacLaren wanted him in any test side that he captained, because, apart from his batting and bowling, there was always the likelihood that he would run out one of the great Australian batsmen.

Gilbert Laird Jessop played in cricket's golden age; more precisely from 1894 to 1914. W. G. Grace, 'Ranji', C. B. Fry, A. C. MacLaren, F. S. Jackson, P. F. Warner, C. L. Townsend, S. M. J. Woods, L. C. H. Palairet, Johnnie Tyldesley, Tom Hayward, Len Braund, J. B. Hobbs, A. A. Lilley, Lohmann, Hirst, Rhodes, Blythe, Barnes, Lockwood, Richardson, Bosanquet, Trumper and Noble, Clem Hill, Joe Darling, Armstrong, Trumble and Saunders; Faulkner, Vogler, Schwartz, Kotze; these were the men that he played with – and against.

During this period many of the best bowlers were to be found among the professionals, or 'the professors' as Jessop and other amateurs called them. This was also the age of the great amateur batsman. Apart from the already-named Grace, Fry, MacLaren, Jackson, Warner, Townsend and Palairet, there were great English players in this category such as R. E. Foster, who scored 287 against Australia in his test match debut, C. J. Burnup, E. H. B. Champain of Gloucestershire, J. N. Crawford, F. G. J. Ford, a great hitter of the ball in ways comparable with Jessop, A. O. Jones, R. H. Spooner, A. E. Stoddart, C. I. Thornton – another tremendous hitter – A. J. Webbe and Major E. G. Wynyard. Next to WG the chief stars in the galaxy of batsmen were Ranjitsinhji, Fry, and Jessop. Fry to some extent modelled himself on Ranjitsinhji; Jessop was a nonpareil.

The son of a country doctor, Gilbert Jessop was born on 19 May

1874 at 30 Cambray, Cheltenham. He had no inherited ability as a cricketer; he was a natural with an enormous dedication to the game. In his delightful and joyous autobiography, *A Cricketer's Log*, he writes of his boyhood:

> To us cricket had no season. Any old time and any old place was good enough. Some of our most exciting matches were played after darkness had set in, played in an underground passage with a candle behind the wicket at one end, another behind the bowler and one in the middle of the pitch. I'm not sure that this was not the most difficult wicket upon which I have ever played.

At the age of eleven, he went to Cheltenham Grammar School, and he was in the school first eleven two years later. Gilbert left school at fifteen on his father's death and taught for six years before going up to Cambridge. He was in fact appointed Senior Resident Assistant Master at Alvechurch Grammar School at the age of sixteen. What was more to the point, he was able to play plenty of cricket. Before going up to Cambridge in 1896 he spent a year teaching at Beccles College in Suffolk, known locally as Hockey's. It was the custom in those days for school teams to be strengthened by the inclusion of masters, and Jessop duly played for Beccles College in 1895. *Wisden's* (1896) records his astronomical batting average (132) and his bowling figures of 100 wickets for 2.44 runs each.

Jessop played in his first match for Gloucestershire on 31 July 1894 at Old Trafford. Gloucestershire were bowled out for 99 but Jessop hit Mold for 4 off his first ball, and scored 29 in no time. 'Well, we've found something this time,' said the Doctor. His diagnosis was correct.

In 1895 Jessop scored 51 out of 53 against Yorkshire in eighteen minutes. The following year he went up to Cambridge, but although he got his blue, he did nothing out of the ordinary. The first of his great years was 1897. In the varsity match, which Cambridge won by 179 runs, he took 6 for 64 in Oxford's first innings and made 42 in Cambridge's second innings. This is how one of the Oxford bowlers, F. H. E. Cunliffe, described Jessop's innings:

Jessop started by hitting Hartley's first ball smash up against the wall of the pavilion whence it rebounded far into the field of play; he followed this up by hitting everything we gave him and for five or six overs we had a lively time. We reckoned afterwards that he had only received 15 balls, but he got 42 runs off them, and it was a relief to see him caught at cover point!

University fixtures completed, Jessop played during the last half of the season for Gloucestershire. At Bristol he scored a marvellous century against the Philadelphians, and at Edgbaston when all seemed lost, against Warwickshire, he scored 126 out of 176 in ninety-five minutes and nearly won the match for Gloucestershire. A few days later, against Yorkshire, in a fantastic display of hitting, he scored 101 out of 118 in forty minutes and despite the terrific pace of his innings, gave no chance.

Wisden's chose him as one of the five Cricketers of the Year for the 1898 issue, and wrote of him, 'We have never before produced a batsman of quite the same stamp. We have had harder hitters, but perhaps never one who could, in twenty minutes or half an hour, so entirely change the fortunes of the game.' The section devoted to Gloucestershire in the same issue of *Wisden's* refers to him as rivalling the feats of great hitters such as C. I. Thornton, G. J. Bonnor, H. H. Massie and J. J. Lyons and makes the compelling assertion that 'until he was disposed of no one could say what was likely to happen'. All this when his career had barely started.

In June 1899, he was selected to play for England against Australia at Lord's – chiefly for his ability as a bowler, Tom Richardson being off form and Lockwood unfit. In a match that Australia won by 10 wickets Jessop bowled 37.1 five-ball overs in the first innings, despite a severe back injury at the start of the game, taking 3 wickets for 105, his victims being Gregory, Trumble and Howell. He scored 51 of England's first innings total of 206, enjoying a partnership of 95 with F. S. Jackson.

In 1900, Jessop was reaching the zenith of his career. He was appointed captain of Gloucestershire in succession to W. Troup, who had taken over the previous year from WG and who now had to return to India. Jessop remained captain until 1912. 'I cannot honestly say,' he wrote, 'that I found my duties unduly harassing. For one thing – and a very big thing too – my relations with the Committee during thirteen seasons' association were always of the friendliest.' The cares of captaincy certainly did not affect his individual prowess, and he celebrated his first year of office by scoring over two thousand runs and taking over a hundred wickets. He was at the time only the third person in the game to have done so; the other two were W. G. Grace and C. L. Townsend, both of Gloucestershire. The following season he scored 2,323 runs in first-class cricket; this was the highest aggregate in his career.

It was on Wednesday, 13 August 1902, at Kennington Oval, in the fifth test against Australia, that Jessop played what has been described as the greatest innings in the history of cricket. England had been set 263 to win on a wicket that was helpful to the Australian bowlers. The score was 48 for 5, the game it seemed, as good as lost when Jessop went in to bat. For the space of an hour and a quarter he proceeded to savage the Australian bowling. There were two streaky shots before he had made 30; after that there was no holding him. Field adjustments were in vain, for in this mood no one could set a field to him. George Hirst, who was with him for ten minutes while 30 runs were scored, never forgot the amazement on the faces of the Australian bowlers. When Jessop was out, he had scored 104 out of 139 in seventy-five minutes and England went on, amid mounting excitement, to win by 1 wicket. Describing his innings years afterwards, Jessop wrote that he was chiefly pleased with the restraint that he had shown when batting against Trumble; it is interesting to conjecture what would have been the views of Trumble himself on this matter.

This, of course, was Jessop's greatest innings. It was possibly the greatest innings that any cricketer has ever played; even so, his 93 against South Africa in the first test at Lord's in July 1907 must bear comparison. England were 158 for 5 when he joined Braund; Jessop scored his 93 out of 145 that the pair put on in seventy-five minutes. He was batting against the South African googly bowlers for the first time, and playing them without difficulty; but the most astonishing thing about his innings was the way that he hammered and pulled the fastest balls that the formidable Kotze could send down.

'Scores and Biographies' sums up the innings with dramatic brevity; 'Fourteen 4's, scored off 39 of 69 balls received.' England made 428 in that innings, but the match was drawn.

On 1 July 1909, at Leeds in the third test against Australia, Jessop strained the muscles of his back so badly that he was unable to play for the remainder of the season. He was right back on form in 1911, scoring 1,907 runs for an average of 42.37. In 1912, the year of the Triangular Tournament, he played in two test matches against South Africa.

Altogether in first-class cricket Jessop scored 26,698 runs – including 53 centuries – for an average of 32.63; he took 851 wickets at an average of 23 runs each; he took 451 catches and he ran out a remarkable number of batsmen who learnt too late that a quick single to cover point was not on if Jessop happened to be the fielder.

The longest that Jessop ever batted was against Sussex at Bristol in 1907, when he scored 240 out of 337 in three hours and twenty minutes. His highest score was also against Sussex; this was in 1903 at Brighton when he made 286 out of 355 in five minutes under three hours. He made 234 against Somerset in 1905, 233 against Yorkshire in 1901 and 206 against Nottinghamshire in 1904; on all three occasions he was at the wicket for about two and a half hours.

Four times he scored a century in each innings; on twelve occasions he scored a hundred in under an hour. It is astonishing that a high proportion of his fifty-three centuries were scored without his giving a chance. In 1901 he scored 66 out of 66 in twenty-eight minutes – Sussex were again the sufferers. He made 76 out of 79 against Nottinghamshire in 1901; 81 out of 89 in forty minutes against Somerset in 1903; and so it went on. In 1904 at Bristol, he hit Len Braund for 28 in an over – 446446. This was off a good over from Braund when he was one of the best slow bowlers in the country. According to C. J. Britton, for the fourth ball Braund posted a man at square leg and bowled a faster ball on the leg side, whereupon Jessop stepped back and cut the ball for four.

It should be mentioned that the law about 6's was not changed until 1910; up to that time the ball had to be hit out of the ground rather than simply over the boundary for a 6; otherwise many of Jessop's huge number of 4's would have been 6's.

G. L. Jessop was no village slogger. He was a great batsman with massive powers of concentration; he had the eyes of a hawk, the heart of a lion and the timing of an angel. His genius lay in the split-second thinking that enabled him to choose from an armoury of strokes to deal with anything that Rhodes or Trumble or Kotze or a hundred others could bowl.

Of course, sometimes he failed. A ball that kept low in his first over might bowl him – a glorious sweep to leg intended – when a lesser player would prod and survive. Test selectors were sometimes grieved at his over-exuberance and suggested a more cautious approach; but a cautious Jessop would have been a contradiction in terms.

Although nearly every stroke he made was an attacking stroke he showed remarkable flair for avoiding risks. Nor is this surprising; the international racing driver knows more about safety precautions than the average motorist. Jessop himself has this to say about C. B. Fry in *A Cricketer's Log*: 'The elimination of risks he reduced to almost an exact science. He saw that the most fruitful method of a bowler's devices lay in his power to entice batsmen to flick across the off ball, and he set himself to remove all temptation in this way.'

Here is clear indication of Jessop's own interest in the elimination of risk. Further evidence is to be found in the ways that he was out. In first-class cricket Jessop made 836 visits to the crease; he was caught 517 times and bowled 193 times. On only 62 occasions – an average of three times a season – was he stumped and, most remarkable of all for someone who was always anxious to keep the scorers busy, in twenty years of cricket he was only run out eight times. Despite his astonishing stroke play, such as cutting balls outside the leg stump, he was out hit wicket – twice! Fewer than half a dozen times in his career, he relates, was he dissatisfied with an umpire's decision.

Tragically, G. L. Jessop suffered massive heart damage in 1914, owing to an accident in a Turkish bath, and was an invalid for the remaining forty years of his life.

There will never be another Jessop. A gentle, friendly and amusing companion, he dominated the game when he was on the field; the better the bowler and the tougher the odds, the more he liked it. Peaked cap on head, sleeves rolled up, stocky, fearless and five feet seven, he faced the bowler, prepared for death or glory. And it was pretty often glory. Gilbert Laird Jessop, the Rupert of the cricket field, was surely the most exciting cricketer of them all.

POSTSCRIPT It has been said of Jessop 'There's never been anyone like him.' Probably that was true in 1975, but is it true since the eruption of Ian Botham, who did astonishing things at the peak of his career? Botham played in 102 tests compared with Jessop's 18, but this was at a time when test matches were plentiful. Different in personality, his achievements have been compared with Jessop's and with good reason. In a test match at Old Trafford against Australia in 1981 his innings of 118 in 123 minutes – six 6's and thirteen 4's – earned immediate comparison with Jessop. Robert Brooke, cricket statistician, who has made an in-depth study of their achievements, writes 'I would say that over a long period Jessop was by far the better batsman, but during his comparatively short peak period Botham was at least his equal.'*

* Letter to the author, 23 September 1993.

CHAPTER 8

The Unplayable Jeeves

In the late summer of 1910, my father, then Warwickshire secretary, was on a walking holiday in his native Yorkshire and stayed one night in the village of Hawes. Using his murderous cut-throat razor, he had mistimed a stroke while shaving; a visit to the local doctor was necessary. The doctor, having dealt with the cut, prescribed a visit to the afternoon's cricket match, and here, on the lovely ground at Hawes, my father saw a young cricketer whose effortless grace as a bowler told something of his potential. At the end of the innings he said to him 'How would you like to play for Warwickshire?' That was how the Jeeves saga began.

In those days there was a two-year qualification period in force so in 1911 – when Warwickshire won the championship for the first time – he played no first-class cricket. In 1912, the year of the Triangular Tournament, he played for Warwickshire against the Australians. He failed with the bat, making 1 (run out), and 0, but did better with his bowling, taking 2 for 35. 'Tiger' Smith gave him his first wicket, snapping up the obdurate Kelleway.

The seasons 1913 and 1914 were to be Jeeves's years of glory.

In 1913, playing in his first championship game at Edgbaston, against Leicestershire, he made 46 and 23. Opening the bowling with F. R. Foster he took 3 for 24 and 5 for 37, playing a major part in his team's victory. This early season promise was fulfilled. His fast-medium deliveries, with their lightning speed off the pitch, yielded a rich harvest: 106 batsmen, including J. B. Hobbs, were victims to his flowering genius. He was top of his county's bowling averages, his wickets costing 20 runs apiece.

In 1914 Percy Jeeves went from strength to strength. Playing for the Players against the Gentlemen he took 4 for 44, his scalps including those of Spooner and Fry. Michael Falcon, who played in the match, had vivid memories of Jeeves's deliveries biting into the soft pitch, and throwing up pieces of turf – 'I said "Hullo, here's someone!"' In the last match that he ever played at Edgbaston, he took 5 for 52 in Surrey's first innings, clean bowling Surrey's opening batsmen, Tom Hayward and Jack Hobbs. He was showing marked ability, too, as an aggressive middle-order batsman; in a lively 70 against Yorkshire he hit one bowler out of the ground and into the Edgbaston road. Chief of all, it was expected that he would develop into a bowler of world class.

Percy Jeeves became engaged to Annie Austin, younger sister of George Austin, the Warwickshire scorer. When war broke out against Germany, Jeeves joined the Warwickshire Regiment, and was killed in the battle of the Somme on 22 July 1916. Annie Austin, who lived into her eighties, never married.

What is the connexion between these two who share the name Jeeves, the inimitable butler – 'Not the yellow spats, sir' – and the splendid bowler? After forty years the question that had often been vaguely in my mind took definite shape: had P. G. Wodehouse chosen the name as a result of seeing Percy Jeeves in the cricket field?

In 1967 I had adapted *The Code of the Woosters* into play form and was producing it at a school in Norfolk, and during the same period I was also writing a feature article for *Wisden*, 'Warwickshire the Unpredictable'. It seemed at that time that I was perpetually face to face with Jeeves. Was there a connexion? After all, Conan Doyle got the name for Sherlock Holmes from a Derbyshire cricketer named Shacklock; could not Wodehouse, who was in the Dulwich XI of 1900, have followed a similar course?

If anyone knew it would be the Master himself, so I looked up his address in *Who's Who* and wrote to him, asking if he had named Jeeves of the Junior Ganymede after Percy Jeeves of the Warwickshire Cricket Club. Back came the reply from Remsenburg, Long Island, almost in less time than it takes to say 'How's that?':

Yes, you are quite right. It must have been in 1913 that I paid a visit to my parents in Cheltenham and went to see Warwickshire play

Gloucestershire in the Cheltenham College Ground.

I suppose Jeeves's bowling must have impressed me, for I remembered him in 1916 when I was in New York and starting the Jeeves and Bertie saga, and it was just the name I wanted. I have always thought till lately that he was playing for Gloucestershire that day. (I remember admiring his action very much.)

Warwickshire did, in fact, play Gloucestershire at Cheltenham in 1913: Percy Jeeves took 0 for 43 in 17 overs, and 1 for 12 in 7 overs – evidently bowling without the luck that even the best player needs, but bowling well enough for P. G. Wodehouse to remember his action three years later.

Excited at the news about Jeeves I took the liberty of sending PGW a Warwickshire tie. In a delightful letter of acceptance he wrote that the tie was much admired in the family and that it is 'the only one I wear nowadays'. Naturally, I thought that this statement was simply an example of Wodehouse's courtesy. However, when Michael Davie went out to the States to interview him for the *Observer* colour supplement in connexion with PGW's ninetieth birthday, it was interesting to see from the photographs that he was indeed wearing the Warwickshire tie. Michael Davie noticed that the tie was a little worse for wear, having been singed in places by embers from the Master's pipe. Hearing of this, Leslie Deakins, the Warwickshire secretary, sent him another tie, which was pleasantly acknowledged.

To go back a little: a couple of years after my Jeeves discovery I had a teaching appointment in Hunstanton, where I learnt that Wodehouse was related to the L'Estrange family of Hunstanton Hall, and that he used to rent the Hall for periods before the Second World War, or stay as a paying guest – he was known in the L'Estrange family as 'PG'. He was often seen cycling through the streets of Hunstanton, generally to the swimming baths, and was liable to be wearing odd socks.

I was told by a Wodehouse fan who was something of an authority about Hunstanton that Bernard L'Estrange of Hunstanton Hall, a relative and friend of Wodehouse, was the original Bertie Wooster.

This seemed to be too good to be true, but there was no harm in checking, so I wrote again to PGW. He replied from Remsenburg (18 April 1970):

How nice to get a letter from Hunstanton! No, Bernard was not the original of Bertie Wooster. I started the Jeeves stories in 1916 and did not meet Bernard till 1925. I don't think Bertie was drawn from anyone, unless it was George Grossmith. He was just the ordinary stage dude at the start of his career, and only took on a character of his own a good deal later. I am wearing the Warwickshire tie as I write this. It is generally admired.

My last letter to him was written to congratulate him on his ninetieth birthday (15 October 1971). He probably received several hundred letters on this occasion, answering a hefty batch every day. He wrote on 27 October: 'Many thanks for your birthday greetings. It is so nice to know that one's readers are wishing one well. I feel pretty good for an old fossil of ninety and I'm going to try for that hundred!' On the back of the envelope was a printed cartoon of a dog, outlined in blue, standing behind a tall, thin cat, all in blue and twice the height of the dog.

The personalized sticker on the front of the envelope was different from previous ones. His name was actually printed as P. C. Wodehouse (which would have amused him) and 'Remsenburg' was printed as 'Rensenburg'. Perhaps the order for this particular batch of stationery had been given over the telephone, with insufficient clarity, by his wife, who was an enthusiastic pet lover.

Alas, P. G. Wodehouse didn't reach his hundred, but died in February 1975 at the age of ninety-three. He had not visited England since 1946. His self-imposed exile can be all too easily explained. Captured in France in May 1940, he had given in 1941 five broadcasts from Berlin while an internee, the intent of which was completely misunderstood, and he became the victim of a campaign of utterly unwarranted vilification that left him scarred for life.

Between May 1940 and June 1941 he was interned in five camps altogether, chiefly at Tost, Silesia, where he received a great many letters and parcels from the United States, at that time neutral. When in June 1941 it was suggested to Wodehouse, who was nearly due on account of his age for release from the camp (though not from Germany), that he might like to broadcast to the States as a way of thanking his American readers, he replied that it would be a good idea. He gave five broadcasts to America between June and August 1941; the same five talks were broadcast to England in August of the same year.

The broadcasts are quoted in full in Iain Sproat's admirable book *Wodehouse at War*. These broadcasts – vintage Wodehouse – aroused a tremendous furore in England. He was denounced by Anthony Eden, then foreign secretary, for having 'lent his services to the Nazi war propaganda machine', and by Quintin Hogg (Lord Hailsham) who compared him with Lord Haw Haw. Duff Cooper, then minister of information, induced William Connor (Cassandra of the *Daily Mirror*), despite protests from the BBC, to broadcast one of the most appalling pieces of vilification that has ever appeared in the English language. A. A. Milne and E. C. Bentley assailed him in the press. Two people were outstanding in their refusal to join in the orchestrated hate campaign – Evelyn Waugh and George Orwell defended him lustily.

Wodehouse had become a victim to the kind of civilian war fever that had raged in the first war, and that Robert Graves so vividly portrayed in *Goodbye to All That*. For instance, in his first broadcast Wodehouse referred to the friendliness of German soldiers who would frequently drop in for a bath at his house. Obviously he was stating with gentle irony that his house had been virtually commandeered, yet numerous listeners misinterpreted what he had said, proclaiming that he was a traitor; they were perhaps unaware that in the first war he had twice volunteered for military service, and had been rejected because of his weak eyesight.

Wodehouse, accustomed to the imaginary world of the Drones Club rather than to the real world of hate propaganda, was horrified when he realized how his well-meant cameos of internee life had been received, and saw too late the unwisdom of what he had done in good faith.

He and his wife were living in Paris in 1944, and when Paris was recaptured in August of that year, he immediately reported to the Allied authorities. He was interrogated extensively by Major E. J. P. Cussen of the Intelligence Corps: there was no evidence that merited prosecution. Wodehouse's legal innocence was explained in the House of Commons to Quintin Hogg, who wanted him to be prosecuted. But though his legal innocence was clear, no effort was made to establish his undoubted moral innocence.

It was Iain Sproat, then MP for South Aberdeen, who put the record straight. After years of trying, in 1980 he finally got the Home Office file on Wodehouse made public, and in his book *Wodehouse at War* established once and for all that his innocence was crystal clear. Though Wodehouse did not live to see this book published, it was through Iain Sproat's efforts that, on the recommendation of Harold Wilson, Wodehouse was knighted in January 1975.

As for Percy Jeeves, I like to think that my correspondence with P. G. Wodehouse, about the match at Cheltenham, helped in some measure to heal the scars caused by the wiseacres who seemed almost to be wilfully ignorant of Wodehouse's good (albeit misguided) intentions in 1941.

He wore the Warwickshire tie for the remainder of his life; he sported it at his ninetieth birthday celebrations and, when he received a second one from the Warwickshire secretary, he had virtually become an honorary member of the club that played its home matches only an hour's drive from the Cheltenham ground where he saw the inimitable Jeeves.

CHAPTER 9

The Bear and the White Rose

Between 1895, when Warwickshire became a first-class county, and 1994, Warwickshire have played 164 games against Yorkshire in the county championship. Warwickshire have won 25, lost 72 and drawn 67, winning on average one game in seven and losing three times as many games as they have won. Three of the victories have been by very narrow margins; two of the drawn games have made their place in cricket history. Ten of these 164 matches, in their different ways, were exceptionally interesting, and are the subject of the present chapter.

In May 1896 at Edgbaston, Yorkshire made 887 in their first innings. These are the details:

YORKSHIRE – FIRST INNINGS

The Hon. F. S. Jackson c Law b Ward	117
Tunnicliffe c Pallett b Glover	28
Brown c Hill b Pallett	23
Denton c W. G. Quaife b Santall	6
Moorhouse b Ward	72
Wainwright run out	126
Peel not out	210
F. W. Milligan b Pallett	34
Lord Hawke b Pallett	166
Hirst c Glover b Santall	85
Hunter b Pallett	5
Extras	15
Total	887

These were the days of five-ball overs, and 274.3 overs were bowled.

Why did Lord Hawke allow Yorkshire to go on batting? Declarations were not then permitted until the third day, but there was nothing to prevent batsmen throwing their wickets away and giving themselves time to get Warwickshire out twice. As it was, Warwickshire were all out for 203 and only lost one wicket in their second innings. The seventh Lord Hawke, descendant of the victor of Quiberon Bay in 'the glorious year' of 1759, was generally keen enough on Yorkshire winning, to the extent that in 1901 he vetoed the choice of Hirst and Rhodes to tour Australia under A. C. MacLaren, on the grounds that a long tour would be detrimental to their effectiveness for Yorkshire in 1902.

The answer seems to be quite simple: evidently Lord Hawke wanted to cock an aristocratic snook at the arch-enemy, Lancashire, who had scored 801 against Somerset in 1895. 'Snubs to you, we can score more than you can,' was Lord Hawke's attitude, even though this record hunting might have cost Yorkshire the championship (in fact it didn't), drawing a game they might easily have won. Yorkshire took two days to score 887; Lancashire got their runs in eight hours, MacLaren making the record county championship score of 424 (which stood until Brian Lara scored 501 not out for Warwickshire against Durham in 1994), and won easily with time to spare. But Lord Hawke was quite happy about it all; only one ball was used in the innings of 887, and it was in good condition at the end of the second day. The ball was given to him by the Warwickshire club; he had it cut in half and mounted on an inkstand. (I have noticed, and it may be a Freudian connexion, that there always seem to be cars in the Edgbaston area bearing registration numbers which include 887.)

It was not until 1904 that Warwickshire recorded their first championship victory against Yorkshire. The match was played at Huddersfield. Warwickshire, going in first, lost 7 wickets for 79, but Santall and Moorhouse (the latter a Yorkshire exile) put on 71 for the eighth wicket. It was this stand that turned the tide in Warwickshire's favour, the innings closing for 164 in 58.3 overs – six-ball overs were now being bowled. On a treacherous pitch – sunshine after rain and no wicket covering in those days – Yorkshire were all out for 116, Frank Field taking 7 for 63 and Hargreave 3 for 27. Warwickshire could only manage 82 in their second innings and on Saturday, 13 August, Yorkshire went in needing 131 to win. Six wickets were down for 66 and amid mounting tension Ernest Smith, who was captaining Yorkshire, and Schofield Haigh put on 48. The eighth wicket fell at 120. When Yorkshire had 9 wickets down, and were 7 short of their target, Hargreave clean bowled Myers; Warwickshire had won by 6 runs.

It so happened that the Warwickshire secretary had been watching the game from the popular side, the only Warwickshire supporter among hundreds of Yorkshiremen. As the ball clicked against the stumps and the bails flew in the air, with a cry of joy he threw his straw hat exultantly skywards, evoking glares of silent disapproval from all around him.

In 1911, when Warwickshire won the championship for the first time, they lost the game against Yorkshire at Edgbaston, but they won the return match at Harrogate in no uncertain manner. Warwickshire batted first and made 341, to which Yorkshire replied with 310. In their second innings Warwickshire made 225, Frank Foster scoring 101 – he had made 60 in the first innings and taken 4 wickets when Yorkshire batted.

Yorkshire started the third day requiring 257 to win. Foster, who, with a few friends from Huddersfield, had been rousing the night owl with a catch, had gone hazily to bed not much before 7 a.m., at which time Frank Field, and the Warwickshire 'trainer', whoever he was, woke him up, put him into a bath, pumped and pummelled him, and ordered a beef steak and a pint of beer for his breakfast. As Frank Foster said in his reminiscences, he could hardly crawl to the wicket when the day's play began. The wicket was bad and the ball flying off the pitch. Yorkshire were all out for 58. One Yorkshire batsman was reported to have told a colleague 'get thy pads on – I've a wife and children to look after'. Another went out without an appeal being made, saying that he had had enough. Yorkshire were out in an hour, Foster and Field bowling unchanged, Foster taking 2 for 33 and Field, who must have been unplayable, taking 7 for 20 in 10 overs.

In the years between the wars Yorkshire won the county championship twelve times. When Warwickshire played them they were liable to be at the rough end of Holmes's and Sutcliffe's bats, or falling victim to the bowling of Waddington, Macaulay, Robinson, Roy Kilner and Wilfred Rhodes, but Warwickshire were able to spring some surprises.

In 1923, at Edgbaston, Warwickshire's well-loved Harry Howell – 'Put 'Arry 'Owell on!' was the advice that F. S. G. Calthorpe frequently received from the spectators on the Rea Bank – achieved the greatest performance of his career, taking all 10 wickets in a Yorkshire first innings of 113; Holmes and Sutcliffe were both caught at the wicket in quick time, Oldroyd scored 44, but apart from that no one got anything, Howell's analysis reading:

O	M	R	W
25.1	5	51	10

To my lasting regret I didn't see Howell's performance, but I did see the great fight for a first innings lead. The crowd was spellbound and the atmosphere electric: Macaulay did the hat trick, and Warwickshire were all out for 110. Yorkshire were 59 for 5 in their second innings; Warwickshire were still in the hunt, but thanks to Kilner and Leyland the visitors were able to declare at 162 for 6 and hustled Warwickshire out for 81.

1927 brought a surprising Warwickshire victory. When the team arrived at the Hull ground on 21 May it was to play a Yorkshire side that was one of the strongest that ever represented the county: Holmes, Sutcliffe, Oldroyd, Kilner, Rhodes, Robinson, Macaulay, Waddington, Major A. W. Lupton, Dolphin; furthermore Yorkshire had not been defeated for seventy matches. They had lost against Surrey in 1924, and had been undefeated in 1925 and 1926. It is unlikely that they regarded the forthcoming game with any anxiety.

Going in first, Yorkshire made 272, an adequate, unsurprising score. Warwickshire had a good batting side – when they came off, and on this occasion they did. Everyone except the nineteen-year-old Kemp-Welch reached double figures in a score of 393. Jack

Parsons scored a splendid 136, the fifty-five-year-old, diminutive Willie Quaife a stolid 59. When Yorkshire batted again, and Sutcliffe was out for 2 – he had made 1 in their first innings – it was the beginning of the end. They were all out for 162. The untiring warhorse Danny Mayer took 4 for 51, Willie Quaife took 3 wickets, and so did the brilliant, erratic Reggie Santall. Warwickshire had thirty minutes – the extra half hour – in which to score 42: they got home by eight wickets with eight minutes to spare.

This was one of the matches in which brother played against brother. Norman Kilner, who couldn't get a regular place in the Yorkshire side, qualified for Warwickshire, and scored sixteen thousand runs for them between 1926 and 1937. Norman Kilner's elder brother, Roy, one of the great Yorkshire stalwarts and one of the world's great left-arm slow bowlers, died at the age of thirty-seven, less than a year after this match was played. So big a place did he have in the affection of Yorkshire hearts that a hundred thousand people lined the route to his funeral.

A nail-biting match at Scarborough in 1934 ended in a Warwickshire win by 1 wicket. Yorkshire, batting first, made 101, George Paine, a left-arm spinner, late of Middlesex, taking 8 for 61. Warwickshire did a lot worse and were all out for 45; Jack Buckingham, with 14 not out, was the only man to reach double figures. Yorkshire made 159 in their second innings; even so, they were helped by dropped catches.

Yorkshire seemed to have the match wrapped up, but Norman Kilner and Jack (he had become the Revd J. H.) Parsons, who was captaining the side, thought otherwise. Kilner made a sturdy 58, Parsons, playing possibly the best innings of his career, scored 94 out of 121, hitting three 6's and twelve 4's in the course of his superlative driving. Even so, it took Warwickshire 96 overs to get the 216 runs required.

Leslie Duckworth, in *The Story of Warwickshire Cricket*, gives an evocative account of one of the concluding stages of the match. When Parsons looked as though he was likely to get Warwickshire home, the Yorkshire slip fielders started chattering while the bowler was running up to the wicket. At one stage, Parsons walked away from the wicket and said 'I wish you chaps would keep quiet.' This brought the comment 'Tak' no notice of t'bloody parson,' from one of the Yorkshire players. Again the talking broke out as the bowler started to run up to the wicket, again Parsons moved away. Brian Sellers, the Yorkshire captain, came up and asked what was the trouble. On being told, he replied 'What can I do about it? You know what they are.'

Parsons was out when Warwickshire were 12 runs short of victory. With 9 wickets down, and Macaulay bowling to Danny Mayer, Warwickshire needed 4 to win. Eric Hollies, white-faced, was at the non-striker's end. As the game had been slipping away from Yorkshire, Macaulay was using words that Hollies didn't even know existed. Having taken 4 wickets for sixty-odd, he now started on his thirty-fifth over. Mayer hit the second ball for 4. Macaulay threw his cap on the ground and jumped on it: the Yorkshire players went off the field without a word. This is how Leslie Duckworth recounted the immediate aftermath:

> The story goes that when it was all over and the Warwickshire players were celebrating in the dressing-room, Hollies, still white and shaken, sat alone in a corner until someone noticed him and asked him how he'd liked facing Macaulay.
>
> 'It wor 'is bowlin' wot frit me,' said Eric, still the Black Country boy, 'it were 'is language. It were fearful. It's all over now, but I shor forget this day if I live to be thousands. I cor repeat what 'e said. 'E come out wi' words I'd never 'eard at Old 'Ill.'*

In 1951 Warwickshire won the championship for the second time. In this 'extraordinary team of ordinary cricketers' Tom Dollery, Warwickshire's first professional captain, and Eric Hollies, leg-spinner and googly bowler, were the mainstays of the side. Not only did Warwickshire win the county championship but, perhaps a more difficult feat, they won their first double over Yorkshire since becoming a first-class county.

At Huddersfield, on a rain-affected pitch, Warwickshire

---

* Leslie Duckworth, *The Story of Warwickshire Cricket.*

struggled to 171. Yorkshire found Hollies and Grove too much for them, but Warwickshire in their second innings could only muster 92. Yorkshire were all out for 49 in their second innings, Hollies and Grove revelling in the warm sun shining on a sticky wicket. Grove took 4 for 25, Hollies, now thirty-nine, turned in what he considered to be the best performance of his career:

O	M	R	W
20.5	12	12	5

The return match at Edgbaston was near the end of the season, and Warwickshire were beginning to look favourites for the championship. Yorkshire in this match had three batsmen – Hutton, Lowson and Watson – away on test duty. Yorkshire batted all of the first day for 249. On the second day a crowd of 28,000 saw Warwickshire score 362, Dollery making 111 – it should be mentioned that Yorkshire's bowling was at full strength. The wicket was now showing signs of wear. Hollies and Ray Weeks – a young left-arm spinner playing in his first season – swept Yorkshire away for 97, and Warwickshire had won by an innings and 16 runs.

August 1967 saw one of the most sensational games in the history of county cricket: it was a game that evoked great emotion at the time, brought cricket into disrepute, and caused Brian Close, the Yorkshire captain, to lose the captaincy of England. It was only in the last half-hour that all the hoo-ha took place.

Yorkshire won the toss and batted first. Against good bowling they made 238; Jack Hampshire 102, Boycott 57. Warwickshire replied with 242. Yorkshire in their second innings made 145 at rather less than two an over, leaving Warwickshire 102 minutes to score 142 runs. Warwickshire, of course, went for the runs. Amiss and Jameson kept Warwickshire up with the clock. The hundred was up, with 3 wickets down, in eighty-two minutes – 42 needed in twenty minutes. Then the fun began; prolonged ball drying, lengthy field setting, time-wasting tactics by the bowlers. Only two overs were bowled in the last twenty-two minutes: once, during a shower, the Yorkshire players ran off the field leaving the batsmen, and more important the umpires, on the field of play. Trueman's last over contained two no-balls, three bouncers and one wicket. Hutton bowled the last over, and play ended with Jameson (36) and B. A. Richardson (o) at the crease: Warwickshire, with five wickets down, were still 9 runs short of victory. The fielding side returned to the pavilion, in some cases angrily unprepentant, in others, ashamed. The scoring system in the county championship being what it then was, Yorkshire got two points for a draw, which they would not have done had they lost – this was the root cause of Close's time-wasting tactics.

Warwickshire made no official complaint after the match; however, so great were the repercussions that the MCC held a committee of inquiry which included A. E. R. Gilligan and A. B. Sellers, who had captained Yorkshire when Jack Parsons steered Warwickshire to victory in 1934. After a two-hour hearing the committee of inquiry came to the unanimous decision that Yorkshire had used deliberate delaying tactics that constituted unfair play; they severely censured Close, whom they held entirely responsible. The Yorkshire club sent a letter of apology to Warwickshire, but Close, who lost the chance of taking the MCC to the West Indies in the autumn, never apologized as he didn't consider that he had done anything unfair. Cricket, to Brian Close, was war without bullets; there seemed to be something of a similarity in temperament to that of D. R. Jardine, to the effect that the result of the game could on occasion be more important than the way it was played.

When the counties issued their respective reports for *Wisden* on the season's play, Warwickshire made no reference to the match. This is what J. M. Kilburn wrote, in his report on Yorkshire:

> Only two points could be salvaged at Edgbaston, where Yorkshire's behaviour in the field created the sensation of the season. To prevent Warwickshire scoring 142 runs in one hundred minutes in the fourth innings Yorkshire indulged in blatant time-wasting tactics which brought down the wrath of spectators and disapproval of the critics. Reports of this conduct raised an enquiry by the county advisory executive committee which

resulted in a public censure for the team with full responsibility laid on the Yorkshire captain.

One last impression: in 1991, when England were playing India, towards the end of one of the tests, an Indian batsman was evidently employing time-wasting tactics. One of the commentators expressed himself forcefully. It was very sad, he said, to see a player deliberately wasting time: it brought the game into disrepute. The commentator's name was Freddie Trueman.

On 25, 27 and 28 June 1983, Warwickshire played Yorkshire at Edgbaston, in probably the most exciting contest that has ever taken place between the two counties. The game was played on an experimental relaid pitch and the ball frequently kept low: *Wisden* used the startling phrase 'most deliveries not bouncing at all'. The Yorkshire team was: R. Illingworth, G. Boycott, R. G. Lumb, C. W. J. Athey, S. N. Hartley, J. D. Love, D. L. Bairstow, P. Carrick, G. B. Stevenson, S. J. Dennis, P. W. Jarvis.

Yorkshire won the toss and batted first. They made an unfortunate start, Boycott mistimed a hook off Willis and was caught on the boundary by Asif Din for a duck. Lumb and Athey fell to Chris Old, and they were 35 for 3. Then came the biggest stand of the match: Hartley and Love put on 125; Bairstow waded in with 48 and Yorkshire finished on 239. On the morning of the second day Warwickshire fared disastrously, losing 5 wickets for 26, and a follow on was very much on the cards; however, a stand of 65 by Amiss and Ferreira saved the situation and Warwickshire achieved the relatively respectable total of 125.

Yorkshire went in again 114 ahead. The ball was still keeping low, Bill Athey had one or two horrible daisy-cutters to deal with (not that there were many daisies on that pitch). However, the first seven Yorkshire batsmen all reached double figures, and when the score was 165 for 5, Warwickshire's chances seemed less than nothing. In the event, the tail didn't wag, and at close of play, Yorkshire, at 184 for 9, were 298 ahead.

Illingworth declared; Warwickshire had all of the third day to get

299 – and Yorkshire had all day to get Warwickshire out. I don't think many people on the ground when play was resumed thought that Warwickshire would survive until tea or that they could hope to get more than half of the runs required. Geoffrey Humpage, who was to bat for nearly four and a half hours on the third day, told me that the pitch was like crazy paving.

I reached the ground, via the Pershore Road entrance, just before play started, and watched the first hour from one of the benches near the groundsman's premises, behind long-on.

The first half-dozen overs were almost unbearably tense: a quick Yorkshire breakthrough could well presage humiliating defeat. Andy Lloyd and K. D. Smith were opening. Lloyd looked fluent and unruffled. Smith was ill at ease, but hung on – hung on, that is, until 27, when he was caught at the wicket by Bairstow off Stevenson. Next came Kallicharran, on this occasion wary and suspicious of every ball. The fifty went up without further loss, and I dared to move to my normal seat on the pavilion balcony. At 56 Illingworth bowled Kallicharran.

At 80 for 2 Warwickshire were still in the fight; at 100 for 5 they seemed pretty well out of it. 'All over by tea time' was the general opinion. Andy Lloyd, K. D. Smith, Kallicharran, Dennis Amiss and Asif Din had all gone.

Ferreira joined Humpage, who had gone in No. 5. I think that this sixth-wicket stand was the turning point of the match. Both Humpage and Ferreira, noted smiters of the ball, batted defensively and with much discretion, but their stand of 36 runs in an hour or so took its toll of the Yorkshire attack. At 136 Ferreira was lbw to Illingworth, and Tedstone, the Warwickshire reserve wicketkeeper, joined Humpage, who had knee trouble and was playing as a batsman only. Tedstone was twenty-two and relatively inexperienced, but he had batted well against Northants a week previously. He batted watchfully, concentrating on survival. Humpage, who had been at the wicket now for an hour and a half, had got the measure of the bowling and had started to accelerate. (Was the long afternoon very hot, or was it just the excitement?)

At 178 Tedstone was lbw to Stevenson: his 8 runs were worth

many a half-century. The seventh wicket had put on 42. Old, going in at No. 9, could hit the ball around when he got going. He began briskly, hitting in the direction of where the two-decker stand used to be. Stevenson picked it up near the boundary as Old started on a third run, threw in with violent accuracy and Old was run out. I heard Illingworth's delighted shout 'Oh, well done, Rocket!' (Cricketers often devise apt nicknames for each other, and Rocket, for a fast bowler named Stevenson, is a case in point.)

It was 180 for 8; Gifford and Willis, No. 10 and No. 11, were both great bowlers, but neither had set the Rea on fire as batsmen. Gifford joined Humpage at the crease. He was still there at tea time (3.40), and I had to go home to receive the electrician, thinking that it would be all over before he had detected the fuse. However the electrician soon completed his work, and I rang up for the score, expecting the worst. 209 for 8: they were still in. Should I go down to the ground, or would that be tempting fate? I went down to the ground. I braced myself and gave an agonized glance at the Delphic oracle: 217 for 8.

I sat down near long-off at the pavilion end, where Dennis was fielding. A spectator was asking him about Arnie Sidebottom, who was on the injured list, and Dennis answered reassuringly. I scented shy whiffs of hope, but Gifford was bowled by Jarvis for 14: 238 for 9 – they had put on 58 for the ninth wicket but still 61 runs were required to win. Dennis, I noticed, joined in the applause for Gifford as he walked back to the pavilion.

Willis went in. Hope hung by the slenderest of threads. Gifford had been out to the last ball of Jarvis's over. Humpage would be facing Dennis, who was bowling from the pavilion end.

Let Geoffrey Humpage take over:

Bob Willis came up to me and said 'What d'you think we should do then, Geoff?' Well, he was the club captain. I said I could have a go at Dennis, and he was quite willing to play it that way. I think we got about thirty in the next three overs, and their heads were down.*

* Conversation with the author, November 1992.

Humpage, who was in the nineties when Willis went in, soon got his hundred. Willis was using his reach, playing the forward defensive stroke, occasionally prodding the pitch, like a pondering stork. Once or twice he belted the ball, but kept it down. Nerves were fraught: a hazardous shot caused a girl in the row behind me to scream.

'I'm sorry,' she shouted. 'I'm sorry, I just can't *help* it!'

The new ball held no terrors. Soon there were no vultures in the slips to menace the stork, and there were eight fielders on the boundary. Later on in the season I heard a spectator describing this phase of the match to a friend. 'The situation grew so desperate,' he said, 'that at one stage Illingworth was seen talking to Boycott.' At 294 the strain briefly was too much for both Willis and Bairstow: Willis swiped and snicked a chance, and Bairstow, who hitherto had kept wicket with textbook perfection, missed the catch. At 298 the scores were level. Then Humpage hit Illingworth for 4, and the impossible had been achieved. I looked at the Yorkshire fielders: as Humpage, 141 not out, and Willis, 16 not out, walked back to the pavilion every single one of them was applauding wholeheartedly. If ever there was a man of the match it was Geoffrey Humpage.

CHAPTER 10

Some Warwickshire Cameos

E. J. (Tiger) Smith   1886–1979

In his later years, referring to Blackham and Lilley, Tiger Smith spoke of 'an enthusiasm which is more than dedication'. He was too modest to claim this for himself, but, when, at sixteen, he lost the tips of two fingers in a works accident at Cadbury's, it was this quality which gave him the confidence to apply for a job at Edgbaston, as a wicketkeeper, taking care when interviewed to keep his hands behind his back. He was successful, and at eighteen was playing against the South Africans in the googly summer of 1904. 'I can remember the South African side to this day,' he was fond of saying, with or without provocation, 'Shalders, Tancred, Hathorn, Frank Mitchell, Sinclair, Llewellyn, Schwartz, White, S. J. Snooke, Hallewell and Kotze. Am I right?' He was right.

Tiger was lucky to be trained by Dick Lilley, and, indirectly, by Blackham. He played in the championship-winning side of 1911, and then went to Australia, keeping wicket to Foster and Barnes. It was said that he was the only wicketkeeper who could take Foster with his amazing swing and speed off the pitch. He was thirty-three when cricket restarted in 1919, and he continued playing until 1930. A reliable opening batsman, he was one of the triumvirate who scored centuries when Warwickshire made 392 for 1 in four and a half hours to defeat Sussex.

Following his retirement he became a first-class umpire, later becoming Warwickshire coach. He was still officially on the staff when he died at the age of ninety-three. 'The gatemen are getting to know me now,' he would quip when in his eighties. At this stage of his life not only Warwickshire players, but batsmen from other counties would come to him with their problems. 'Let's see you in the middle first,' Tiger would say. Then, with the intuitive flair of

III

the born teacher he would put his finger on the weak point and indicate the remedy. Mike Brearley was one of several distinguished cricketers who sought and benefited from Tiger's advice.

Like all old cricketers he would maintain that cricket isn't what it was. 'When we played we would like to discuss the match afterwards over a drink. Nowadays they just go home,' he would say, followed, like as not, by 'When did you last see a proper late cut?' He had an immense knowledge of wicketkeeping and batting techniques; he loved the rigour of the game and reminiscing about hard-fought battles when 'it was "good morning" when you met, and "how's that" for the rest of the day.' He would often hark back to the Australian tour of 1911–12. 'I suppose I was pretty good then. Mind you, you had to be good if you went on to the field in Melbourne and there were forty thousand people watching you.'

Canon J. H. Parsons   1890–1981

Jack Parsons was engaged by Warwickshire at the age of nineteen, and by the outbreak of the First World War was making his name as a batsman. He joined the Army as a trooper, and rose to the rank of squadron sergeant major. His regiment was badly cut up at Salonika and he was commissioned to the Warwickshire Yeomanry, taking part at Beersheba in the last cavalry charge ever made by the British Army. He won the Military Cross and was mentioned in dispatches. The war over, he had his sword, together with one picked up from the Turks, converted into a ploughshare, which helped to provide corn for bread to be used at Holy Communion.

Between the wars he attacked bowlers with the same zest with which he had attacked the Turks. His chief weapon was the straight drive – runs scored by deflection he considered unethical. In 1928, at Edgbaston, he hit Scott, the West Indian spinner, for four successive 6's; two of them went over the pavilion and into the Tally Ho ground, and another landed in the refreshment room, where a lady suddenly found herself holding only the handle of her teacup.

Jack Parsons and his wife used to worship at St Anne's church, Moseley, where the Revd. R. S. Lound was the vicar. The latter, seeing Parsons batting with his customary vigour, exclaimed 'This man has great character, he should take Holy Orders.' A few days later, having scored a rapid 70, he was invited into the secretary's office, where he was greeted by the Archdeacon of Coventry, who said 'Parsons, we have been talking a lot about you, and think you ought to become a parson.' He was a bit nonplussed at this, as, although a regular churchgoer, the thought of being ordained had never crossed his mind. He was persuaded, however, went to college at Birkenhead in the winter and came back to play cricket in the summer. He was ordained in 1929 and played for Warwickshire as an amateur. He was a fine slip fielder, but on Saturdays F. S. G. Calthorpe allowed him to field in the deep so that he could prepare his sermons.

In the course of his career he played for both the Gentlemen and the Players. He scored 18,000 runs in first-class cricket at an average of thirty-six. Against Solihull school in their quatercentenary season, at the age of seventy, he made 65 in forty-three minutes.

In the Second World War he was a chaplain to the forces. Torpedoed in the Mediterranean, he was in the water for several hours. He was rescued, brought ashore, tidied himself up and then gave Communion to twelve hundred German prisoners of war.

Hon. F. S. G. Calthorpe   1892–1935

Frederic Somerset Gough Calthorpe was one of the last of the genuine amateurs playing cricket between the wars. It is said that during his three years at Cambridge he never met his tutor. He found Fenner's quickly enough, winning his blue in 1913, 1914 and 1919: he also became a scratch golfer. He was captain of Warwickshire from 1920 to 1929; his family owned the Calthorpe estate on which the Edgbaston ground stands. (The name Calthorpe, incidentally, is pronounced with the first syllable rhyming with 'tall' and not with 'shall': as a five-year-old I formed the impression that people who pronounced the name incorrectly didn't go to heaven.)

Freddie Calthorpe was a glorious batsman when he got going,

with a lyrical array of strokes which included straight 6's over the pavilion. He was a fast-medium bowler with an intriguing cork-screw run up to the wicket: there was always about him a careless aristocratic grace. As a captain he was inclined to lack the killer instinct; hence letting Hampshire off the hook when they were out for 15 in the first innings. In 1924, a South African stand was assuming titanic proportions when Len Bates was discovered lying down, apparently asleep, between the overs. 'Look at this,' said Calthorpe, with simulated fury, to two or three of the fielders, 'here are we, toiling all the afternoon, and he goes to sleep.' Then, addressing Len Bates, 'You can jolly well bowl next over.' Len Bates – he had no claims to be a bowler – got up, took the ball, and broke the partnership.

But there were tense situations that even Calthorpe couldn't endure. Warwickshire, set 270 to win against Lancashire, had 8 wickets down and a few still to get. Calthorpe sat in one of the committee room wicker chairs, looking out on to the field and closing his eyes at each delivery; a friend sitting next to him told him the outcome of each ball until Warwickshire were home and dry.

Calthorpe was my hero. I had often heard him laughing in the distance, but had never heard him actually speaking, until one day I saw him in the pavilion with Ted Leyland, the Warwickshire groundsman and father of Maurice Leyland. I stood some yards behind them as they remained in silence, watching the play. Then Calthorpe turned towards Ted Leyland; I was going to hear my hero speak:

'Well, Ted, have you got anything for the 3.30 at Kempton Park?'

F. S. G. Calthorpe died prematurely of cancer in 1935. My father wrote on the funeral wreath: 'In memory of happy days and unforgotten laughter.'

L. A. (Len) Bates   1895–1971

Len Bates was born in the pavilion at Edgbaston. You couldn't have better birth qualifications than that. His father, John Bates, was groundsman for many years, and the groundsman's cottage was part of the main pavilion building. Len's elder brother Harold played a few matches for Warwickshire, but was killed in action in 1916. Len Bates served throughout the war and played most of his games between the two wars.

He was a beautifully stylish batsman. He had all the strokes in the book and batted with great elegance. He once made a century in each innings against Kent, and twice he carried his bat throughout the innings. He always looked as though he were a test batsman, but 19,000 runs and an average of twenty-eight was not a satisfactory return for such ability. Perhaps there were times when he preferred artistry to the prosaic business of getting his head down. Maurice Leyland seemed to think so. 'He'd have played for England, only he played too pretty,' he once observed.

He retired from first-class cricket in 1935 and became coach and head groundsman at Christ's Hospital, Horsham, until his retirement in 1963. Here he was a great success and very much liked. One of his pupils, whose potential he was quick to spot, was John Snow, the Sussex and England fast bowler.

The last years of his life were marred by ill health and both legs were amputated. This did not prevent him tending his garden from a wheelchair or from taking up water-colour painting.

R. E. S. Wyatt   b. 1901

R. E. S. Wyatt, a descendant of the poet Sir Thomas Wyatt, played for Warwickshire from 1923 to 1939, and for Worcestershire from 1946 to 1951. He scored 40,000 runs in first-class cricket at an average of forty. He took nine hundred wickets and could make the new ball swing like a ping-pong ball. As a nine-year-old, I saw the first innings that he played for Warwickshire. Going in No. 7, when the runs were not coming too easily, he made a fluent and confident 37; he walked back to the pavilion, touching his cap shyly to receive a rapturous reception from a crowd of four thousand. 'He'll be playing for England one of these days,' we told each other, and four years later he was wearing the England blazer. He played forty times for England, sixteen times as captain.

Bob Wyatt had a reputation for dourness as a batsman; it was said of him that he parsed and analysed each ball. Dour he certainly could be, but there were many facets to his play. Set 236 to win in two hours against Middlesex, he and Norman Kilner put on a hundred for the first wicket in fifty minutes. His courage against fast bowling was legendary. In the last test match of the MCC tour of the West Indies in 1934–35, his jaw was broken in four places by a ball from Martindale. Wyatt was unable to speak and had to get Errol Holmes to deputize for him in replying to the toast at an official dinner. Wyatt sent a message to Martindale in which he emphasized that it was a fair ball, that he attached no blame to him and that he had the greatest respect for him as a cricketer. A few days later Wyatt was taken from hospital to the boat at Port Antonio. Martindale had travelled five hundred miles to be there to see him off.

There were occasions when Bob Wyatt could be positively hilarious on the cricket field. I well remember his duels with big Jim Smith in a match against Middlesex. He was bowling slow stuff to Jim Smith who, deciding to hit him out of the ground, gave a colossal swipe and failed to connect. Wyatt, pretending that Smith had skied the ball a mile high, looked up to the heavens and, cupping his hands against his forehead, ran about thirty yards in a quarter circle, before bringing off a brilliant 'catch' somewhere near mid-wicket, exuberantly throwing a non-existent ball into the air, while Jack Buckingham, the wicketkeeper, stood expressionlessly waiting, the real ball in his gloves. During the remainder of the over Jim Smith glowered and made Herculean swipes, whilst Wyatt brought off imaginary catches. These were the days when the crowds flocked to see Gilbert and Sullivan, and Sir Henry Lytton himself could hardly have excelled this virtuoso performance.

F. R. Santall   1903–1950

Reggie Santall first played for Warwickshire within a month of his sixteenth birthday. Here, it was felt, was an England cricketer in the making. Crisp, straw-coloured hair, vivid, rubicund complexion, athlete's figure; like Tom Sueter of Hambledon, 'the ladies' pet'. He achieved some brilliantly exhilarating innings; in his early twenties he was showing parallel promise as a centre threequarter for Moseley.

He played five hundred matches for Warwickshire – nearly as many as Dennis Amiss. He had the potential to do great things, but he lacked the necessary application and self-discipline. Once, against Sussex, he got to 75 with scorching drives and cuts: against fast bowling – three slips and a bouncing pitch, a cavalier flick of the wrist sent the ball crashing against the boundary fence. Next ball, another scintillating late cut and another 4. The third, again a flash of the wrist, and second slip was throwing the ball triumphantly in the air. True, he had made 83, but he had thrown his wicket away through over-confidence and lack of concentration. Only too often a careless stroke ended his innings before it had started to flower. Jack Bannister refers to 'a flamboyant style and extrovert character which never allowed him to make the most of his talents'.*

Every now and then – his 173 before lunch against Northants – there were glimpses of the world-class genius that he might have been, but his final tally of twenty-one centuries and a batting average of twenty-four was in no way commensurate with his potential.

Eric Hollies   1912–1981

Several references have been made to Eric Hollies in other sections of this book, but to leave him out from a chapter specifically about Warwickshire cricketers would be analogous to producing *Hamlet* without the Prince. (Interestingly enough, Hollies said he remembered Stratford-upon-Avon as the place where he once opened the batting for Warwickshire's second eleven.)

He took 2,323 wickets in first-class cricket; he was world class both as a leg-spinner and a leg-puller. With his broad grin and his razor-sharp quips, he was a joy for any captain to have in his side. If

---

* Jack Bannister, *The History of Warwickshire County Cricket Club* (Helm).

Warwickshire were fielding on a batsman's paradise, the day scorching hot, his Black Country witticisms would almost make fielding a delight and he himself would be happy to bowl on and on and on. J. C. Clay praised him thus:

> When the wicket has been too hard for Alf, too soft for Bert or too dead for Perce the ball has been handed to Eric and he has carried on. For here lies his merit – an ability to bowl effectively, untiringly, cheerfully, no matter what the conditions.

In 1946 he took all 10 wickets for 49 against Notts – 7 bowled, 3 lbw. As a batsman he fitted naturally into the order of going in – one above the extras. In 1954 he made 47 against Sussex. Asked if he was hoping for promotion in the batting order he replied that he preferred to bat in his usual place at No. 11, because he could then see what the situation was and adapt his style accordingly. A latter-day Tom Emmett, he had jokes for every occasion.

But he was no joke to the Aussies. Once – with parental permission – Keith Miller kidnapped Tom Dollery's five-year-old son and took him to the Australian dressing-room. Eric Hollies was bowling. 'That's my godfather,' said the five-year-old proudly. Big Bill Johnston glanced at the bowler. 'That's not your godfather,' he said. 'That's the devil.'

Peter Cranmer 1914–1994

There was a favourite advertisement in the late 1940s which ran 'What *you* need is Schweppervescence!' Schweppervescence was undoubtedly what Peter Cranmer had. As a fast-running threequarter with a steepling crosskick be played for the Harlequins, Moseley, Oxford University and England. In January 1936 it was he who set up Obolensky's famous try against the All Blacks.

In 1938 he was appointed as Warwickshire cricket captain, his mission to infuse an adventurous approach to the game which, rightly or wrongly, the committee considered had been lacking. He captained Warwickshire for the two years before and for two years immediately after the Second World War. Exuberant, ebullient, exciting, exhilarating, never giving a thought to popularity, he was none the less the most popular captain Warwickshire – perhaps any county for that matter – ever had.

For the two years before the war he had the loyal support of R. E. S. Wyatt, but the two post-war years were difficult ones, as half a dozen Warwickshire stalwarts had retired from county cricket: in 1946 it was often a case of Cranmer, Dollery, Hollies and Ord supported by club cricketers garnered from all over the county. There was an away match for which Cranmer was given a player whose CV he knew nothing about, so he asked Eric Hollies to try him out at the nets. Hollies came back with gloomy relish – 'Well, he cor bat and he cor bowl, so you'd better sort it out.'

Peter Cranmer excelled in this kind of situation. Defeat by an innings he would dismiss with insouciance – 'Well, it didn't quite work out.' A target of 500 would be 'a good match to win'. An apparently casual approach never prevented him from straining every nerve and muscle, and from getting the best out of an inexperienced side. He did two stints as captain of the second eleven, which he described as 'a cross between a nursery and a geriatric hospital' – there was always a grain or two of truth among his chaff. He finally gave up the reins at fifty-eight.

An entertaining freelance journalist and broadcaster, he excelled as a raconteur; he had a knack of bringing comic scenes so vividly to life that you felt that they were happening all round you.

A stroke followed by leg amputations did nothing to impair his mental faculties or his sense of humour. Should he meet Job and Jeremiah in the next world he will soon have them helpless with laughter.

H. E. (Tom) Dollery   1914–1987

Above all things, Tom Dollery was famous for his leadership of the 'extraordinary team of ordinary cricketers' that won the championship in 1951. Born in Reading and educated at Reading School, he first played for Warwickshire in 1934 and became Warwickshire's first professional captain in 1949. He was a first-class batsman and an excellent fielder; in these matters he led by example: what was most important was his leadership, intuitive flair and understanding both on and off the field. It was said that when he went into the dressing-room in the morning he could sense which of his bowlers would be getting among the wickets. His judgement, his cricketing awareness, his knowledge of how the pitch was behaving were all typical. Like all good generals, he had luck. None of the championship side of 1951 was required for representative matches and none was plagued by injury.

His batting often influenced the game; for instance his centuries against Lancashire and Yorkshire at Edgbaston in 1951 – matches that brought in crowds approaching 30,000. On the field, like Mike Brearley at a later date, he had the ability to make things happen. A judicious declaration could cause an over-eager side to lose early wickets, then, when they shut up shop, Eric Hollies, accidentally on purpose, would bowl one or two loose balls, interest would be reawakened, a stand broken, and Warwickshire victory achieved.

In 1953, against the Australians, Dollery declared twice – the only captain to have the temerity to do so. In Warwickshire's second innings, he surprised his own side by declaring at 76 for 3, setting the Australians 166 to win in 170 minutes: he had spotted that the pitch was deteriorating, and his cricket genius nearly produced what would have been a sensational victory almost immediately before the final test on which the Ashes depended. The Australians could not afford to lose, but they very nearly did. In the event they scored 53 for 5 in 58 overs; only Hassett, who went in first and made 21 not out, could cope with Hollies.

Like most cricketers Tom Dollery had his superstitions. He seldom wore his cap until 1951, when he started to wear it as a good luck talisman; then, feeling that Warwickshire were going to command success, throughout the season he never played without it.

M. J. K. Smith   b. 1933

If you were to question M. J. K. Smith about his cricket career he would probably observe of his 205 against Cambridge that he should have been caught behind the wicket for a duck, and tell you with relish, of his debut in county cricket, that he was out caught Fiddling bowled Nutter 0, but would fail to mention that he once scored 3,245 runs in a season, that for six years in succession he topped the 2,000 mark, that he scored sixty-nine centuries, made 593 catches, played for England fifty times, half of these as captain. He and R. H. Spooner are the only two England cricketers of this century who have also played for England at rugby football.

Mike Smith, or MJK as he is now generally referred to, captained Warwickshire from 1957 to 1967, a period when the county came near to winning the championship on two or three occasions and won the Gillette Cup in 1966. Jack Bannister, who played under him during these years, found that he was able to get the best out of players without any fuss and easily sustained the difficult balance between being 'one of the boys' and maintaining the unswerving respect of his players. Off the field he maintained the tradition of Warwickshire having a happy dressing-room, which he described with typical understatement as 'seeing that things were reasonably amicable'. His vagueness could be deceptive. Non-abrasive, and a good psychologist, he knew the difference between saying 'I want you to do this' and 'Can you do this?'

Like Tom Dollery, as a batsman and a fielder, he led by example. If the opposition didn't get him out early, then heaven help them. Most of his catches were made in the forward short leg area. For one who found spectacles a necessity his close-in, on-side fielding was quite amazing: one dismissal of Boycott was possibly the catch of his career. His advice to the aspiring professional is that if you don't enjoy fielding you had better find some other occupation. He enjoys travel and enjoyed his cricket tours, getting on with the game and avoiding involvement in any political matters.

Now retired from cricket, like Sir Colin Cowdrey, Clive Walcott and Alan Smith he works hard – he pretends to hate work – on the administration of the game.

Groucho Marx would have appreciated MJK's sense of humour, so would PGW, who created a cricketer named Psmith. He enjoys telling the story of the boy who returned, wild with delight, from a

Lord's one-day final. Asked what was the high spot of the day the boy replied that it was the singing in the train coming back.

MJK led an MCC team to Australia in 1965, at a time when Ian Smith, the Rhodesian prime minister, was threatening a Unilateral Declaration of Independence. The British prime minister, Harold Wilson, would have been somewhat surprised to receive a telegram from the departing MCC to the effect that 'Any Smith declaration will be in England's favour'.

Dennis Amiss   b. 1943

Now Warwickshire's chief executive, as a player Dennis Amiss scored 102 first-class centuries and played in fifty tests for England. He played his first match for Warwickshire at seventeen, against Surrey in 1960. He didn't bat in that game, but may have learnt a bit from Fred Gardner and Norman Horner, watching them make their unbroken stand of 377 for the first wicket. He made his first century for Warwickshire in 1966, against the West Indies, and in 1967 scored his first century in a county championship match. He had been learning a lot about the game from Tiger Smith, Tom Dollery and Derief Taylor, finishing the season easily top of the Warwickshire batting averages.

In 1972 his career reached a watershed: out of form at the beginning of the season he couldn't find a place in the first eleven. Eventually, in mid-June, he got a chance as an opening batsman and literally seized it with both hands; with glorious cuts and drives he scored 151 not out against Middlesex, immediately followed by 156 not out against Worcestershire. Soon afterwards he shared in a second-wicket stand of 318 in three hours with Rohan Kanhai which he followed with a match-winning hurricane century against Kent. At the end of August he played in the first three limited-overs matches against Australia. Batting with exhilarating confidence he scored a century at Old Trafford, receiving the award as the England Man of the Series. In 1973 he played the innings of his life, against the West Indies, in the second test at Sabina Park. Batting with steely concentration for nine and a half hours, he made 262 not out to save the game. So far as county cricket was concerned he had the reputation, year after year, of getting Warwickshire out of trouble.

A front-foot batsman with strong forearms, he liked picking up a good-length ball off the toes, flicking it with plenty of right arm somewhere between mid-wicket and fine leg. He has been compared with Barrington for his pertinacity, with Boycott for his dedication and with Graveney for his elegance. More recently Robin Smith has been compared with Dennis Amiss.

Equable and modest, Amiss has the gift of being self-analytical without being self-absorbed. He knows how narrow for a batsman can be the difference between success and failure: 'When I played in the Prudential Trophy match at Old Trafford the first ball that I had from Bob Massie missed my glove by a quarter of an inch. If it had been a fraction nearer I might never have gone on that tour to India and Pakistan.'

There are many other Warwickshire figures who should not be forgotten; space permits the inclusion of a mere half-dozen.

George (Chico) Austin   1890–1963

George Austin was connected with the club for nearly sixty years. He began as an office boy in 1904; in 1911 he was offered the job as scorer, and scored every run for and against the county for the next fifty-two years, until he was taken ill shortly before his death in 1963. On the outbreak of war in 1914 he tried to join the Warwickshire Regiment, but was rejected because of his diminutive stature. He persuaded the Marines to take him on, and landed with his contingent at Gallipoli, five weeks too early: there was no cover. Taking the unspeakable conditions in his stride, he was soon writing to the secretary in the metaphor of the cricket field:

I expect you have heard we have had the first match with the Turks just over a fortnight ago. We made a good show; there was some big hitting and runs were plentiful. I don't think the Turks had seen such big hitting before, and they must have been glad when the innings were closed.

The war over, he continued as Warwickshire scorer, with a salary less than princely: 'We were poor,' said his daughter Joan, 'but that didn't matter because we had humour.' Between the wars teams travelled by train and, like most county scorers, George was also baggage manager. There were times when the baggage went astray and he would be marooned until the early hours on station platforms. No doubt he told himself it was better than Gallipoli. On the other hand there were times when he was involved in knockabout comic situations, such as when the team, staying in a Leicestershire hotel, came across a chest containing a variety of fancy dress costumes; guests returning from a hunt ball found themselves greeted, *inter alia*, by Elizabethan courtiers and Regency bucks. Then there was the hotel in Bristol, where George and Eric Hollies were room-mates. The trouble here was that the floor gave way.

Cricket meant more to George Austin than the recording of runs and wickets; his kindly personality thrived on the dramas that unfolded in front of him, and there were many who found him a good friend and a wise counsellor.

Romilly Lisle Holdsworth   1899–1976

R. L. Holdsworth was in the Repton XI and captain in 1917. At Oxford he got a blue as a freshman for cricket and soccer. He played thirty games for Warwickshire between 1919 and 1921, with a best score of 141 against Worcestershire in 1920. In the team photograph for that year, five amateurs are seated on wooden chairs in the front row. F. S. G. Calthorpe is flanked on the right by George Stephens and R. L. Holdsworth, on the left by Commander C. F. Cowan and Gerry Rotherham. No two blazers alike; they stare with quiet confidence into the future. No self-doubters here. Holdsworth, dark hair well brushed; possibly aided by Rowland's Macassar Oil, could well have been on a film set for some cricketing version of *Chariots of Fire*. He played later for Sussex and afterwards in India, where he became headmaster of the Doon School, Dehra Dun. *Wisden* says of him that, playing ability apart, his charm and his quiet sense of humour made him a welcome member of any eleven.

He will chiefly be remembered for climbing Mount Kamet, when as botanist of the 1931 Kamet Expedition he reached the summit – the first peak of over 25,000 feet ever to be climbed – and, having reached the summit, in the rarefied atmosphere, proceeded to smoke half a pipe of tobacco.

Edward Pearson Hewetson   1902–1977

Hewetson went to school at Shrewsbury; he excelled in all games, especially cricket, where he was a fast bowler and a ferocious batsman. Winning a cricket blue, he savaged the Cambridge attack in 1923. *Punch* devoted a page of cartoons to the varsity match, the cartoonist writing – with appropriate illustrations – 'the excitement of the match did not really commence until E. P. Hewetson "took the field". After hitting everything that came his way – including nine boundaries – he eventually sent a ball right over the pavilion – causing havoc among the flappers enjoying their ice creams.' According to Lord's folklore, Albert Trott is the only batsman to have cleared the pavilion. Did Hewetson's 6 bounce on the roof first? The subject was to crop up recently in Brian Johnston's *Trivia Test Match*.

E. P. Hewetson played twenty-nine matches for Warwickshire, on several occasions getting among the wickets. He and C. A. F. Fiddian-Green shared an unbroken last-wicket stand of 89 in forty-five minutes against the Australians in 1926, Hewetson's share being 37.

After teaching for some years at St Edward's, Oxford, he ran The Craig preparatory school, Windermere, for thirty years. In the summer he used to take the senior boys to climb Helvellyn, in time to reach the summit by sunrise.

Robert Cooke   1900–1957

In 1925, this medium-paced bowler achieved the hat trick and 4 wickets in 5 balls at Tunbridge Wells against Kent; his full figures were 5 for 22. Cooke, who had come into the side from parks cricket, never did anything like it again in the two seasons he played for Warwickshire. On his day of triumph in Kent he had made the ball nip off the pitch disconcertingly, but said afterwards that he didn't know how he did it. He could bowl a length, though: of the 209 overs he bowled for Warwickshire, 59 of them were maidens.

Derief Taylor   (?)1908–1987

Taylor, who never let on about his actual date of birth, was born in Jamaica and died in Jamaica. Derief met Tom Dollery in the Eighth Army, and followed him to Edgbaston in 1948. A left-arm spinner and a left-hand batsman, as a night watchman in 1949 he scored a century against Leicestershire. In 1951 torn shoulder muscles put an end to his playing career. In a workout at the nets, trying to get fit, he found himself coaching three or four youngsters. Tiger Smith was impressed with the way he did it, and an amazed Derief Taylor was offered the position of assistant coach – the first black man, he mused, to be engaged in coaching white cricketers.

For the next thirty years he was coaching the youngsters; a boy of eight named Dennis Amiss, David Brown, Tom Cartwright, Alan Smith, Colin Milburn (who escaped the Warwickshire net) – up to fifty or so more went on to play county cricket. Derief had become a pied piper leading the young into the Warwickshire side. He was probably the best coach of the under-18 age group in the country. Leslie Deakins considered his success was due to dedication, to infinite patience; perhaps, most of all it was due to his infinite capacity to understand the adolescent mind.

He was held in great affection by cricketers world-wide. At Edgbaston, in the course of a year, literally thousands would have greeted him 'Well, Derief, how are you?' His reply was always the same, mock-lugubrious expression belied by the mischievous glint in his eyes, the long-drawn-out word 'S-t-r-u-g-g-l-i-n-g!'

Hilary Pole   1938–1975

Hilary Pole was the daughter of a cricketer, and mad on cricket. She was educated at King Edward's High School for Girls, Edgbaston. Her Latin was erratic and she was liable to climb through the window during history lessons, but she was a good gymnast. After a three-year course at a physical education college, she taught PE and dance for a few months, when she was stricken with the rare disease myasthenia gravis, a disease that prevented nerve impulses reaching the muscles. She could not breathe without a ventilator, she could not speak or open her eyes; her mobility was restricted to a slight movement of her big toe.

Help came when the POSM* (Possum) research foundation developed an electronic device for Hilary that could control several machines, the most important being an electronic typewriter enabling her to write at speeds up to forty words per minute, so releasing her keen but imprisoned mind. Listening to test matches on the radio she was able to write about commentators thankful for mice and sparrows and cups of tea, and wrote an appropriately hilarious parody of a commentator desperately ad libbing while Mike Procter walked the long trail to the beginning of his run-up.

In 1963 the Warwickshire Cricket Club, knowing of her passionate love of the game, arranged for her to see a test match. This was a major undertaking. She was brought in by ambulance near the Thwaite scoreboard, where the necessary socket had been installed. Hilary drank in with delight the wild atmosphere of the West Indies test and, when the weather intervened, returned to hospital overjoyed at having felt the rain on her cheeks for the first time in three years.

Thanks to Possum she was able to use her administrative ability

* Patient Operated Selector Mechanisms.

to great effect; for instance she organized a concert for the disabled at the Albert Hall. She worked with happy dedication for the disabled, she kept up a flow of correspondence; using her Possum typewriter she held lively conversations with her many friends who called. Norah Deakins, wife of the then Warwickshire secretary, spent several hours with her every Friday, and was amazed at her zest and energy.

Once a staff nurse, teasing her affectionately, said 'Well, Hilly, I'm going to lock you in, so that your men friends won't be able to come in.'

Fast as lightning came the reply on Possum. 'All the men have got keys.'

CHAPTER 11

Cricket and Gamesmanship

YORKSHIRE *v* WORCESTERSHIRE.
Played at Bradford,
Wednesday, Thursday, Friday, 12, 13, 14 July 1922.
Worcestershire, first innings 116
Yorkshire, first innings 214 for 4
(innings declared closed)
Worcestershire 2nd innings

F. Bowley c Kilner b Waddington	4
F. Pearson b Rhodes	34
Mr H. L. Higgins not out	52
Mr J. B. Higgins c Dolphin b Macaulay	1
C. A. Preece c Oldroyd b Rhodes	0
Mr J. P. Davies c Kilner b Rhodes	1
Major W. Wallace b Waddington	10
C. V. Tarbox not out	28
F. Root b Waddington	2
Extras	17
Total (for 7 wkts)	149

This account comes first in my collection of gamesmanship stories because of the vividness with which H. L. (Laddie) Higgins recounted it, only obliquely referring to his own part in saving the game, but telling with relish of the mounting tension and frustration among the Yorkshire team as they tried all they knew to break the Worcestershire eighth-wicket partnership.

In 1922 Yorkshire won the championship for the eleventh time, winning nineteen of their thirty matches: they would almost certainly have won this one were it not for the rain and for the obduracy of Higgins and Tarbox. Worcestershire were skittled out for 116 in their first innings. The rains came and Yorkshire declared 98 runs ahead, Worcestershire commencing their second innings on the afternoon of the third day. The pitch was soft and not too difficult; on the other hand the Yorkshire bowling line-up consisted of such warriors as Robinson, Waddington, Macaulay, Kilner and Rhodes. Seven wickets were down for about 70 when Tarbox joined Laddie Higgins. When they went out for the final session after tea there were still 30 or so needed to avoid an innings defeat, and only three wickets to fall.

Higgins and Tarbox batted imperturbably, and Yorkshire were getting desperate. At one stage, at the end of an over, Herbert Sutcliffe walked up to HLH and enquired 'Have you ever hit a 6, Mr Higgins?' This was the story of Reynard the Fox over again, translated into cricketing terms. Had Chaucer, Boccaccio or Aesop been playing for Yorkshire on this occasion any of them might have said exactly the same thing. However, Higgins was no crowing, vainglorious cock, nor, for that matter, was he a rabbit. He scored a thousand runs and a couple of centuries for Worcestershire in 1922. He had a distinguished war record, and was so badly wounded that his sister was told he would be in a wheelchair for the remainder of his life. Eighteen months later he was playing fly-half for the Barbarians. HLH was too wise to get himself caught out trying to hit 6's. His reply to Herbert Sutcliffe was 'Yes, but I'm all right as I am, thank you.'

A few overs later Higgins saw Rhodes go up to Macaulay, saying 'Here, let me have the ball.' Geoffrey Wilson, the only amateur in the Yorkshire side, and therefore captain, ran up, in a face-saving exercise, saying 'Will you have an over, Wilfred?' Rhodes glared at him, said nowt, and took the ball.

At half past six, Worcestershire were 51 runs ahead and Yorkshire did not claim the extra half hour. The players walked in amidst the raucous silence of the crowd.

Ploys such as 'Have you ever hit a six?' sometimes do work. Peter Cranmer, Warwickshire captain in the years immediately before and immediately after the Second World War, told me how he was caught out against Worcestershire in more senses than one. Cranmer, like H. L. Higgins, was also a fine rugger player, at which game he had captained England. As a batsman he delighted in having a go. In one of his early games for Warwickshire he went in to bat when his side were really up against it. Accordingly, instead of batting in the exuberant uninhibited manner that he preferred, he played successfully for a time with extreme caution, treating the inviting slow bowling of Howarth with great respect.

After twenty minutes or so of this, Reg Perks, the Worcestershire captain, played the Reynard the Fox gambit:

'I thought this chap was a hitter!' he said in audible tones to Howarth.

'Yes, so did I,' said Howarth.

'I lashed out,' recalled Peter Cranmer, 'and I was caught at extra cover. Perks and Howarth threw themselves on the ground and howled with laughter. We've often laughed about it together since.'

W. G. Grace, of course, was the supreme master of gamesmanship and verbal warfare, just as he was in putting his bat to the ball. The most dramatic of his gamesmanship achievements actually involved two matches on the same day, on two cricket grounds – Lord's and the Oval – before play in either match had begun.

This saga chiefly concerned Grace and the Australian cricketer W. E. (Billy) Midwinter, who was a member of the Gloucestershire playing staff, and who, in 1878, was also expected to help out with the Australian tourists. In his biography of WG, Eric Midwinter, a descendant of W. E. Midwinter, explains how it all came about:

> [W. E. Midwinter] was the phlegmatic mercenary plying his craft wherever it paid best, but in what was still a confused situation over fixture lists and eligibility, Midwinter got entrapped into a confrontation. He was doubtless under the impression that Gloucestershire with only thirteen fixtures in 1878 would have made some arrangement with the Australian

management, and when on 20 June he sat padded up at Lord's he thought that the only immediate problem would be the bowling of the opposition.

Not so. Arriving at the Oval, WG had been furious at finding his county a man short. He called a cab. It was a case of 'To Lord's, to Lord's like fury', and, with his brother EM and Bush the gargantuan wicketkeeper, WG strode into Lord's where he literally hijacked Midwinter, having talked him into joining them in their waiting cab which then transported them to the Oval. This episode was described by *Cricket* as Midwinter's 'severance from the colonial players'.

The drama was far from over:

John Conway, the Australian Manager, organised a group of vigilantes to recapture 'Mid'. David Gregory [the Australian captain] accompanied the posse, as did 'Mid's' boyhood friend, Harry Boyle. They just managed to overtake the renegade at the Oval gates, and, to the delight of the crowd, a furore took place in which, among other epithets, Grace condemned his opponents as 'a damned lot of sneaks.' He claimed they had caused Midwinter to break his engagement by promise of higher pay.*

Grace ultimately apologized for his 'stormy language', and the situation gradually became defused. Later in his memoirs Grace, whose flair for meiosis was comparable with Clement Attlee's, described the affair as 'a curious incident'.

Second only to the Midwinter affair was the occasion on 30 August 1878, when WG, while batting at Clifton against Surrey, found the ball lodged in his shirt. He ran several before being collared by a posse of fielders who brought him to a standstill. WG pleaded that, had he removed the ball, the fielding side might have appealed for 'handled the ball'. After a brief discussion it was agreed that three runs should be allowed.

Age could not wither nor custom stale his infinite variety.

---

* Eric Midwinter, *W. G. Grace* (Allen & Unwin).

Inexperienced home captains were made aware of his genius for winning the toss. 'Woman', he would call as the coin spun in the air, landing with either Queen Victoria or Britannia face upwards. In either case he would say 'Right, we'll bat.'

Once, when bowling on a sunny day, 'Look at those pigeons!' he called, pointing heavenwards. The batsman looked up, the light dazzled and he was bowled. Another time, when he was palpably out, WG detected indecision in the umpire, so he called out genially, 'Well, let's get on with the game!' and settled himself down to continue his innings.

He didn't always get away with it. C. J. Kortright, reminiscing over the wireless, recalled clean bowling WG, who tried the old gag of saying he wasn't ready and that he had started to move away. The umpire ruled in his favour. Kortright bowled again, and bowled him out again. This time WG had to walk, and he had no answer to Kortright's valediction: 'What, you're not leaving us so early, are you? There's one stump still standing!'

Some umpires were afraid to give him out. There is a nice story of an exception. WG, batting, played and missed. One of the bails fell on to the ground.

'Windy, isn't it?' called WG, jovially replacing the bail.

'Yes,' said the umpire, 'but I'm not. You're out.'

I. A. R. Peebles described WG as the patron saint of points, surpassing all others in physical and psychological prowess. The position, now virtually obsolete, wrote Peebles, had unrivalled advantages in the matter of gamesmanship. Point, besides being bang in the batsman's line of vision, was just within earshot for his muttered asides, such as 'Can't play spinners', 'Bit out of practice', and so forth. WG would take full advantage of his opportunities. A callow batsman missing a ball well outside the off stump would immediately prompt WG's anxious enquiry of his wicketkeeper 'Where did that one go, Board?' and Board, alert to the situation, would reply 'Just over the top of the middle, sir.'

WG was often childlike in his fun. Witness his games of 'Mummy, Daddy and the Baby' that he played with W. L. Murdoch and Alec Bannerman in his London County days. Using an oval zinc bath for this hilarity, WG with his high-pitched voice played Mummy, W. L. Murdoch was Daddy and the diminutive Alec Bannerman the Baby. Tiger Smith, who played both for and against him when London County flourished, remembered one of WG's simpler forms of gamesmanship. 'Do you know what he would do if he thought you weren't any good? He'd go out and buy a rabbit and put it in your cricketing bag.'

'Did he ever cheat?' asked Neville Cardus of an old Gloucestershire professional.

'Bless you, sir, never on your life! Cheat, no sir – he were too clever for that.' Like Warwick Armstrong, and other old sweats of the game, he exploited loopholes in the laws to his own advantage.

Gamesmanship, if too overt, can lead to changes in the laws. For instance, Warwick Armstrong's time-wasting tactics in 1909 led to the abolition of trial balls from bowler to wicketkeeper:* in 1926, Robertson Glasgow, playing for Somerset, bowled four wides and four no-balls in an over, so that Yorkshire reluctantly reached 200, and Somerset could claim a new ball; since 1926 the overs bowled and not the runs scored have been relevant.† Brian Close's delaying tactics in 1967 resulted in twenty overs being always available in the final stages of county championship matches. Mike Brearley's ploy of placing a helmet at short mid-wicket, in the hope that the lure of 5 runs for hitting the helmet would cause the batsman to hit a catch, resulted in the regulation that unworn helmets can only be placed immediately behind the wicketkeeper.

'Cricket ain't fun,' said Wilfred Rhodes. Not only that, it can be downright murder. R. W. V. Robins remembered, in his first season for Middlesex, going in to bat against Yorkshire when he was on a pair, and Rhodes was bowling. The latter, greeting him with a show of sympathy that the Walrus and the Carpenter would have envied, said he believed Robins was on a pair, and was going to give him

---

* See p. 32.

† In the 1920s a new ball cost seven shillings and sixpence. After use, at Edgbaston, they were available for five shillings. I remember my father giving me one, saying, 'Here you are, Jack Hobbs made a hundred off that yesterday, now see what you can do.'

one off the mark. Robins took his guard, Rhodes signalled the fielders to move back a yard, and bowled one of his unplayable specialities. Robins had got his pair. Experience is cheap at any price, and he was to become pretty good at the art of gamesmanship himself.

But if cricket wasn't fun for Wilfred Rhodes, there were times when it could be fun for a good many of the Yorkshire eleven. I. A. R. Peebles, playing for the MCC against Yorkshire in 1936, made a duck in his first innings, and then unwisely told Brian Sellers, the Yorkshire captain, that he had never made a pair. 'Right!' said Brian Sellers ominously. When in the second innings Peebles went in ninth wicket down, he found his partner was Bill Bowes – on this occasion playing against Yorkshire. Peebles, having survived a confident lbw appeal, then pushed the ball to extra cover for an easy single, possibly for two. He cantered happily up the pitch, to find horror in the shape of his partner, Bill Bowes, wearing an evil grin, and standing well behind his own crease. Peebles frantically tore back and just got home. The next ball he snicked. Turning hastily, he saw that the ball had gone over second slip, and, much to the regret of the conspirators, was rocketing away to the boundary.

Ticker Mitchell, at gully, summed it all up: 'Eeh, Mr Peebles, tha's spoilt bludy morning.'

Another story in which Bill Bowes figures was retailed to me by Peter Cranmer. Tom Dollery was going in to bat No. 5 for Warwickshire against Yorkshire; Bill Bowes was the bowler. On his way to the wicket Dollery was met by R. E. S. Wyatt, the Warwickshire captain, who was at the non-striker's end.

'Do you mind them short and fast on the leg?' said Wyatt to Dollery.

'No, skipper, that's all right.'

A few minutes later, Wyatt, who also happened to be the England captain, said to Bowes 'Did you know we're thinking of picking you for England?'

Bowes, very much interested, confessed his ignorance.

'Well, we are.' A pause for reflection. 'Of course, you're not really fast, are you?' This had the desired effect. Bowes increased his speed and lost his length, and Warwickshire caught up with the run rate.

There are different ways of coping with fast bowlers. In 1937 Warwickshire suffered at the hands of the fiery redhaired Derbyshire bowler Bill Copson, whose late swing and pace off the pitch was too much for them, Copson taking 8 for 11 in 8.2 overs in a total of 28. Next year Warwickshire were doing nearly as dismally; set 259 to win, they had lost 5 wickets for 39, with Copson again on the rampage, when Jack Buckingham went in to join Dollery. Jack Bannister recalls how

> Copson was known to dislike any disparaging remarks about the colour of his red hair, so imagine the effect when, as Buckingham passed Dollery, he said – loudly enough for the bowler to hear: 'Don't worry about "Ginger". I'll deal with him and if you see to the rest of 'em, we'll soon get the runs.'*

Copson, maddened by Buckingham's audible comment, became faster but more erratic, Dollery, 134 not out, played the innings of his life, 'the Duke' scored a maiden century – and Warwickshire were home and dry.

Mike Brearley finds verbal warfare perfectly legitimate, but bids us beware of the slide into sledging:

> I am sure there is a legitimate space here for tactical grumbling, sarcasm and conning – I am reminded of the story told of R. W. V. Robins, confronted by a newcomer to first-class cricket. After the youngster had taken guard, Robins held the bowler up. 'Wait a minute,' he said publicly. 'This fellow can't hit the ball there; or there; or there.' And one by one the fielders were brought in to close-catching positions. This strikes me as entirely legitimate and enjoyable. Bowlers' threats can be simply nasty or malicious; but they can also be good-humoured, as when Fred Tueman said to me 'Good shot, son, but tha' won't do it again.'

One of Brearley's most long-drawn-out experiences of verbal

---

* Jack Bannister, *The History of Warwickshire County Cricket Club*.

warfare involved his luring Derek Randall, always a bad starter, into making a pair at Trent Bridge in 1981:

> He knew well that I would tell our fast bowler, Simon Hughes, to bowl a bouncer early on. Indeed, Derek Randall and I had had long conversations in Australia about his compulsive hooking before he had played himself in. Sure enough, in the Notts first innings the second ball Randall received was a bouncer; he went for the hook, and was caught by Radley running back from deepish square leg. Randall had several days to wait before his second innings, including an evening that I spent at his house. I stayed the night, and we drove to the ground together next morning. There was a certain amount of verbal fencing about which ball the bouncer would be later that day. I told him I might well counter-bluff, by getting Hughes to bowl it on Randall's second ball. He did. Randall hooked. Radley caught.*

Ian Botham, of course, is not the man to be left out from this sort of charade. This story, of which Vic Marks is the sponsor, describes him in playful mood:

> Richard Ellison was batting for Kent at Taunton, resisting stoutly, but being extraordinarily fussy about movement around the sightscreen. Time and again he halted Botham in his run up because of spectators apparently moving around. Eventually, Botham had had enough. He stopped in his run up and bellowed towards the River Stand – at wide extra cover – 'Will you keep still in the River Stand please' – to considerable hilarity. Next ball he ran up – tongue hanging out, and Ellison was lbw.†

These samples of what occurs on the pitch, of warfare, courteous, ingenious, psychological, provocative, deceptive, humorous, wildly hilarious, illustrate the complicated nature of the game. Whoever masterminded the affair of the Trojan horse would have made an admirable county cricket captain.

* Mike Brearley, *The Art of Captaincy* (Hodder & Stoughton).
† Letter to the author, August 1993.

CHAPTER 12

Cricket and Literature

This chapter does not deal with cricket journalists, as such, but is concerned with poets, playwrights and prose writers who have written about cricket or have been cricketers themselves.

The intention has been to write of them in one of these three categories: poets, playwrights and novelists. Of course, it is possible for a writer to belong to all three. Masefield, for instance, has written poems, plays, and prose work, but he is easily placed, as a poet laureate. Not so Conan Doyle, famous for Sherlock Holmes and for historical novels; however, among his many poems is the delightful account of how he captured the wicket of WG, so that fact settled the issue so far as this chapter is concerned.

Let us start with the poets.

William Blake, who was born about the time of the formation of the Hambledon club, and died a few years before the publication of Nyren's *Young Cricketer's Tutor*, was the first of our great poets to write about cricket, with a pleasant lyric, 'The Song of Tilly Lally'.

William Wordsworth, though chiefly committed to walking and fell climbing as his outdoor activities, can be claimed as a passive cricketer, and probably, for the occasional half-hour or so, as an active one. Numerous scholars, athletes and divines are included among the members of the Wordsworth family. His nephew Charles Wordsworth, who became Bishop of St Andrews, played for four years in the Harrow eleven; Charles's younger brother, Christopher, Bishop of Lincoln, played for Winchester. Charles continued his cricket at Oxford, where he had much to do with organizing the first Oxford *v* Cambridge match in 1827; whilst in 1829, in the same week, he rowed in the Boat Race and appeared for Oxford against Cambridge at cricket. Christopher Wordsworth, playing for Winchester against Harrow at Lord's, caught out Henry Manning, the future Cardinal. When Charles Wordsworth left Harrow for Oxford, he sent Manning his bat, provoking this acknowledgement:

> The bat that you were kind enough to send
> Seems (for as yet I have not tried it) good;
> And if there's anything on earth can mend
> My wretched play, it is that piece of wood.

With two such enthusiastic cricketing nephews – they visited him in Grasmere – William Wordsworth must surely have been conscripted into single-wicket games with them, perhaps – why not? – with Simon Lee, Harry Gill and the odd leech gatherer in the outfield.

Thomas Hood's poem, 'The Dream of Eugene Aram', concerns a schoolmaster at King's Lynn in Norfolk, a distinguished scholar studying Chaldee, Hebrew, Arabic and Celtic dialects. In 1745, with an accomplice, he murdered a Knaresborough shoemaker to gain a small amount of property. Aram was greatly loved by his pupils, to whom he obsessively recounted murder stories. For fourteen years he continued as a teacher at Lynn, melancholy and haunted by his crime, before he was found out, arrested, tried and hanged.

In the opening stanzas of 'The Dream of Eugene Aram', Hood contrasts the joyous innocence of the schoolboys with the guilt-ridden melancholy of the schoolmaster in charge of them:

> 'Twas in the prime of summertime,
> An evening calm and cool,
> And four and twenty happy boys
> Came bounding out of school,
> There were some that ran and some that leapt
> Like troutlets in a pool.
>
> Away they sped with gamesome minds
> And souls untouched by sin
> To a level mead they came and there

They drave the wickets in:
Pleasantly shone the setting sun
Over the town of Lynn.

Lord Byron played for Harrow against Eton in 1805. This was the first Eton *v* Harrow match, and most of the arrangements on the Harrow side were made by Byron himself. After the match he wrote in a letter to C. O. Gordon:

We have played the Eton and were most confoundedly beat; however it was some comfort to me that I got 11 notches the 1st innings and 7 the 2nd [batting with a runner because of his club foot, he actually got 7 and 2] which was more than any of our side except Brockman & Ipswich could contrive to hit. After the match we dined together, and were extremely friendly, not a single discordant word was uttered by either party. To be sure, we were most of us rather drunk and went together to the Haymarket Theatre, where we kicked up a row as you may suppose, when so many Harrovians and Etonians meet at one place.

A day or so after the match the Etonians sent this quatrain to their opponents:

Adventurous *boys* of Harrow *School*,
 Of cricket you've no knowledge,
You play not cricket but the fool,
 With *men* of Eton *College*.

Harrow's reply is attributed to Byron:

Ye Eton wits, to play the fool
 Is not the boast of Harrow School;
No wonder, then, at our defeat –
 Folly like yours could ne'er be beat.

Byron enjoyed his cricket, and in 'Hours of Idleness', published when he was nineteen, wrote twenty-six lines of rhyming couplets chiefly about the game, in which he referred to 'cricket's manly toil'.

As for his poem 'Lara', we would be in deep waters to comment on this in the context of cricket.

The casual spectator might have been surprised to see, on an August day in 1831, the delicate and beautiful Miss Elizabeth Barrett playing on a pitch of uneven bounce, at Colwall Green, in the shadow of the Malvern Hills. Elizabeth Barrett Browning, as she became, made three references to cricket in her diary for 1831, written when the family were living at Hope End in Colwall.* She was one of twelve children of Edward Moulton Barrett, and at the time was twenty-five years old. Her favourite brother, Edward (Bro), was twenty-four, and had been educated at Charterhouse. The second son, Samuel, was nineteen. Both these brothers were keen cricketers.

On 10 June Elizabeth had written:

> Bro and Sam are engaged in the Colwall Green cricket match this evening; and the minor boys are to accompany them. Good fun to them! – Now I must go and read Pindar.

On 2 August she wrote with some feeling:

> The boys, save Stormy [Charles, the third son] and the girls, save nobody, to Colwall this evening, to play cricket and drink tea. I wish a little shyness and obstinancy cd have kept me at home with the only *saved* person.

Elizabeth evidently regretted having allowed herself to be press-ganged. Very likely the game was also played on Colwall Green. (I played cricket many times at Colwall Green in the 1930s, when the pitch was unpredictable. Heaven knows what it would have been like in the 1830s.) On September 13 she wrote:

> So Sam came home in an irrational unchristian state from the Cricket match last night! Henrietta heard him carried upstairs, & was very much frightened. Neither he nor Bro appeared at

---

* The diary quotations are from *The Barretts at Hope End*, edited by Elizabeth Berridge (John Murray).

breakfast; for Bro went out to shoot, & he went to Mathon – & the farther he goes the better.

The best that can be said of Lord Tennyson's knowledge of the game is that it was sketchy. It is doubtful whether his grandson, Lionel, who captained Hampshire and England, ever read 'The Princess'; if he did he would have been puzzled by the sentence 'a herd of boys with clamour bowled / And stumped the wicket'.

Lewis Carroll's *Alice in Wonderland* first saw the light in 1865, which is about the time that the county championship got going. One would have thought that the general ethos of cricket would have appealed to Lewis Carroll, both to his imagination and because of the mathematical eccentricities embodied in the game. He excelled himself in his description of a crazy croquet match: perhaps he felt that the law makers of cricket had hoist him with his own petard. As it was, he wrote twenty grumpy lines, chiefly in the medium of the heroic couplet, about cricket in the deserted Parks at Oxford.

Sir Arthur Conan Doyle's collected poems are not as well known as his Sherlock Holmes stories. However they contain a delightful account of how he got WG caught off his bowling when 'wicket-keep' Storer made sure of a terrific skier from a ball that the doctor had diagnosed incorrectly. *Wisden's* said of Conan Doyle that he could hit hard and was a slow bowler with a puzzling flight. Playing for the MCC against Cambridgeshire he took 7 for 61 in 1899, and in 1901 carried his bat for 34 against a strong Leicestershire eleven.

He made a considerable study of cricket: like R. J. O. Meyer he came up with some original ideas. Shortly before his death, he wrote the story of Spedegue's 'dropper' – a lob flung high enough in the air for it to come down at the pace of a fast bowler; it was like fast bowling coming from above. Accuracy attained, Spedegue won a famous match for England against Australia. In one of his Brigadier Gerard stories Conan Doyle describes the French officer's calamitous efforts at the game as a prisoner of war.

Conan Doyle had strong views on the subject of left-handers, contending that left-hand batting should not be permitted, as it held up the game.

Francis Thompson, who wrote 'The Hound of Heaven', started work, as a boy, selling scorecards at Old Trafford. 'At Lord's', his evocative piece of trafficking in cricket nostalgia, recalls the Lancashire opening batsmen of his boyhood, the volatile 'Monkey' Hornby and the stonewaller Barlow:

> For the field is full of shades as I near the shadowy coast,
> And a ghostly batsman plays to the bowling of a ghost,
> And I look through my tears on a soundless clapping host,
> As the run stealers flicker to and fro.
>   To and fro:-
> O my Hornby and my Barlow long ago.

Sir Henry Newbolt was born in 1862, two years after Francis Thompson. His poems 'He fell among Thieves' and 'Clifton Chapel' were included in *The Oxford Book of English Verse*; others, such as 'Admirals All', were just the stuff to inspire boys at their prep schools. His poem 'Vitaï Lampada', written about the time of Queen Victoria's Diamond Jubilee, is supremely and splendidly awful. Nobody who wished to ridicule cricket could have done better; but Newbolt was being deadly serious when he wrote:

> There's a breathless hush in the Close tonight –
> Ten to make and the match to win –
> A bumping pitch and a blinding light,
> An hour to play and the last man in,
> And it's not for the sake of a ribboned coat,
> Or the selfish hope of a season's fame,
> But his Captain's hand on his shoulder smote –
> 'Play up! Play up! and play the game!'

Well, what can you do when you go in No. 11, with 10 runs wanted, beyond trying to stay in and help get the runs? Playing the game, as surely the shoulder-smiting Captain should have noticed, doesn't come into it. What most school cricket captains would say – if anything – at such a juncture would be something like 'Good luck, Ricky. Watch the spinner.'

Rudyard Kipling, who described cricketers as 'flannelled fools', told P. F. Warner that he imagined a cricket ground in hell would be like the Wanderers ground in Johannesburg. PFW, like a good many cricket lovers, had a soft spot for the Wanderers ground as it then was, with its arena of red sand and its peacock-coloured matting wicket. I have vivid memories of a day there in 1929 when the Transvaal were batting against Western Province, and how, time after time, the crowd applauded 'Tuppy' Owen-Smith's brilliant fielding in the covers. The garishly attractive buildings in the near and far distance gave it a magical appeal. It may have been hell to Kipling; to many it was heaven.

John Masefield, poet laureate for thirty-seven years, brought to life, in '85 to Win', the last dramatic hours of the test match between England and Australia at Kennington Oval on 29 August 1882, in the days of four-ball overs, when England slipped agonizingly from 51 for 2 to 77 all out, thanks to the demonic efforts of F. R. Spofforth, who took 7 England wickets. England went in to bat at four o'clock on a wild afternoon when rain had cleared to sunshine and mad wind. Masefield tells this heart-stopping tale – literally in the case of one spectator – in a little less than two hundred lines: a shorter poem than 'Reynard the Fox', it is no less compelling. This is what he has to say of Spofforth:

> Then when he bowled, he seemed a thing of Hell
> Writhing; grimacing; batsmen, catching breath,
> Thought him no mortal man but very Death;
> For no man ever knew what ball would come
> From that wild whirl, save one from devildom.

Of the poets largely connected with the First World War, four, Rupert Brooke, Siegfried Sassoon, Edmund Blunden and Robert Graves, were not only cricket lovers, but were themselves competent players.

Rupert Brooke played for Rugby School at both cricket and rugger. He was in the cricket eleven of 1906, playing on Big Side in the school's home matches, and at Lord's in the 'needle' match against Marlborough. Having got his 'Eleven', Brooke would wear the peaked light blue cap and light blue shirt that the Rugby capped players wore. Top of the bowling averages, he took 19 wickets in 65 overs at an average of 14 per wicket. He was assessed at the end of the season as 'a slow bowler who at times kept a good length and puzzled the batsmen. A safe catch.' As he had a strike rate of a wicket every twenty balls the comment seems a little ungenerous. As a batsman he was not so good, averaging 7 with a highest score of 16. In the Lord's match against Marlborough, Rugby won easily, but Brooke didn't have a good match, taking 0 for 35 and scoring a duck. He made two catches in Marlborough's second innings. From Rugby Brooke went on to King's College, Cambridge. King's has never had a reputation as a sporting college, and it was written of him that 'Rupert Brooke was good at rugger and cricket, but only turned out if the team was short.'

Siegfried Sassoon was the author of *Memoirs of a Foxhunting Man*. He was also a cricket lover, and had the wisdom to select as an aunt a lady who possessed a Persian cat named Ranji. He himself, as a ten-year-old, had watched spellbound while Ranjitsinhji scored about 175 at Canterbury. He was only thirteen or so when he was chosen to play for his village against their rivals in the Flower Show match, notching the winning single to ensure victory by one wicket in a game described at length in the *Memoirs*. From prep school he went to Marlborough, and was in the house team for two years. While still at school he had his first poem accepted – by W. A. Bettesworth, the editor of *Cricket*. During a reluctant year at Cambridge he discovered he couldn't do Law, couldn't read History and couldn't win the Chancellor's Medal. However, he could write poetry – and, for that matter, prose – and he could play cricket:

> The Blue Mantles averages in my scrapbook [he wrote] show that in the years 1910 and 1911 I had 51 innings with 10 not outs and an average of 19. This I consider quite a creditable record for a poet.

Sassoon, who won the MC and was recommended for the VC in the First World War, went on playing cricket until well into his seventies.

Edmund Blunden, not only a poet, but also an Oxford Professor of Poetry, was perhaps more scarred by his experiences in the trenches than was his friend Siegfried Sassoon. Blunden got some of the horrors of trench warfare out of his system in his autobiographical work *Undertones of War*, but the spectres of no-man's-land never left him. Michael Davie 'was fleetingly taught Eng. Lit. by Edmund Blunden – my first encounter with a cricketer-poet', and wrote:

> It would indeed be true to say that on several occasions the greater part of an hour's tutorial with Blunden was spent playing cricket. I always read my essay first. Less serious-minded under-graduates may well have suggested a little practice *before* reading their essays, because they hadn't actually brought an essay to read ... You could well be right about his love of cricket helping to keep him sane ... He hated the war. He hated war *per se*. Possibly the cricket practice took his mind off things. He was a sweet man.*

Blunden was a competent batsman who could let fly at times, and he was also a good wicketkeeper, who sometimes played for J. C. Squire's Invalids – of whom more anon. He helped other people to take their minds off the second war with his gently nostalgic book *Cricket Country*, published in 1941.

Robert Graves (1895–1985), poet, historical novelist and short story writer, when a schoolboy at Charterhouse, tried to get cricket demoted from being the chief summer game at the school, not because he disliked cricket, but because he disliked Charterhouse traditions. In his diary for 24 June 1915 he described a bizarre cricket match when, as an officer of the Royal Welch Fusiliers, he was billeted at Vermelles. He reproduced this extract in his autobiography, *Goodbye to All That*:

> This afternoon we had a cricket match, officers *versus* sergeants, in an enclosure between two houses out of observation from the enemy. Our front line is perhaps three-quarters of a mile away. I

* Letter to the author.

made top score, twenty-four; the bat was a bit of a rafter; the ball, a piece of rag tied round with string; and the wicket, a parrot cage with the clean, dry corpse of a parrot inside. It had evidently died of starvation when the French evacuated the town.

Cecil Day Lewis, writing his first thriller under the pseudonym of Nicholas Blake, gives an account, in *A Question of Proof*, of a prep school fathers' match so exciting that a member of the staff is able to murder the headmaster without anyone noticing. Dylan Thomas loved John Arlott's cricket commentaries, and also played cricket after his own fashion. Inviting a friend to take him on in 1946, he said, 'I have a cricket bat and hard ball and choice of lawns.'

Alan Ross, who represented Oxford University at cricket and squash, editor of the *London Magazine* and also of the *Cricketer's Companion*, achieved a poignant cameo, in free verse, of Barnes and Rhodes, octogenarians, at a Lord's test match; Barnes guiding his blind companion down the pavilion steps.

John Betjeman, in 'Cricket Master', wrote about an ignoramus getting a post as master in charge of cricket: he does not know the fielding positions or how many balls there are in an over. Evelyn Waugh did this kind of thing superlatively in *Decline and Fall* – Paul Pennyfeather teaching the organ at Llanabba Hall – but Betjeman's effort is too predictable. Other writers recently to have written cricket poetry include Edward Brathwaite, Brian Jones, Vernon Scannell, Kit Wright and Egbert Moore, whose 'Victory Calypso' sings the praises of Ramadhin and Valentine. Philip Larkin, a passive cricketer, when librarian at Leicester University, used to watch cricket at Grace Road.

Gavin Ewart has written two cricket poems of outstanding quality. 'The Sadness of Cricket – Many facts from *The Golden Age of Cricket 1890–1914* by David Frith' – depicts the summer game from a dark wintry aspect. Some of the cricketers from the Golden Age died prematurely through illness – Victor Trumper, 'Tip' Foster: 'Time can out trump a Trumper' – and through suicide – their playing days over, life held nothing for them.

Strength, talent gone – then what to do?
Great Albert Trott, like Relf was gunned down too
By his own hand in Willesden, very sad but true.

'His powers waned in 1904'
The record says – and just £4, no more,
Was found, his wardrobe left to landlady.

Johnny Briggs, Arthur Shrewsbury, Aubrey Faulkner, A. E. Stoddart, and others, Gavin Ewart tells of their suicide: like it or not, this is one of cricket's greatest poems.

Ewart's Pindaric Ode on the Headingley Test of 1981, when England, following on 227 behind, won by 18 runs, is a pulsating epic to keep us breathless on the edge of our seats:

Well Gatting was batting and Yallop came in at a gallop
to save a single . . . we could mix and mingle with a loud
crowd, on our telescreens we saw the best match ever to
be called a Test Match . . .

Don't be abrupt, don't interrupt,
just keep quiet, don't riot, sit still and listen,
hear the Umpire's bell – I'm ready to tell
a story of glory and the unfading laurel crowns that glisten.

And he does so. Even if we know the scorecard of that tremendous match off by heart, we are still at fever pitch until Willis knocks out Bright's middle stump.

A playwright can be a cricket enthusiast: he can play cricket; he can write cricket for films; but he will find it difficult to introduce cricket into a play. R. C. Sherriff, who made his name in *Journey's End*, in a later play *Badger's Green*, ingeniously introduced five minutes' cricket, seen from the pavilion, during which a property developer saves his soul, loses his fortune, through missing his train, and wins the game for his side: a lot can happen in the last over.

Ben Travers, creator of the famous Aldwych farces, was a cricket enthusiast all his life. At the age of fifteen, as he vividly relates in his autobiography *94 Declared*, he saw Jessop's century in 1902, when England beat Australia by 1 wicket. His farce, *A Bit of a Test*, starring Robertson Hare and Ralph Lynn, was produced at the Aldwych Theatre at the height of the bodyline controversy in 1933.

J. M. Barrie, as related in Chapter 3, was on friendly terms with the Australians of the Armstrong/Collins vintage. A practised after-dinner speaker, in his welcome to the 1926 Australians he delighted the tourists with a piece of mock rodomontade in which he threatened them with an unplayable England fast bowler named W. K. Thunder: as for the England batting line-up – J. B. Hobbs would be the twelfth man.

Barrie founded a team of literary cricketers that played villages in the Home Counties. As they advanced upon Shere for their first match, he discovered, during the train journey, that he had to coach several members of the side in the finer points of the game, such as which side of the bat you hit with. He asked one of the team, a travel writer, the 'African' for 'heaven help us', and was told 'Allah Akbar', so they called themselves the Allahakbars, later becoming the Allahakbarries. They fared abysmally in this game, but the next year they beat Shere, having picked up a soldier they found outside a pub, sitting with two ladies. The soldier carried them to victory. The last they saw of him he was sitting outside another pub with another two ladies.

Once the Allahakbarries hijacked an artist whom they found in a field painting cows: occasionally they won matches by surreptitiously introducing outsiders. Conan Doyle was their star regular; the others included E. V. Lucas 'who unfortunately had style', Jerome K. Jerome, who once hit two 4's, Owen Seaman, Maurice Hewlett, Augustine Birrell and A. E. W. Mason, a very fast bowler, who was liable to hit square leg in the stomach. Barrie has a charming cricket passage in *The Little White Bird*.

Lord Dunsany was a writer of enormous output, whose many plays included blood-curdling thrillers such as *A Night at an Inn*. The family home for about eight centuries had been Dunsany Castle, in the village of Dunsany, about eighteen miles from

Dublin. He was vivid, maverick and unpredictable. It was not unknown for him to shoot at the doorbell with his revolver, in order to apprise the butler of his arrival. A friend of Synge, Lady Gregory and that coterie, he was often with them, but hardly of them; he was at home with the hunting, shooting and fishing fraternity.

He learned cricket at Eton: the affable violence of the game appealed to him. He loved its illogic; its vigour; its subtleties; its poetry – above all, its glorious uncertainty. His team at Dunsany would take on sides such as I Zingari, the Free Foresters, Trinity College, Dublin, any regiments that were around. He had a good eye as a batsman – an aggressive hitter; he was an exciting slow bowler and a good slip fielder. Among his multitudinous efforts with the pen is a short story, 'How Jembu played for Cambridge', concerning an African chieftain whose magical powers enabled him to score half-centuries at will. He also composed felicitous light verse on the subject of cricket.

A. A. Milne is famous nowadays for *Winnie the Pooh*, and many prep schools, unprovoked, repeatedly stage *Toad of Toad Hall*. His domestic comedies, such as *Mr Pym Passes By*, *The Dover Road*, *Ariadne* and *Wurzel-Flummery* are out of fashion, presumably because they are dated. I hope that one day they may return to fashion, because they are excellent plays.

In *The Day's Play* Milne revelled in the ambience of cricket. His saga about *The Rabbits*, concerning the activities on and off the field of a band of cricketers whose enthusiasm outruns their ability, is joyously fascinating. His beach cricket reporting is marvellous; you can smell the seaweed. A. A. Milne played for Westminster in 1899 and 1900. He was a far more able cricketer than he pretended to be. Against a strong Oxford University Authentics eleven he made the second highest score of 44 in a total of 250 for 8; against I Zingari he clean bowled A. J. Webbe.

Milne himself was far too modest to mention these achievements, but in an article for *The Cricketer* (1921) he tells us that his greatest *tour de force* as a cricketer was when, playing against Incogniti, he bowled a maiden to the great F. G. J. Ford. Colin Blythe, Milne explains, used to puzzle the opposition by keeping his bowling hand hidden for as long as possible. Milne, so he claims, in this match bowled several yards behind the crease, and then hastily side-stepped behind the umpire. This happened six times: Ford could see the ball coming, but where was the bowler? Thoroughly rattled, he could only pat the ball back. Next over, Ford's partner hit a single, then Ford hit five sixes and the Incogniti captain declared. The story has an element of truth behind it. Against a Westminster score of 260 (Milne c&b Ford 17), Ford made 101 not out, Incogniti scoring 156 for 2 in 44 overs; Milne bowled 6 overs, 3 of which were maidens, taking 1 wicket for 12.

J. C. Squire, editor, essayist, dramatist, author of the remarkable play *Berkeley Square*, once wrote that one of his great ambitions had been to play cricket for England, and that he often imagined himself, having completed a superb innings, walking proudly off the field, batting gloves in hand, waving his bat in acknowledgement of the crowd's applause, and striding up the pavilion steps as spectators rise to salute his magnificent batsmanship.

Squire did play a lot of cricket, but not for England. He was founder and captain of the Invalids, a team run on similar lines to the Allahakbarries, consisting mainly of literary men, playing their matches in the Home Counties. In his saga, *England, their England*, A. C. Macdonnell gives an amusing account of the Invalids in action.

Terence Rattigan, modest and highly popular author of such plays as *The Winslow Boy* and *The Browning Version*, was as keen on cricket as J. C. Squire, but played it rather better. He opened the batting for Harrow in 1930.

Samuel Beckett made his name in 1953 with *Waiting for Godot*, the mysterious stranger who makes an appointment with two tramps which he never keeps – a play translated into twenty languages and produced from Tokyo to Warsaw. Beckett played for Trinity College, Dublin in their tour of England. Michael Davie has pointed out that Beckett is the only Nobel prizewinner for literature mentioned in *Wisden*. In his preface to the *Faber Book of Cricket*, Davie refers to Beckett reading the sports pages of a newspaper all the way on a flight from London to Berlin, right down to the schools cricket results. The Irish writer James Stern told Davie that when he met Beckett in Paris in the 1930s they talked only about boxing and cricket. Stern claimed that Beckett bowled right-arm tweakers with a rather contorted action. Sad to relate, in 1984 he was to write that he had lost all interest in the game.

Tom Stoppard, one of the outstanding playwrights of the present day, Czech by birth, took readily to cricket with his googly sense of humour. This is Moon speaking in *The Real Inspector Hound*:

'Sometimes I dream of revolution, a bloody *coup d'état* by the second rank – troupes of actors slaughtered by their understudies, magicians sawn in half by indefatigably smiling glamour girls, cricket teams wiped out by marauding bands of twelfth men.'

Harold Pinter established himself with his first full-length play, *The Birthday Party*, which he followed up with the enigmatic drama *The Caretaker*, with its concentrated language and rhythms of colloquial speech; the setting a dilapidated house in West London. Since 1960 he has done much for stage, screen, radio and television.

He has a deep knowledge of the cricketing scene. Here he is describing the Australians in the Lord's test, 1948:

After lunch, the Australians, arrogant, jocular, muscular, larking down the pavilion steps. They waited, hurling the ball about, eight feet tall.

When he was forty, Pinter said, 'I am a batsman who has never fulfilled his promise. What's more, I've never made 50. My highest score is 49.' He was coached at the Alf Gover cricket school, and then by Arthur Wellard at the Middlesex school. Wellard, who played for Somerset for twenty-three years (once for England), joined Pinter's club, the Gaieties – a wandering side that plays club cricket, as did Barrie's and Squire's, in the Home Counties. This is Pinter's account of Wellard, aged 72 and partially blind, playing in appalling light against Banstead in 1973:

So Arthur prepared to face what we knew had to be the last over, with one run to win. The Gaieties side, to a man, stood, smoked, walked in circles outside the pavilion, peering out at the pitch through the gloom. It appeared to be night, but we could discern Arthur standing erect, waiting for the ball. The quickie raced in and bowled. We saw Arthur's left leg go down the wicket, the bat sweep, and were suddenly aware that the ball had gone miles, in the long-on area, over the boundary for four. We had won.

It is tempting to end this section on dramatists with a quote from George Bernard Shaw, who was born three years before the first overseas tour of an English eleven, and who died three years after Bradman's last tour of England. Midway between the two wars any newspaper reporter asking Shaw a topical question could expect a pretty bright answer: for instance, returning from a visit to the States and asked for his first impression of America, he replied 'They call me the master of irony, but even I could hardly bear to see the Statue of Liberty in New York.' Yet, about the same time, when a reporter bowled him an innocent half volley, he had Shaw playing and missing:

REPORTER: Who do you think will win the test?
BERNARD SHAW: What are they testing?

Obviously, it was a test to see which was the better side, in this case England or Australia. The *Shorter Oxford English Dictionary*, which makes about a hundred allusions to cricket, defines a test:

Short for test match 1908. One of a series of matches played between representative teams to test the cricketing strength of the countries which they represent.

Bernard Shaw would have known what a test match was, but for once a bright *riposte* eluded him. He might at least have said 'You Never Can Tell'.

Prose writers on cricket fall into four main groups: first, those who wrote of cricket in its early days; second, those who have written novels and short stories in which cricket plays a central part; third, those who have devoted a chapter or section of a novel to an account of a cricket match; fourth, writers who have enriched their narratives with the use of cricket metaphors, jargon or casual references to the game, and in so doing show that they can tell a hawk from a handsaw.

First, the early writers: we can do worse than begin with a quote from Gilbert White of Selborne, in a letter written in 1786:

> Little Tom Clement is visiting at Petersfield, where he plays much cricket. Tom bats, his grandmother bowls, and his great grandmother watches out!

Mary Russell Mitford, in the 1820s, was the first of the village cricket writers. William Hazlitt, in a vignette of an old cricketer, wrote 'The very names of cricket bat and ball make English fingers tingle.' In 1837, the twenty-five-year-old Charles Dickens enlivened the year of Queen Victoria's accession when the complete *Pickwick Papers* was published. Dingley Dell played All Muggleton* and Alfred Jingle related, in boisterous staccato, his single-wicket achievements in the West Indies. Anthony Trollope died in 1882: his novel *The Fixed Period* contains a test match fantasy in which England play Britannula in 1980.

The Cricket Match, by Hugh de Selincourt, is outstanding among novels about the game. In this narrative of Tillingfold's match against Raveley, in a book of 250 pages, we get 71 pages for Tillingfold's innings, 24 for the tea interval, 38 for Raveley. This is the story of a serious village cricket match, with all its loveliness, kindliness and compassion, a novel beautifully and sensitively written, a period piece depicting life in a Sussex village in 1921, the year in fact when Armstrong's Australians were ravaging the land.

The Amateur Cracksman, by E. W. Hornung is the story of Raffles, an uppercrust burglar, the Sherlock Holmes of the criminal profession, who is known to the general public as a formidable spin bowler and a cavalier cricketer. George Orwell wrote a piece about Raffles in 1944 in which he said that cricket is an upper-class game and

* The match is currently illustrated on the back of Bank of England £10 notes.
Pickwick Papers was originally published in monthly parts from April 1836.

expensive to play – both statements wide of the mark. However, he makes interesting points about the ethics of cricket – 'its rules are so ill defined that their interpretation is partly an ethical business', concluding that 'in making Raffles a cricketer as well as a burglar, Hornung was not merely providing him with a plausible disguise; he was also drawing the sharpest moral contrast that he was able to imagine'.

One of P. G. Wodehouse's earliest literary efforts was the cricket novel *Mike*, published early in the reign of Edward VII. Mike Jackson, the youngest brother of a fine cricketing trio, gets into the Wrykin Eleven – as a replacement – to bat impressively and take his side to victory in the derby match against the rival school Ripton. The book has been republished several times: in 1968 it was republished as *Mike at Wrykin*, in a somewhat confusing manner. The Edwardian breakfasts – in the school holidays – remain: 'I say,' says Mike, at the beginning and end of the book, 'what's under that dish?' The jolly ripping schoolboy slang of Edwardian England remains as it was – but the names of great cricketers such as Ranji and Jessop have been replaced by those of England players of half a century later – May and Compton and Freddie Trueman. But it doesn't spoil the story, as it doesn't spoil Shakespeare when Puck appears wearing an Old Harrovian tie. Wodehouse wrote several other early books in which cricket features prominently and the debonair spinner Psmith joins forces with Mike Jackson, and later takes the central part in *Psmith in the City*.

Wodehouse was in the Dulwich College elevens of 1899 and 1900. A fast bowler, in his first year he took 7 for 50 against Tonbridge. In the House final of 1900 he finished off his opponents' innings with a hat trick; all clean bowled. The school magazine (the *Alleynian*) reports somewhat scathingly of him in 1899: 'bowled well against Tonbridge, but did nothing else. Does not use his head at all. A poor bat and a very slack field.' In 1900 the *Alleynian* reports that P. G. Wodehouse 'Has wonderfully improved in the field, though rather hampered by his sight.' So it was eye trouble, not slackness, that hampered his fielding. This same eye trouble prevented his enlisting in the first war; he volunteered twice. It is interesting that the great N. A. Knox, then aged fifteen, was playing in the Dulwich side with Wodehouse, though he was then regarded primarily as a batsman.*

Other cricket novels include *Willow the King*, by J. C. Snaith, a prolific and popular novelist who was also a talented all-rounder, a left-handed batsman and bowler (he played twice for Nottinghamshire at the turn of the century); *A Mother's Son*, by B. and C. B. Fry and *That Test Match* by Sir Home Gordon. More recently, three novels with a test match background are *Matheson at Melbourne*, by William Godfrey, *A Sky Blue Life* by Maurice Moisevitch, and *Testkill*, by Ted Dexter and Clifford Makins – the latter an *Observer* sports journalist.

As for the authors who have concentrated a cricket match into a section or chapter of a book, in Thomas Hughes's immortal *Tom Brown's Schooldays*, it is the end of term and Rugby are playing the MCC:

> 'Only eighteen runs and three wickets down.'
>
> 'Huzza for old Rugby!' sings out Jack Raggles, the long-stop, toughest and burliest of the boys, commonly called 'Swiper Jack'; and forthwith stands on his head, and brandishes his legs in the air in triumph, till the next boy catches hold of his heels and throws him over on to his back.

A good time is had by all, including young Arthur, who is playing not because of his off-drives, but because Tom Brown thought it would be good for him. In the event he does make a good off-drive, evoking cries of 'Well played, Young 'Un!'

H. A. Vachell's *The Hill* contains an exciting account of an Eton–Harrow match, Harrow winning by two runs as the result of a heroic runout by the Harrow captain. This was quite a match. At one stage 'grey-headed men threw their hats into the air; peers danced; lovely women shrieked.' E. M. Forster's novel *Maurice* was

---

* In 1906, his best year, Knox bowled devastatingly for Surrey and was probably as fast as Kortwright or Larwood in their prime. J. B. Hobbs said of him 'He was the best fast bowler I ever saw.' His career was curtailed through sore shins and consequent lameness.

completed in 1914 but not published until 1971. His presentation of a village cricket match is stylish, thoughtful and somewhat muted. The hero of Ernest Raymond's first and bestselling novel, *Tell England*, achieves glorious success in a match against the masters when he bowls out the great Middlesex batsman, Radley, a fictional cricketer who was playing for Middlesex before the real Clive Radley, of Middlesex and England, was born.

There is a sundrenched and convincing account of a village match, played shortly after the First World War, in Edward Bucknell's *Linden Lea*. George Mordyn, a spinner who a dozen years before had taken wickets for Winchester against Eton, is persuaded into the match. He takes 8 wickets; he knows what spin bowling is about, and so does Edward Bucknell.

In his poignant novel, *Fate Cannot Harm Me*, J. C. Masterman makes no bones about including a lengthy tale of a cricket match wholly irrelevant to the main issue. An Oxford don, he had played cricket at most levels; this fictitious story of country house cricket introduces Lt.-Col. Murcher-Pringle, a gloriously foul character, who criticizes his captain and the competence of everyone else on the field. Murcher-Pringle's behaviour provides a lurid contrast to the amiability of the other players.

In *The Go-Between*, one of the outstanding novels of the last fifty years, L. P. Hartley sets his story in high Norfolk, at the time of the Boer War. The story is centred round thirteen-year-old Leo Colston, a guest at Brandham Hall. The game between Brandham Hall and the village is a beautifully evocative period piece: young Leo, fielding as substitute at the end of the match, has his moment of glory when he takes a blinding catch at square leg to dismiss the lusty tenant farmer Ted Burgess, who had nearly run away with the game.

Geoffrey Household's novel *Fellow Traveller* concerns the maverick activities of a university player who becomes, spectacularly, a prisoner in the Tower of London. While on the run he gets involved in a village cricket match; his peculiar style as a slow bowler gives him away to a knowledgeable spectator as Wolferstan, the man who spun Oxford to a notable victory. The cricket match in

John Hadfield's *Love on a Branch Line* is great fun; bucolic, amatory and Bacchanalian.

E. V. Lucas wrote a dozen novels and many books of essays. His light verse includes a lovely poem on the three Graces, but it was in some of his essays that he chiefly wrote on cricket. In her charming book, *Portrait of E. V. Lucas*, his daughter Audrey describes a match which EVL contrived to arrange at Downe House (once the residence of Charles Darwin), where Audrey Lucas went to school, in which his side played an eleven captained by J. M. Barrie. Which side won 'this most excellent match' Audrey Lucas did not remember, but thought that the favourite was 'George Morrow, who, if not brilliant, was most endearingly industrious, and the sight of whose behind disappearing in search of the ball through a hole in the hedge gave rise to hearty cheers.' A group photograph shows the players wearing cricket flannels or informal clothes. They include J. M. Barrie, EVL, A. A. Milne, Maurice Hewlett, George Morrow, Walter Frith, Denis Mackail and Harry Graham.

Some of the great English novelists of this century, without recounting fictional cricket matches, none the less show by casual phrases, brief paragraphs and passages, comments and conversations, a knowledge of the game that is better than average.

John Galsworthy in his later Forsyth novels peppers his pages with cricket metaphors. He is also fascinatingly ironical in *The White Monkey* on the subject of Elderson, a much-respected City man who is suddenly suspected of being a financial shark of the deepest water. Sir Lawrence Mont cannot believe the mounting evidence against a man who used to go in No. 3 for Winchester.

> 'If Elderson could do such a thing, well – really, anything might happen. It's a complete stumper. He was such a pretty bat, always went in first wicket down. He and I put on fifty-four against Eton.'

But Elderson *could* do such a thing; Sir Lawrence learns that Elderson has Levanted.

Evelyn Waugh did not share his father's or his brother Alec's love of cricket. He played at least one match for Squire's Invalids, recording that he was out second ball and missed a catch. He wrote an amusingly unenthusiastic article about cricket in the *Cherwell*. In *Brideshead Revisited* Nanny Hawkins accuses Sebastian Flyte of 'cricketing all day long', and Father Mackay, visiting the dying Lord Marchmain, asks Charles Ryder if he saw Tennyson's recent half-century.

References to cricket in Anthony Powell's twelve-volume saga *Dance to the Music of Time* are rare, but they are brought off with deft assurance. Charles Stringham, at Eton, describes how he goes into the shop, where the Eton eleven are ragging about after a match. Widmerpool, no cricketer, is standing by himself with a glass of lemonade in front of him. The cricket captain throws a skinned banana at one of the team, misses – and hits Widmerpool. 'Characteristic of the eleven's throwing-in,' observes Nicholas Jenkins.

The charmingly devious Sunny Farebrother takes his cricket bat and pads with him on his travels, not in order to play cricket, but because it creates a good impression. Towards the end of the saga Widmerpool gets hit again: this time at a dinner-table cricket game, by a peach.

For Graham Greene, in his autobiography *A Sort of Life*, there were two kinds of cricket – the game he enjoyed playing with a few friends, as a little boy, and the compulsory cricket he played at Berkhamsted, which he hated. As a seven-year-old, filling in a questionnaire, in answer to the query 'Which is the cricketer you most admire?' he wrote 'Herbert Greene'.

> My eldest brother was the only cricketer I knew, so my praise was not exaggerated. I remember how at Overstrand I went with him to a county match, and he asked me to collect the autographs of the team, who he thought would be more amenable to the request of a little boy. The captain used my head as a desk to write on . . . Only once, on a later occasion, did I collect a signature, when I ran, in my school cap, after G. K. Chesterton, as he laboured like a Lepanto Galleon down Shaftesbury Avenue.

*

A last look round at writers with a cricketing theme.

It must be admitted that D. L. A. Jephson (1871–1926) is known more as a cricketer than as a writer. A Cambridge blue, he played for Surrey from 1891 to 1904, captaining the side in 1901 and 1902. In 1899 he changed from fast overarm bowling to lobs and took 6 for 21 in the Gentlemen *v* Players match at Lord's. He made nine centuries for Surrey. In 1900, against Derbyshire, he and Bobby Abel put on 364 for the first wicket, Jephson scoring 213. In his last season he did the hat trick with his lobs against Middlesex. Briefly on the Stock Exchange he later turned his attention to writing. Among his publications was a book of light verse, *A Few Overs*; another effort, *A Song of Cricket*, was set to music. He wrote numerous short stories and essays.

E. F. Benson's *David Blaize* tells of a perky prep school cricketer; and there is plenty of cricket in Ian Hay's *Pip*. Stacey Aumonier wrote a wistful short story in 1916 about a village cricket field. Shane Leslie, in *The Oppidan*, wrote briefly about an Eton *v* Harrow match; Lou King Hall, in *Fly Envious Time*, about the wife of a county cricket secretary; Christopher Hollis in *Death of a Gentleman* writes convincingly on county cricket. Dorothy Sayers – *Murder Must Advertise* – makes Lord Peter Wimsey try to bat inelegantly; John Creasey's whodunit *A Six for the Toff* has the Oval as its background.

The Hampdenshire Wonder, by J. D. Beresford, begins as a cricket novel, and turns into something quite different. 'Ginger' Stott, a first-class bowler, has his county career cut short because of an amputated finger. He now wants his infant son to become a world-beater; and so he does, but not as a cricketer. By the age of three the boy's IQ has rocketed beyond human understanding. He assimilates, in a few hours, the history of mankind, and finds it chaotic. His potential is apparently boundless. Then the three-year-old is found drowned. Was it murder?

John Moore, who made his name after the Second World War with *Portrait of Elmbury* and *Brensham Village*, writes affectionately of Mr Chorlton, his prep school master, who had played for Somerset when MacLaren made his 424. From prep school Moore went to Malvern, where he hated the 'regimented cricket'. He paints a sympathetic picture of Gloucestershire's maverick Charlie Parker, in the 1920s the best left-arm bowler in the country, but he was a poor fielder, and could be a difficult man to deal with.

Numerous present-day writers touch on cricket. Simon Raven and V. S. Naipaul have written knowledgeably on the subject. Alice Thomas Ellis, in *The Sin Eater*, takes a cautious look at the annual set-to between Llanelys and The Visitors, played, appropriately enough, on the Elysian Field: 'The morning of the cricket match dawned dust grey and saddening,' she observes triumphantly, and contents herself with describing the awful quarter of an hour in the pavilion area before the match starts:

> Michael looked nervous. He juggled a little with his bat and did a few dance steps. It was extraordinary how much it mattered to them, thought Rose.

Gavin Lyall, in *The Conduct of Major Maxim*, takes us to a prep school match when young Chris Maxim scores a fluent 32 before being caught in the slips. Major Maxim and Agnes Algar have been watching:

> 'You know what they say in Yorkshire,' Maxim offered, 'Never make a late cut until September, and then only on alternate Tuesdays.'
> 'You've said that before, Daddy.'
> 'I'll say it every time I see you contributing to the Slips' Benevolent Fund.'

It seems appropriate to conclude this chapter by quoting from Thomas Keneally, Australian novelist and Booker prizewinner. Keneally believes that Australia's sense of nationhood developed through cricket: the first flickerings of desire for independence burnt in 1878, when they first defeated England. And he tells us 'No Australian had written *Paradise Lost*, but Bradman had made 100 before lunch at Lord's.'

CHAPTER 13

Cricket, Royalty and Politicians

The first member of the royal family to take an active interest in cricket was Frederick, Prince of Wales, heir to George II, who played about the time of the formation of the Hambledon club. In 1751, during the course of a match, he was hit by a cricket ball on the temple, and died as a result of the blow, predeceasing his father by eight years.

George IV was an enthusiastic cricketer. In a footnote to an interview with Prince Christian Victor, W. A. Bettesworth relates that the king,

> when riding in the Great Park, at Windsor, once came across a large party of his domestics playing the game near the Lodge. At the unexpected approach of the King the servants began to scamper in all directions, but His Majesty, much amused, sent one of the gentlemen in attendance to desire them to continue their game, and never to let his approach interrupt their sports. The King then continued his ride in another direction, observing to his attendants that cricket was a noble game, and that when he used to play cricket he enjoyed it as much as anyone.*

Edward VII as Prince of Wales showed considerable interest in cricket at all levels. He supported country house cricket at Sandringham and on occasion acted as captain of his Sandringham eleven. Unfortunately the only statistic I have of his achievements consists of the line:

HRH the Prince of Wales   b   Wright   o.

---

* W. A. Bettesworth, *Chats on the Cricket Field*. I am strongly prejudiced in favour of Mr Bettesworth as a historian because when he visited us in 1926, he gave me half a crown, with strict instructions to spend it how I liked.

He was patron of the Surrey County Cricket Club from 1888 until 1901. He was followed, first as Prince of Wales, and then as King, by George V, since when the patron has always been the monarch.

Prince Christian Victor (1867–1900) was a grandson of Queen Victoria, the eldest son of HRH Prince Christian of Schleswig-Holstein and of Queen Victoria's third daughter Helena Augusta Victoria. He played for three years for Wellington College, being captain in his third year. At Oxford he was in the Magdalen eleven and was considered unlucky not to have got a blue. He was a good wicketkeeper and a good batsman; Grace was much impressed by his ability at cutting. He once made 230 in a house match and in a game of regimental cricket in India he scored 205. He was interviewed by W. A. Bettesworth in 1896 as one of the subjects of *Chats on the Cricket Field*. A versatile and amiable young man, while serving as an officer in the Greenjackets he died of enteric fever in the Boer War and was buried in Pretoria.

George V was not an active cricketer, but made numerous visits to test matches at Lord's, when the England and visiting teams were presented to him. Conscientious in all his duties he made it his business to acquaint himself with the salient events of the bodyline tour. According to I. A. R. Peebles he mastered his brief most effectively.

Edward VIII, when Prince of Wales, came to the Australian test at the Oval, possibly because it was the occasion of Jack Hobbs's last appearance for England. This was in 1930. Peebles writes that

> When he arrived Duleep and I were alone in the dressing room and rather dejected, having spent two days in the field and fearing we might well be there for another two. The Prince had obviously been hastily briefed for he said to me 'You have just come down from Cambridge haven't you?' to which I replied 'No sir. I'm still up at Oxford.' There was a slight hiatus and he then said to Duleep 'Of course, you're still up at Oxford' to which Smith [one of Duleepsinhji's nicknames] replied 'No, sir. I came down from Cambridge two years ago.' On the whole we felt that

the occasion hadn't been an outstanding success, but we had gained some insight into the trials Royalty has to bear.*

Bradman's 1948 Australians were guests of George VI and Queen Elizabeth (the Queen Mother) at Balmoral. Their son-in-law the Duke of Edinburgh was president of the MCC in 1949 and again in 1974–75. He was captain of cricket at Gordonstoun. He continued playing cricket in the 1950s. In 1953 he skippered his own team against the Duke of Norfolk's eleven, containing several stars, scoring 18 and taking 1 for 24; when the fixture was repeated in 1957 Prince Philip took 4 for 60 – Tom Graveney was one of his victims. In an article for *Wisden*, 1975, he shows an incisive understanding of the subject that would do justice to any professional cricket writer:

> There is a widely held and quite erroneous belief that cricket is just another game . . . it can be as brutal as rugby and as delicate as chess; it requires all the grace and fitness of athletes, but at the same time it requires the psychological judgement and insight of master politicians.

Queen Elizabeth II has often added charm and distinction to Lord's. She was the first woman officially to have been escorted into the famous Long Room. Unofficially, the irrepressible R. J. O. Meyer, as an undergraduate in the early 1920s, is reputed to have introduced a girlfriend, disguised in male attire, into the holy of holies.

But times have changed. 'Ladies are not normally allowed in the Long Room during the hours of play,' writes Stephen Green, Curator of Lord's cricket museum, 'but the pavilion is frequently used by the fair sex at other times for all sorts of purposes. Almost every day of the year a mixed group, for example, comes to look round the Long Room as tourists.'

The Queen, now a veteran of forty years of test cricket at Lord's, is naturally adept at greeting the England and opposing sides that

---

* I. A. R. Peebles, *Batter's Castle* (Pavilion).

are presented to her. Once – during the Centenary Test, when the teams were being presented – Dennis Lillee produced his autograph book, asking the Queen to 'sign here please Ma'am'. The Queen replied serenely that unfortunately she was unable to do so on such an occasion as this; Lillee was surprised and delighted when a day or so later he received by post a signed photograph of Her Majesty. Even the Queen, however, must have been more than a little surprised, some years later, when the England team were being presented to her and Phil Edmonds, so the story runs, asked with a charming smile 'How did you know that blue was my favourite colour?' In 1994, when the South Africans were playing the Earl of Carnarvon's XI, press photographers showed the Queen trying on David Gower's sunglasses. David Gower was captaining the Invitation XI.

Today several members of the royal family act as patrons of cricket. The Queen is patron of the MCC, Surrey and Lancashire; the Duke of Edinburgh is patron of Middlesex, the Prince of Wales of Glamorgan; the Princess of Wales of Gloucestershire, the Duke of Kent (appropriately enough) of Kent; the Duchess of Kent of Yorkshire – her father, Sir William Worsley, was a former Yorkshire captain and president.

Over to the politicians, and here I have prime ministers chiefly in mind. First, a word about the Lords *v* Commons matches, which have taken place for many years. Owing to the exigencies of parliament, players in these matches have often had to drop out, and replacements from outside the two houses of parliament have not infrequently taken part. In one game a spin bowler for the Commons took two wickets in an over. The noble lord at the non-striker's end congratulated the bowler:

'You bowl very well, you know.'
'Thank you.'
'With a bit of coaching you should become pretty good.'
'Thank you.'
'What team do you play for, by the way?'
'England.'

The replacement bowler was G. T. S. Stevens, of Oxford University and Middlesex, spin bowler, humorist and amateur cartoonist, who played in ten test matches for England in the 1920s.

Nowadays, combined Lords and Commons teams play a dozen or so matches a year in the London area. In 1922, against Conservative Agents, Lords and Commons made 161 for 8 in 30 overs, the Rt. Hon. Tom King scoring 42. A fortnight later they lost to MCC by 57 runs, *Wisden* explaining that Lords and Commons had lost 9 wickets, but one batsman had retired 'due to an appointment with the Prime Minister'. In 1993 (16 June) the match between Conservative Agents and Lords and Commons was cancelled owing to a three-line whip, and on 23 July the match between Fleet Street and Lords and Commons was cancelled owing to a vote of confidence.

Prime ministers have varied in their attitude to cricket. The Duke of Wellington was supposed to have said that the battle of Waterloo was won on the playing fields of Eton. If we can believe that we can believe anything: the Duke of Wellington loathed Eton.

An anecdote relating to Edward Canning, who became foreign secretary in 1822 and prime minister in 1827, is told by Charles Wordsworth, nephew to the poet, who found himself deputizing as host to Canning in a cottage near Rydal Water that his father had rented. Before a dinner party that included Canning, William Wordsworth and Robert Southey, young Charles Wordsworth was asked to show Canning round the garden. He was full of the Eton and Harrow match, and rather tactlessly gave a ball-by-ball account of the game to the Old Etonian Canning:

> While my father went upstairs to arrange his toilette for the evening, I had the honour of showing the great orator and statesman into the garden – a beautiful spot – and he walked by my side with his arm upon my shoulder (I was then a boy of sixteen) listening in the kindest manner and with keen interest to all the particulars I had to tell respecting the grand cricket match – then a novel occurrence – between Eton and Harrow which had been played only a few days before, and in which I had taken such a prominent part, with the result of defeat to Eton and victory to

Harrow; Canning's own sympathies, of course, being with the former, though he was too generous to disclose them.*

Lord Palmerston, another Harrovian, was probably the first prime minister to use a cricket metaphor when talking politics. 'It's our innings now!' he said, on an occasion when the Tories weren't doing too well.

The Etonian Gladstone, Palmerston's successor as leader of the Whigs, soon to be renamed the Liberals, cut trees but not cricket balls in his spare time. Disraeli, no cricketer, was surely a spinner manqué.

The fifth Earl of Rosebery, who became Gladstone's successor as prime minister and leader of the Liberal party in 1894, when Gladstone resigned at the age of eighty-five, was a racing man but not a cricketer. His son, Lord Dalmeny, later the sixth Earl, certainly *was* a cricketer and, as he was also a politician, perhaps it is not out of order for him to appear as a substitute for his father. In the Eton eleven of 1900 Lord Dalmeny scored 52 against Harrow and 55 against Winchester. After a few games for Buckinghamshire and then for Middlesex, he captained Surrey from 1905 to 1907. Apart from his uninhibited driving, two events stood out for Surrey in 1905. First, Dalmeny obtained royal permission for the county club to use the Prince of Wales's feathers as their crest. Second, 1905 saw Jack Hobbs's debut as a first-class cricketer. In his second match for Surrey, Hobbs scored a century against Essex; his innings was sufficient for Dalmeny to appreciate Hobbs's potential, and he gave him his county cap at the end of the game. Dalmeny scored two centuries for Surrey, in the first of which he hit fiercely during a sixth-wicket stand of 260 with J. N. Crawford. An exhilarating batsman, in first-class cricket he scored 3,551 runs for an average of 23. As the sixth Earl of Rosebery he was president of the MCC in 1953.

David Lloyd George was prime minister when Glamorgan became a first-class county in 1921. He was a competent golfer, but

---

* Charles Wordsworth, *Annals of my Early Life, 1806–1846* (Longmans, Green).

he didn't play cricket – another spin bowler lost to the game.

Ramsay Macdonald, golfer, was fully aware of the fact that England had a cricket team. When the cable between England and Australia was inaugurated in 1932, he conversed over the sound-waves with the Australian premier, concluding with the quip that he would place no embargo on the return of the Ashes to England. Whether he approved of the methods employed to bring back the Ashes in 1933 is another matter.

Stanley Baldwin (Earl Baldwin of Bewdley) was prime minister during the General Strike, and again during the abdication crisis. English of the English, an equable pipe-smoking man, he loved cricket and had a deep knowledge and understanding of the game.

Stanley Baldwin was born in 1867 and went to Hawtrey's prep school at the age of ten. It was a big break from the home life that he had so loved, but his mother counselled him to stick to work and cricket. From Hawtrey's he went to Harrow. Wearing his first top hat, he was taken to see Harrow defeat Eton, where the largest schoolboy he had ever seen, batting for Harrow, hit his first ball into the old pavilion. The large schoolboy, Rory Neill, Lord Cushendun, was to become a cabinet minister when Baldwin was premier.

During the General Strike in 1926, Baldwin managed to find time to attend a dinner in honour of the Australian touring team. In his speech of welcome he observed that the Prince of Wales once captained an England team and was beaten, but that was two hundred years ago. He continued:

> 'I find it difficult to express to the Australian team what their visit means to old men like myself [he was 58] who ... have followed with the keenest interest from the days of early childhood the performances of the giants of cricket right across the world. To us the mere word "Australia" smacks of romance and we think of our childhood and those great names upon which we were brought up, and we seem to see once more the demon bowler at work – the great Spofforth.'

He went on to refer to other of the Australian immortals –

Turner, Trumble, Ernest Jones, Victor Trumper, Clem Hill, Giffen, Blackham and Bonnor.

Baldwin was in at the death when England defeated Australia at the Oval, to regain the Ashes after fourteen years, among scenes of tremendous excitement. On this occasion, as on many others, he was probably wearing his I Zingari tie. George Beet told me that once when umpiring at Lord's he was sitting in front of the pavilion for five minutes before play started, to accustom himself to the light. Baldwin sat down beside him: 'Well, Mr Beet, your job is very much the same as mine. Whatever decision you make, everyone will say it was wrong.'

In 1938 Baldwin became the first prime minister to be president of the MCC. His daughter Diana married George Kemp-Welch, the Cambridge blue, who played for Warwickshire from 1927 to 1935, and who was among those killed when a flying bomb hit the Guards Chapel during a service in 1944. Earl Baldwin's wife died in 1945, and his widowed daughter Diana Kemp-Welch looked after him until his death in 1947.

Winston Churchill chatted about cricket on one occasion to I. A. R. Peebles. Churchill, it turned out, had retired early from the game, at the age of ten in fact, with a broken thumb. At Harrow, briefly and little to his elation, he was fag to A. C. MacLaren. As related in Chapter 2, he didn't take kindly to General Alexander and Walter Monckton discussing Fowler's match immediately after Dunkirk. In common with other war leaders, he was later to accept life membership of MCC and I Zingari.

Clement Attlee, Labour prime minister from 1945 to 1951, had, like Stanley Baldwin, a deep love of the game. In his autobiography, *As It Happened*, Attlee writes of his prep school in Hertfordshire:

> The real 'religion' of Hall and Poland [the headmasters] was cricket. The ideal in life was to become a first-class county cricketer; the Holy of Holies, the pavilion at Lord's. Every afternoon throughout the summer we played cricket. In the breaks and at odd times we practised with cut-down bats and rope balls, in the paved stable-yard and in the gravel-yard. In the evenings in

the schoolroom we played 'paper cricket', dabbing with a pencil on to a paper marked with runs and cricket happenings, and scoring the results against the names of members of rival teams; not infrequently the Kings of Israel and Judah, the former always being captained by Jehu on account of his driving prowess. We knew the names and scores and the likenesses of all the principal cricketers of the epoch, headed, of course, by W. G. Grace, then at the height of his renown. I never was much use at the game. A good field, nothing of a bowler and a most uncertain bat, I hovered on the edge of the team but never got my colours.

He remembered 'long, lazy afternoons ... meticulously keeping scores and bowling analyses, while we lay stretched on the grass drinking ginger beer, which was always provided on these occasions'.

In 1896 he went to Haileybury, where the headmaster, Edward Lyttelton, of Cambridge University and England, saw to it that Haileybury was a cricket-conscious school. In the same year, Attlee's father bought a country house in the village of Thorpe-le-Soken, Essex, and here Clem Attlee played cricket as a member of the village team.

In later years Pelham Warner was to describe Attlee as 'a first-rate captain of a third-rate team'. At a Lord's test in the late 1940s, according to Allen Synge, 'Shrimp' Leveson-Gower, not the most shrinking of violets, leaned from his perch into a neighbouring box where Warner was entertaining the PM, and loudly enjoined the Labour leader to 'play a straight bat' and forgo his nationalization policy.

Attlee was once spotted in the House of Commons, reading a magazine, his face anything but cheerful.

'What's the trouble,' asked a friend. 'Nuclear bombs?'

'Worse than that,' said Attlee, displaying a cricket periodical, 'Haileybury hasn't got any spin bowlers.'

Since 1950 cricket has tended to become a political football. When Warwickshire won the county championship in 1951, Anthony Eden, as MP for Leamington, sent a telegram of congratulations to the club. He was immediately asked to become a vice president, and accepted the invitation, though he had previously shown little interest in Warwickshire cricket. In the 1955 general election he was intro-duced at one meeting as a Warwickshire cricket enthusiast, and was wearing the Warwickshire tie.

Harold Macmillan (Lord Stockton) was not especially keen on cricket but he attended several matches at a prep school near his home in Sussex and showed evident enjoyment of the game.

Sir Alec Douglas-Home (Lord Home of the Hirsel), Mac-millan's successor, was the best cricket player of all our prime ministers. As Lord Dunglass he was in the Eton eleven of 1921 and 1922. Opening the innings, he scored 30 and 4 against Harrow in 1921; the following year, in a match spoilt by rain, he made top score of 66. He later played a few games for Middlesex and also enjoyed turning out for Eton Ramblers. President of the MCC in 1966–67, he didn't use cricket metaphors in politics (although in one radio election broadcast he made the surprising statement that the Beatles were his secret weapon).

Harold Wilson, coming from the county of the white rose, natur-ally keen on the game, spoke entertainingly about cricket, and, in the course of an election broadcast, referred to Freddie Trueman as 'the greatest living Yorkshireman'.

Edward Heath reacted to Kent's winning of the county cham-pionship in 1970 in more or less the same way that Anthony Eden did to Warwickshire's success. However, as he was actually in office when Kent won the championship, he was able not only to send a telegram of congratulations, but also to invite the Kent team to dinner at 10 Downing Street. Harold Wilson followed Heath for another innings and James Callaghan followed on. In the 1964 general election Callaghan was opposed by Ted Dexter who was Conservative candidate for the Cardiff South-East constituency: Callaghan's majority increased from 868 to 7,814.

Mrs Thatcher, as she then was, not a frequent visitor to Lord's or the Oval, often invoked cricket metaphors, and in particular liked using the expression 'I'm batting for Britain'. It was at the termi-nation of her time as prime minister that the House of Commons almost literally vibrated to the sound of cricketing idioms. Geoffrey

Howe, who had been deputy prime minister and foreign secretary, set the ball rolling by complaining bitterly to a breathless House that his captain had sent him in to open the innings with a broken bat. Mrs Thatcher's riposte that Geoffrey Howe should have got a new bat failed to convince her listeners. At the prospect of Michael Heseltine challenging for the captaincy, she broke into a farrago of cricket idiom, in which she asserted that anybody who tried to bowl her out would be hit all over the ground: none the less, shortly afterwards she declared her own innings closed.

Who should bat next? Michael Heseltine, Douglas Hurd and John Major had all got their pads on. In the event, it was John Major, a keen Surrey supporter, who scored the necessary runs to become prime minister. Since then he has become a member of the MCC, and, following the examples of Stanley Baldwin and Clem Attlee, he watches test matches when opportunity offers.

It goes without saying that any prime minister of Australia has to be interested in cricket. There could be no doubt about Sir Robert Menzies' involvement in the game. A cricket lover all his life and a great ambassador for cricket, Sir Robert was premier of Australia from 1939 to 1944, and from 1949 to 1966. When he retired from active politics he saw a lot of cricket in England; intrigued by what Freddie Trueman was chuntering to himself as he went back to his mark, he reached the conclusion that the Yorkshire fast bowler was quoting iambic pentameters from the ancient classical poets.

There are not many people around with a greater knowledge of Caribbean cricket than Michael Manley, prime minister of Jamaica 1972–80 and 1989–92; he is also the author of a comprehensive *History of West Indian Cricket.*

A century ago there lived a flamboyant Irishman who never became prime minister, but who created more of a stir in the political scene than many politicians before or since. Charles Stewart Parnell (1845–1891), leader of the Irish National Party in the 1880s, could be as highly individual as a cricketer as he was as a politician. Once, having led his team on to the field, he quarrelled with his opposing captain over some trivial details; the latter not complying, Parnell took his side off the field and the match was abandoned.

Sir Home Gordon recounted a story concerning Parnell in America at a time when the Free Foresters were touring in the States. One short, they asked him to play in a match which the American press was erroneously calling England v United States. The protagonist of Irish Home Rule regretfully declined. 'It wouldn't do,' he said. 'If it was in the papers that I had played for a side called England, there would be no end of a row.'

CHAPTER 14

Cricket and Class Distinction

> The rich man in his castle
> The poor man at his gate,
> God made them high or lowly
> And ordered their estate.

So wrote Mrs C. F. Alexander in 1848. This attitude to class distinction, the Alexander syndrome, permeated English social life in the nineteenth century, and although it took hard knocks following two world wars, who can say that it has totally disappeared? The purpose of this chapter is to discuss the Alexander syndrome in its connexion with first-class cricket in England.

> God bless the squire and his relations
> And keep us in our proper stations.

The poor man was not always contented with his lot, though generally speaking he had no desire to castle the rich man. Lines of demarcation were tacit, only when it was considered necessary were practical measures taken to ensure that the toe of the peasant didn't come too near the heel of the courtier.

The early games up to the end of the eighteenth century took place in multifarious venues and circumstances, so that class distinction as such simply existed as part of the social order, rather than as facets peculiar to cricket, which tended to come later. The first Gentlemen v Players match was played in 1806: the sides were simply Amateurs and Professionals – a pity they weren't so named – but the games were run on the same lines as Marrieds v Singles, Over 30s v Under 30s and Smokers v Non-Smokers, which were popular during the nineteenth century.

By the mid-1860s the county championship with its three-day matches had evolved and a certain or rather an uncertain amount of apartheid had become evident. Amateurs and professionals had separate dressing-rooms. For away matches amateurs were generally entertained by the local gentry; professionals were booked in at commercial hotels or bed and breakfast houses, or they might be given not over-generous expenses, with instructions to find their own accommodation. Taking the field, the amateurs would go out first, normally through a separate gate, the captain having pressed a bell connected with the professionals' dressing-room, the pros duly following in the amateurs' wake. Amateurs would be referred to, and addressed on the field of play, as Mister, unless, of course, like Lord Harris, Lord Hawke, Lord Dalmeny and Sir Timothy O'Brien, they were titled. Senior professionals, like RSMs in the Army, were often given the courtesy title of Mister, on formal occasions, by the amateurs, and, of course, by the younger pros. The relationship between amateurs and professionals was in fact very similar to that between officers and other ranks in the Army.

To some amateurs all this was as it should be. Andy Sandham has related that when D. R. Jardine encountered him in the street the latter would walk past him and ignore his existence. There were other amateurs with a similar outlook. The majority of them were more outgoing, addressing the pros by their first names, and – especially in the early 1900s – referring to them collectively as the professors. Amateurs and professionals of both sides could, if they wanted to, meet for a drink in the pavilion bar after close of play, but beyond that fraternization was not customary. 'Ranji' was an exception: he once wrote to the England wicketkeeper, Dick Lilley, who had co-operated with him in a brilliant runout, suggesting that they should meet in London and go to a show.

A. E. R. Gilligan, of Cambridge University, Sussex and England, was one of the most highly popular and respected captains the game has known, and although it was perfectly natural for him to address professionals, especially his Sussex pros, by their Christian names, two-way traffic was just not on the cards. Gilligan would address M. W. Tate as Maurice, but the nearest Tate and the other professionals would get to informality, even over a celebratory drink, would be to call Gilligan 'Skipper': to address him as Arthur would have been unthinkable.

A conversation at the end of the day's play between H. L. Higgins, the Worcestershire amateur, and Harry Howell, the Warwickshire fast bowler (a professional), was told verbatim to me a couple of times by HLH, nearly forty years after the chat had taken place:

'That was a bit cheeky, wasn't it, Mr Higgins, hooking me for four like that?'

'Well, Harry, when it gets to around six o'clock, you're a bit slow.'

Turn the conversation on its head:

'That was a bit cheeky, wasn't it, Higgins, hooking me for four like that?'

'Well, Mr Howell, when it gets to around six o'clock, you're a bit slow.'

This, in 1921, would have been impossible. If Harry Howell had said 'Higgins' without the 'Mr' it would have been assumed that he was being deliberately impertinent, and if HLH had addressed Harry Howell as Mr, the latter would have been deeply hurt, assuming something unkindly meant.

This conversation actually took place at close of play, when HLH had scored 99 not out. The next morning his sister went to the ground to see him make his century. HLH faced Harry Howell, who, with the best will in the world, bowled him a slow half-volley, but had forgotten to tell him he would do so. The result was that Laddie Higgins, playing too early at the ball, spooned a dolly catch to Len Bates, who either knew nothing about the intended gift of a single, or else was taken by surprise, and who made the catch.

Wisden's accounts of matches were meticulously clear in pointing out who were amateurs and who were professionals. This is a typical extract (Somerset *v* Kent at Taunton in 1891):

Alec Hearne and Mr Best opened Kent's innings, and in the first over from Tyler the amateur hit eleven runs and was then finely caught at point, while at 14 Hearne was bowled. Mr Fox and Mr Marchant then freely punished the home bowling . . .

In contrast to this, the Hon. R. H. Lyttelton, in the same issue of *Wisden's*, writing a feature article on the development of cricket, mentions numerous cricketers, amateur and professional, without bothering to differentiate, referring to them simply by their surnames, before making the *avant garde* statement that the scythe, however effectively used, is not comparable with the mower in preparing a pitch.

F. S. Ashley Cooper, writing thirty-two years later in his *History of Nottinghamshire County Cricket*, was also orthodox in his discrimination: the relevant achievements of Mr A. O. Jones and Mr A. W. Carr are recorded, so too are those of Hobbs, Hendren, Hardstaff and Hitch. Team photographs taken before the Second World War, decking county pavilions, generally have the amateurs indicated with the initials in front, and the professionals with the bare surnames.

In the years between the wars several professionals assumed amateur status towards the end of their careers. On the other hand L. C. Eastman, extrovert Essex all-rounder, switched from amateur to professional. Nigel Haig thought seriously of becoming a professional, and had support from, of all people, his uncle Lord Harris; eventually Haig abandoned the idea. What did cause a flutter in the dovecotes, not to mention the Long Room, was when Paul Gibb (1916–1976), a Cambridge blue, signed professional forms, playing for Yorkshire and Essex. He eventually became a first-class umpire, travelling from ground to ground in his caravan.

The attitude of such people as Eastman, Haig and Gibb was in marked contrast to the shamateurism that had prevailed in first-class cricket since the days of W. G. Grace (the greatest shamateur of them all, who received lucrative testimonials in reward for his prowess for Gloucestershire and England), and especially from the 1920s onwards. Amateur status was formally abolished in 1962, cricketers in first-class counties becoming contracted players. Somewhat paradoxically, players coming from what was loosely called the professional classes had been anxious to maintain their amateur status. Owing to the economic conditions following the First World War this was not easily done; indeed it was the economic situation that caused the collapse of cricket in Philadelphia. In England, cricketers accepted posts as assistant secretaries or took up positions as administrative officers in firms where the chief executives were supporters of the county cricket clubs concerned. In 1946 T. R. Reddick was asked by the Nottinghamshire committee whether he wished to play as an amateur or a professional. He enquired which paid better.

My father had quickly become aware of the Alexander syndrome when, at the turn of the last century, as assistant secretary of Warwickshire, his eyes were opened to the fact that at luncheon the amateurs were served with salmon, whilst the professionals, seated with the amateurs at the same table, were given cod, which was then pretty well the cheapest fish on the market. In those days professionals were expected, if required, to bowl to the members in the nets. Jack Shilton, a Falstaffian figure, who with Knack Pallett bowled Warwickshire into first-class cricket, once bowled for over an hour, alone, to a practice-hungry member. At the end of the session, the member took off his gloves and pads, put on his blazer, opened his purse, said thank you, and handed Jack Shilton twopence.

One of the brightest sparks of English cricket about this time was Sir Timothy O'Brien. Born in 1861, appropriately enough on 5 November, he went in No. 6 immediately after F. G. J. Ford in a Middlesex side that generally contained nine amateurs. He made his last appearance for the county in 1898, but in 1914 at the age of 53, playing for Lionel Robinson's XI against Oxford University, he savaged the university attack, batting splendidly for 90 and 111. Sir Timothy was the third baronet.

Sir Timothy preferred the ambience of the Long Room at Lord's to the less salubrious surroundings of the Oval. When playing against Surrey at the Oval he made it quite clear that he was not accustomed to slumming and had no liking for playing among the caitiffs and coistrels that abounded at the Oval, and developed the habit of flicking imaginary fleas from his shirt as he walked from the pavilion on to the field. He would have got on well with Beau Brummell, who resigned from the Army when his regiment was sent to Manchester.

The amateurs' gate, on some grounds a kind of antithesis to the tradesmen's entrance, was likely to have a provocative effect on some professionals. W. G. Quaife was a case in point. This diminutive Warwickshire pro was a great batsman – he scored a century in his final first-class innings, at the age of fifty-six. He was also extremely disputatious. In 1899 he reacted strongly to the rule of the Leyton ground that only amateurs could use the centre pavilion gate and that professionals must use the entrance on the side. Quaife flouted the rule and was reported by the Essex Club for doing so. The Essex crowd, who saw what was going on, had cheered Quaife, and the *Birmingham Post* said 'such incidents and unnecessary insistence on class distinctions between amateurs and professionals cannot be for the benefit of the game'. It is interesting that a Conservative paper like the *Birmingham Post* should have shown overt sympathy with Quaife over the matter. Not so the Warwickshire committee, who expressed their disapproval over Quaife's behaviour.

In the same season of 1899 the Warwickshire committee reacted quite differently to an incident in which A. C. S. Glover, an amateur, was involved. Glover was playing for Warwickshire against Gloucestershire at Edgbaston, and was acting as captain in place of H. W. Bainbridge, who had injured a wrist. Warwickshire were having a bad time of it in the field and a section of the crowd was jeering at their loose fielding. In the late afternoon Glover ran to field a ball which he picked up near the boundary and was then seen to throw it into the crowd, an action which not surprisingly provoked a roar of disapprobation. The ball had hit, though not violently, an old gentleman and an elderly lady, to whom Glover later apologized, explaining that his action had been caused by a very insulting remark made to him by a member of the crowd.

Glover also apologized in a letter to the committee, in which he wrote:

> Some people are hasty and I fear I am one of them – but I consider I was deeply insulted and perhaps I am a little ready to rise at insult . . . I hope the counties will try and prevent so far as possible coarse insults being hurled at players who are doing their best if not successfully . . . I may say I don't fancy myself as captain and would rather be relieved of the duties. It would honestly be better for the county, though I hope an amateur will always hold that post if Mr Bainbridge's wrist fails again.

Glover's explanation was accepted and the Warwickshire committee expressed regret that he had been insulted. What would have happened, one wonders, had Glover been a professional?

Lord Harris, Oxford University, Kent and England, president of the MCC, test selector, moved with some reluctance into the twentieth century. Not only was his word law, but his very existence was a source of terror to many professionals. Once, in the 1920s, when R. J. O. Meyer, the famous Somerset amateur, offered a drink to a professional at the game's headquarters; the latter replied 'Not while his Lordship is in London, thank you, sir.'

On to the 1930s, and a celebratory dinner at the Mansion House, given in honour of Jack Hobbs, who was always a bit of a wag. Jack Hobbs opened his speech as guest of honour with an amiable story at the expense of the Lord Mayor. This was to the effect that the Lord Mayor bet a friend five shillings that the latter didn't know the Lord's Prayer. The friend accepted the challenge and began 'The Lord is my shepherd, I shall not want,' whereupon, said Jack Hobbs, the Lord Mayor put his hand in his pocket, and, producing two half crowns, said 'I've lost.' The remainder of the speech followed on pleasant and conventional lines. When it was his turn to speak, the Lord Mayor immediately expressed the view that 'Mr Hobbs should in future confine himself to cricket stories.' The reason for this highly dismissive rejoinder to Jack Hobbs's joke was that Hobbs, not being a gentleman, was therefore not entitled to make jokes at the expense of his betters. Had the story been told by

H. D. G. Leveson Gower, R. C. Robertson Glasgow or John Daniell, as might easily have been the case, the Lord Mayor would have displayed intense amusement: Leveson Gower, 'Crusoe' and John Daniell, as gentlemen, were entitled to make such jests: Jack Hobbs, a professional cricketer, was not. However, it was not long before Jack became Sir John.

Lord Hawke was a bird of the same feather as Lord Harris: 'Pray God no professional is ever permitted to captain England,' he said in a speech at Lord's. Walter Hammond, who had been a professional for nearly twenty years, changed his status to amateur in the winter of 1937–38, and in 1938 captained England against Australia in the Ashes series. Lord Hawke died later in the same year. Fourteen years afterwards the unthinkable happened: the professional Len Hutton was invited to captain England against India. He had had little experience of captaincy, but had learnt a lot in the days when amateurs and pros had separate dressing-rooms, and had listened carefully when Sutcliffe, Leyland, Verity and Bowes discussed and analysed the mistakes of Brian Sellers, the Yorkshire captain. As Allen Synge points out, this couldn't have happened in an integrated dressing-room.*

On the field of play a professional could be rather more than a private soldier. The senior professional would be akin to an RSM in a regiment. There is a story, probably apocryphal, that illustrates the point. Yorkshire had scored about 400 for 6, and Major Lupton, sensing the possibility of scoring a nice 25, bat in hand, gloved and bepadded, walked out of the amateurs' dressing-room, to find himself touched on the arm by a young professional: 'It's all right, sir, Mr Rhodes has declared.'

After the Second World War there weren't so many amateurs about, and a number of professionals rejoining their counties had been commissioned during the war, so the dividing line became blurred. But the old ideas died hard. Perhaps two final examples of the Alexander syndrome may be permitted.

David Sheppard, later Bishop of Liverpool, in his early days for

* Allen Synge, *Sins of Omission*.

181

Sussex had played a glorious innings against Gloucestershire. As batsman and fielders were walking in to the pavilion Tom Graveney called out to Sheppard 'Well played, David!' The then Gloucestershire captain severely reprimanded Graveney for his familiarity, and assured Sheppard that such an occurrence would never happen again. Sheppard was not impressed.

The second anecdote concerns a match at Lord's in the 1950s, when Middlesex were the home team. Shortly after play had started an agitated voice announced over the intercom that the name of F. J. Titmus on the scoreboard should of course read Titmus, F. J.

Whatever they were printing on the scoreboards, the writing, so far as amateurs in first-class cricket were concerned, was on the wall, and in 1962 they were abolished with a stroke of the pen: first-class cricketers were no longer amateurs or professionals – they were contracted players. This presumably means that all first-class cricketers are professionals, but professionals without – dare one say it – any social stigma attached. If you are a county cricketer today there are no problems about initials – they all go before the surname; there are no provocative amateurs' gates, and as for cod and salmon, cod is nowadays if anything the more expensive of the two.

With the contracted player edict a kind of social revolution had taken place. Cricketers who had been to Oxford or Cambridge or to the top-bracket public schools now spoke with the flattest of flat accents, rather in the manner that university-educated other ranks spoke in the barrack rooms of the Second World War. David Gower's mother once observed that her son had become bilingual. Other parents would have noticed the same thing. However, one wonders whether the Flat Accent Society is any more relevant than the Flat Earth Society. In the past there were doubtless illiterate cricketers about, both old-fashioned amateurs and old-fashioned pros. Today you have to be above average as mathematician, psychologist, diplomat, dietician and map reader; a high standard of driving and maintenance is desirable and often essential – oh yes, and if you can bowl a leg-cutter or do the reverse sweep they won't think any the worse of you for that.

CHAPTER 15

Where Do We Go from Here?

Secretaries' meetings at Lord's to arrange the fixture lists were solemn and formal affairs. Every December my father would sally forth by the London Midland and Scottish Railway to Euston, and thence by cab – they later called them taxis – to Lord's. He would be wearing his silk hat bought at the turn of the century – 'Extra Quality. Hope Brothers Ltd. Ludgate Hill. London.' Ninety years on, it is still in pristine condition.

'Fixture making,' wrote my father, in *Wisden's* 1936 ('Trials of a County Secretary'), '... was an unhurried business, commencing in September, through the agency of the penny post [it had rocketed up to three-halfpence by 1936] and culminating in a visit to Lord's in December where the silk hat and frock coat were *de rigueur*.' Here the final touches were put to the fixture lists at meetings in the committee room that were a cross between a parochial vestry meeting and a stock exchange free for all. It was no good asking for such and such a date with Yorkshire as arrangements for this particular time had been made months if not years ahead. Every county had their traditional fixtures; it was arranging the last two or three that taxed the ingenuity and patience. The meeting over, the secretaries relaxed in the evening at a show. Leslie Henson and Fred Emney, Oscar Ashe in *Chu Chin Chow*, George Robey, 'the Prime Minister of Mirth', these were the stars that entertained them over the years. My father once had lunch with George Robey, who talked about income tax and the coming war.

Silk hats and frock coats are no longer required dress for county secretaries, nor do they meet to draw up their fixture lists; this all comes from the Test and County Cricket Board and is done by computer. The relevant fixture lists are sent to county secretaries, who are asked to comment. They will previously have been asked if they want to play Oxford and Cambridge universities; the TCCB will have acted in the knowledge that counties like to play their local rivals at bank holidays, and that counties with test match grounds don't want a home match immediately before a test or a one-day international.

The county secretary of today has overall responsibility for the ground itself and for the preparation of pitches. An accountant deals with the club's finances; the marketing manager looks after the ever-increasing commercial interests of the club, especially the advertisements – many of them round the boundary fence – and the hospitality tents. Obviously he will be in constant touch with the club's captain and coach; there will be a variety of committees to cope with. His major link is with the TCCB. In his own right he may well be chairman of a club cricket association within the county, and associated with youth organizations; he will also be closely connected with the National Cricket Association, which represents club and school cricket. If a secretary has a test match on his hands, during the preceding months he will be very busy indeed. Although county clubs are very active, they are no longer autonomous, but are subordinate to the TCCB.

Cricket, like the world around us, is always changing. Thackeray, told that *Punch* was not what it was, replied that it never had been. The same could be said of cricket, which is much older than *Punch*, but has survived. Cricket, like the house of Lords, like the monarchy, like Europe, like mankind, stumbles from crisis to crisis, and keeps going.

When the laws were first printed in 1744, there were two stumps, 12 inches apart, and one bail at each end. Stumps were pitched opposite each other at a distance of 22 yards – the length of a farmer's chain. In 1776 a third stump was added to prevent the ball passing through the wicket. In 1787 the Marylebone Cricket Club was formed, and was virtually to control English cricket for nearly two hundred years. The over, of four balls for generations, was changed in 1889 to five, and to six in 1900; in this year the follow on, compulsory for over a hundred years, became optional. The first recorded lbw was in 1795; in 1935 the law was altered, so that a batsman could be out to a ball pitching on the off.

It has been noted in Chapter 11 that laws have been changed when players have used loopholes to their own advantage. Maurice Turnbull and Peter Cranmer were ahead of their time in 1939, when, as opposing captains of Glamorgan and Warwickshire, they had their fingers rapped by MCC for making early and adventurous declarations.

In the first few years after the Second World War crowds flocked to cricket grounds; Compton and Edrich waved their magic wands. In 1950 two million people paid to see county cricket. Then came the joys of television; more people could afford motor cars; the domestic habits of the English were changing. Attendances had dropped by 1966 to half a million. County membership dropped; subscriptions were increased; county membership fell further. First-class cricket in England was now only solvent because of test match profits and the efforts of supporters clubs with football pools.

What could be done?

Amateur status had been abolished in 1962: first-class cricketers became contracted players. There was no longer room for the brilliant part-timer who could bat with freedom because his livelihood did not depend upon it.

A more positive venture was the appointment of a committee under David Clark, chairman and former captain of Kent, to look into the state of the first-class game, and to make recommendations as to its future. David Clark had on his committee four ex-test players: Gubby Allen, Ted Dexter, Doug Insole, who was also chairman of selectors, and Fred Titmus; three players who had won distinction as county captains: Brian Sellers, Stuart Surridge and Ossie Wheatley; Charles Bray, former Essex player and veteran cricket reporter; and four highly-thought-of administrators in Edmund King, Geoffrey Howard, Ken Turner and Mike Turner. They produced a report in 1967 which Graeme Wright has described as 'a brave, intelligent attempt to come to terms with the problems confronting cricket at the time'.* The main proposals were that there should be two separate championships of sixteen three-day and sixteen one-day matches, as well as the Gillette Cup. The proposals were only supported by four counties, and a promising opportunity was lost.

The solution to MCC's main issue of keeping first-class cricket in the black was adventitiously supplied by Harold Wilson's Labour government, which had set up a Sports Council for the purpose of helping sport through the relevant governing bodies. 'To a national game on more than nodding terms with penury,' wrote Graeme Wright, 'the prospect of Government assistance must have seemed to MCC as appealing as donkey-drop bowling to a schoolboy batsman. In place of runs in the book it saw money in the bank – and for the best intentions, such as coaching and youth cricket.'

However, a Labour government was not likely to provide funds for a private club, so, in 1968, MCC set up the Cricket Council in order to gain Sports Council money, and also established the Test and County Cricket Board. In so doing, MCC had sold its birthright.

One-day cricket, in the shape of the Gillette Cup, had already started and was proving a success. The end of the 1968 season saw the beginning of the D'Oliveira affair – a black comedy indeed. Basil D'Oliveira, a South African-born coloured player, had come to England to further a career denied him in his own country. After scoring 158 for England against Australia in the Oval test, in a series of illogical actions that would have had Lewis Carroll playing and missing, he was finally chosen for the impending tour of South Africa. The South African government refused to allow him into the country, the tour was called off, and for over two decades South Africa was excluded from international cricket. The Afrikaans word 'apartheid' became the most important word in the English language. British politicians seized upon it with enormous gusto,

* Graeme Wright resigned after six years as editor of *Wisden* in 1992. Of his book *Betrayal: The Struggle for Cricket's Soul* (M. F. & G. Witherby), Derek Hodgson wrote in the *Independent* that it would become one of the most influential books on cricket this century.

almost invariably pronouncing it incorrectly, rhyming it with 'white' instead of with 'hate'.

Sunday cricket started in 1969 with the formation of the John Player League – each county playing sixteen games of 40-over matches with restricted run ups. When the Benson & Hedges competition was inaugurated in 1972 – 55-over zonal competitions terminating in a knockout competition for quarter finalists – there were now four competitions, three of which were different forms of one-day cricket: the Gillette Cup and the Benson and Hedges Cup involved showpiece finals at Lord's. These innovations brought in the crowds who supported their teams vociferously. With sponsorship came trim-suited marketing officials and their salesmanship jargon. Intensive marketing of the game followed, putting a great deal of money into the coffers of cricket.

And then, in 1975, came Kerry Packer, an Australian tycoon possessing his own television channel. He wanted the exclusive television rights for Australian cricket, which the Australian Cricket Board was not prepared to grant, having already made other arrangements. The immediate result of this refusal was that Kerry Packer, without a syllable being whispered to the English or Australian authorities, set about buying up a number of international cricketers to contest a 'World Series' during the course of the Australian season.

Jack Bailey, an Oxford blue who had played for Essex, was secretary of MCC at this time. For him 'cricket was one of the constant bastions of the ideals we hoped the world would one day live by'.* He felt that the game had been sold down the river. In England, the matter went to the law courts, where Mr Justice Slade declared in favour of Kerry Packer and his mercenaries. Efforts by the TCCB and the ICC to prevent Packer's men from playing test cricket, it was declared, would be unreasonable restraints of trade: the TCCB and the ICC found themselves landed with the costs.

Throughout the 1980s it appeared to many that cricket was being changed from a game into a business. 'All that they need is a good

* Jack Bailey, *Conflicts in Cricket* (Kingswood Press).

captain and a good secretary,' Tom Dollery had observed, but secretaries were being transmuted into chief executives; marketing managers, promotional clichés at the ready, invaded grounds where once had flourished the bearded doctor, Lord Hawke and Lord Harris, Ranji and Fry. *Domine salvum fax regem.* Coaches became directors of coaching; administrative staffs increased. From administrative offices came information packs extolling the virtues of prestigious executive suites, hospitality tents, chalet villages.

During the last decade there has been a plethora of one-day internationals, often tense, sometimes exciting, generally shallow; they have been driving out the test match, as John Woodcock wrote, 'as inexorably as the grey squirrel drives out the red'. Sponsorship has done more to make its presence felt, and it seems only fair that the sponsors should be able to advertise themselves. The problem is to what extent it is reasonable for them to do so. Graeme Wright put the cat among the pigeons in his valedictory editorial notes for the 1992 issue of *Wisden*, when he observed of the Cornhill logos on the outfield during test matches, 'It is a symbol of the level to which English cricket has to go to earn a crust.'

Sponsorship in the Arts and leisure activities is now widespread. Quite recently an RSC production of *Hamlet* was sponsored by a detergent company – though it could have been argued that their slogan 'Persil washes whiter' would have gone down better in *Macbeth*. But this is no new trend: Shakespeare was sponsored four hundred years ago by the Earl of Southampton.

My own feelings about Cornhill logos are ambivalent. The advertisements round the boundary bring money into the game, so although not inspiring they are presumably necessary. Sponsors' advertisements on players' clothing are now part of the cricket scene: it is to be hoped that Alan Ayckbourn's quip about cricketers wearing advertisements for contraceptives on their boots can be taken as satire rather than prophecy. As for the use of sightscreens for advertising in alternate overs, surely even the atmosphere of a test match should at times be relaxed and leisurely, at least for the spectators. White-painted sightscreens form a restful and attractive part of the cricket scene, and should not be turned into horrific robots clamouring for attention.

Cricket in the 1980s was off to a controversial start when the TCCB decided that the wicket should be fully covered: the object was to control seamers bowling on green pitches, but in fact the decision made life more difficult for spinners.

In the autumn of 1984, Charles Palmer – he had scored 85 for Worcestershire against the Australians in 1948 – was commissioned by the TCCB to chair a committee of inquiry into the standards of play of English test and county cricket. A former president of MCC and chairman of TCCB, Charles Palmer presented the report and recommendations of the inquiry in 1986. Eight of the nine members of this committee had played test cricket; their sane and sensible proposals for the restructuring of the fixtures programme were supported by only four counties. Two Sunday League divisions of eight teams each, for instance, were proposed with the laudable intention of cutting down cricketers' travel; action was taken, however, about the recommendation for greater use of the Lilleshall Recreation Centre, and the TCCB was caused to think seriously about the minutiae of overseas tours and their management.

Meanwhile, as David Clark wrote in 1993, the fully covered wickets of the 1980s

> reduced the need for good technique for batsmen and the skill to use different conditions for bowlers.
>
> The worst decision made was to form a pitches committee which had the right to ban a county pitch if reported as unsuitable by umpire or captain. The fear of a bad report has made the groundsman play safe. It is easy to prepare a flat slow wicket which will last three or four days (and which will produce dull and slow cricket: how often do we hear it's difficult to score runs because the ball doesn't come on to the bat). It is much more difficult to prepare a hard fast pitch without the risk of it breaking up and taking too much spin too early in the game.*

---

* Letter to the author, 5 November 1993.

In August 1991 the TCCB set up a working party to study the format of the competitions composing the first-class fixture list. Mike Murray, the chairman, had a very different team from those who composed the Clark and Palmer inquiries, who were mainly experienced test and county cricketers. Mike Murray had only one test player, C. J. Tavaré, in his team. The rest, although they had only a dozen first-class games between them, were all keen cricketers. Chosen for their financial, administrative and marketing expertise, they included Sir Ian MacLaurin, who was chairman of Tescos, a director of NatWest bank and of Guinness brewery. Their report was completed in April 1992, their all-or-nothing recommendations adopted in 1993. The Murray committee had six hot potatoes on their plates – test matches, one-day internationals and the four competitions chiefly affecting the first-class counties.

With regard to international matches in England, test matches were to be promoted in preference to one-day matches, and six test match slots with three one-day international matches (four in a double tour year) were to be the norm. Test matches are still immensely popular in England. 'Only in Britain perhaps would cricket crowds carry on watching the national game in vast numbers when they were losing heavily,' wrote Christopher Martin-Jenkins in the *Daily Telegraph* (25 November 1993). 'Last season's crowds for the Cornhill test series, won 4-1 by Australia, totalled 420,000, an increase of 22 per cent on the numbers who watched the six tests of the previous home series against Australia in 1989.'

Of the six potatoes on the working party's plate, the question of three- or four-day cricket was the hardest nut to crack. The three-day game had been the backbone of first-class cricket in England since the 1860s. A mixture of three- and four-day matches, recommended in the Palmer Report, had been adopted experimentally in 1988, the counties playing six four-day and sixteen three-day matches. Now, it was felt that it should be one or the other.

In the Murray Report's 32-page pamphlet 'A Blueprint for the First Class Game', the pros and cons of the two time-spans were outlined with apparent impartiality, coming down in favour of an all-play-all county championship of sixteen (now seventeen) four-day matches. What had destroyed the three-day game's chances of survival was that games tended to be played on dead pitches; deals appeared to be negotiated at earlier stages of matches with the result that many games were played as 'limited over' affairs on the third day. An analysis of results in 1991 revealed that over 20 per cent of the three-day match programme appeared to involve 'joke' bowling, whilst no incidence of 'joke' bowling appeared in the four-day matches played in the same year.

The Murray Report's comments on negotiated deals leading to what were virtually yet more 'limited overs' matches is highly relevant, but perhaps the pitches were more to blame than the captains. This is what the report achieved:

Britannic Assurance County Championship A seventeen-match four-day championship. Among the points in favour of four-day matches it was felt that bowlers' techniques would be improved with a greater emphasis on wicket taking: spinners would be assisted by matches of longer duration. Batsmen would have a longer period in which to build an innings: longer matches would be helpful to younger middle order batsmen.

NatWest Bank Trophy Retained in its present format. There were no problems here; a fact triumphantly proved in the 1993 final, when Warwickshire beat Sussex in what must have been one of the greatest games of cricket ever played since Nyren's time.

Sunday League In an effort to lift the League from the doldrums, 50-over matches with unlimited run ups were prescribed, each county playing seventeen matches. Coloured clothing to be worn, players to be identified by names on their shirts; white balls and black sightscreens. Axa Equity and Law agreed to sponsor the League.

Benson & Hedges Cup Zonal rounds abolished and the competition to be played on a straight knockout format.

All this was accepted by the TCCB, and the three-day game, which had flourished since W. G. Grace was a boy, became a thing of the past. Matthew Engel, the new editor of *Wisden*, wrote in the Editor's Notes for the 1993 issue:

Cricket at the highest level has acquired a unique and insoluble problem by turning itself into two separate sports. There is traditional cricket, a game that has stood the test of time as a satisfying pastime and way of life but which finds it increasingly hard to get an audience. And there is one-day cricket, which is popular among spectators but is regarded with varying degrees of contempt by the professionals forced to play it, administrators forced to stage it and journalists forced to report it.

Matthew Engel further asserted that since 1989 the counties have been forced to play three-day games on four- or five-day pitches: any miscalculation in favour of result wickets has been punished by the threat of a 25-point deduction for an unsuitable pitch.

Alan Lee, cricket correspondent of *The Times*, and E. W. Swanton, for thirty years cricket correspondent of the *Daily Telegraph*, were asked to put the case for and against the Murray Report in *Wisden* (1993). Alan Lee, in favour, wrote that the four-day game, which was overdue, would improve quality at the expense of quantity, would get rid of 'joke' bowling, and give a better chance to spinners. Under the new system the better team would usually win. 'Mike Murray,' he concluded, 'has served the game admirably, his working party consulted extensively throughout the game, and there is so much logic behind their conclusions that they are fully worthy of their three-year trial.'

E. W. Swanton, on the other hand, wrote that three-day cricket on uncovered pitches produced outstanding county teams and greater England teams for a century or more, until full pitch covering was introduced in 1981. In England, maintained Swanton, experience on difficult surfaces refines techniques and often makes for intriguing, sometimes heroic cricket. Early batsmen will play fewer innings, there will be correspondingly fewer chances for young cricketers. First-class cricket must entertain with positive, attacking play. A four-day diet will put initiative and variety at a discount. It is arguable that an all-play-all system will be a fairer way of determining the champions. The more matches played the less will be the influence of the weather. Swanton conceded that under the new system there would be less travelling for players.

The 1993 season passed: time and the hour runs through the roughest day. The Cornhill test series against Australia, as already stated, went well enough for England financially, if not in the middle.

What have been the first fruits of the Murray experiment in domestic cricket? The first complete season of four-day county cricket has at worst proved a qualified success.

> There is always a weighing of pros and cons [wrote Mike Brearley], the best thing about 4-day is the possibility of such dramatic fightbacks (as Glamorgan *v* Middlesex 1993). At its best 4-day can have greater range and less artificiality. At worst it can be very boring. I think I come down in favour of 4-day on balance since the sides that can bowl teams out will win more often.*

> I am not pessimistic about the future of county cricket [wrote Charles Palmer]. It has for a century or more been periodically decried in critical cricket writings but still flourishes. However, even more effort must be made to ensure that it is not irretrievably overtaken in public affection by ever increasing competitive leisure activities ... Bearing in mind how cricket has evolved during the last two decades or so I think the 4-day 'experiment' (with suitable wickets!) correct at least for the trial period of the Murray Report.†

E. W. Swanton feels that county cricket has not been the game that it was since the covering of wickets in 1981. All things considered, the first full year of the four-day programme has been satisfactory. A lot will depend on the captains.‡

David Clark is not over-optimistic:

> It is probably right to give it [four-day cricket] a try but I have

---

* Letter to the author, 4 November 1993.
† Letter to the author, 8 November 1993.
‡ Conversation with the author, 18 November 1993.

doubts as to whether it will raise the standard of batting and bowling which is the reason for trying 4 days. Over time it may encourage the use of slow bowlers and reduce the amount of dreary medium pacers. I fear one of the results of 4-day cricket will be to reduce the art of captaincy which is lacking in county cricket today – there is likely to be an attitude of *laissez faire* to wait and see what happens rather than to have a strategy to win.*

How wise were the TCCB and their Murray men not to interfere with the format of the NatWest competition. It was not only the exhilarating batting by both Sussex and Warwickshire in the final of 1993 but the spirit in which the game was played that was so splendid. In the photograph, taken immediately after the match, of the Warwickshire players celebrating in their dressing-room, it was interesting to see the cheery figure of Norman Gifford, ex-Warwickshire captain and now manager of Sussex, who had looked in to congratulate his former team.

The new Sunday competition, the Axa Equity and Law League – other Refuge have I none – 50 overs with unrestricted run ups, was not a success and, in 1994, went back to a 40-over game. The coloured clothing, unpopular with county members, but highly popular with county treasurers – 70,000 T-shirts were bought by ecstatic youngsters so that they could flaunt the colours of their heroes – will remain at least until 1995. The white ball, though it swings less, has been given the thumbs up.

The Benson & Hedges Cup, shorn of its zonal rounds in order to cause less disruption to the early championship matches, became a watered-down version of the NatWest competition. However, it will return to zonal rounds in 1995, which will give members more for their money and will not displease the county treasurers.

Leaving the domestic scene for a while, it is encouraging to see how the game is flourishing overseas. Sir Colin Cowdrey, who was

---

* Letter to the author, 5 November 1993.

president of the MCC in 1986–87, recently completed a four-year stint as chairman of the International Cricket Council (founded in 1909 as the Imperial Cricket Conference).

Cowdrey saw cricket as a game of national aspirations. Gone were the days of the paternalism of the Marylebone Cricket Club; so, as Graeme Wright pointed out, with all roads no longer leading to Lord's, he went on the road as a roving ambassador and 'became the Henry Kissinger of cricket, embarking on a diplomatic shuttle to solve the game's problems'. The ICC, no longer a toothless tiger, now had considerable bite. Apart from Cowdrey's personality and dedication to the game, and apart from national interests, the airways had brought the nations closer. England to Australia was a day's trip, not a voyage of several weeks; England to South Africa a twelve-hour flight, not a seventeen-day journey on a Union Castle liner. Not the least of Cowdrey's achievements was to get the countries of test match status to agree to the institution of match referees with the authority to administer reprimands, fines and suspensions on the spot: sledging and intimidation of umpires – Pakistan and Australia are the worst offenders according to E. W. Swanton – while not things of the past, are certainly being contained. The fight for law and order in cricket, at any rate, is being won. E. W. Swanton reminds us of Law 42: 'The captains are responsible at all times for ensuring that play is conducted within the spirit of the game as well as within the laws.' Swanton gives Graham Gooch full marks in this respect.

Cricket world-wide is prospering. Not only is the game holding its own in countries where it had already established itself, but it has also taken root in other areas of the globe. The International Cricket Council now boasts nine full members, twenty-one associate members and eleven affiliate members.

Full members of the ICC are the two foundation members, Australia and UK, plus India, New Zealand, Pakistan, South Africa, Sri Lanka, West Indies and Zimbabwe; associate members, not of test match status, but where cricket is fully established and organized: Argentina, Bangladesh, Bermuda, Canada, Denmark, East and Central Africa, Fiji, Gibraltar, Hong Kong, Ireland, Israel,

Kenya, Malaysia, Namibia, Netherlands, Papua New Guinea, Scotland, Singapore, United Arab Emirates, USA and West Africa; affiliate members, where cricket is played in accordance with the Laws of Cricket; Austria, Bahamas, Belgium, Brunei, France, Germany, Italy, Japan, Nepal, Spain and Switzerland. The affiliate members were elected between 1984 and 1992.

The twenty-one associate member countries competed for the ICC Trophy in Kenya (March 1994), Matches of 50 overs were played in groups. In the semi-finals the United Arab Emirates beat Holland, and Kenya beat Bermuda. UAE beat Kenya in the final. Holland will be competing in the NatWest competition in 1995.

In the USA, where once the Philadelphians flourished, cricket has been enjoying a boom, owing to the influx of immigrants from cricket-playing countries. There are now over seven hundred cricket clubs in America, and exhibition matches played in New York by international stars including Imran Khan, Malcolm Marshall, Richie Richardson and Sachin Tendulkar have been well attended, but it is the leagues across the country that form the source of major strength; and there are now nearly 20,000 active cricketers in the States.

With regard to the affiliate countries, the Belgian League had twelve teams competing in 1994, and the national side will be playing a three-day test match with France. Touring clubs visiting Belgium have increased both the standard of play and the bar takings. The languages used in Belgian cricket vary from English through Urdu to Flemish. French teams in France use their own terms, including *guichet* for wicket, *lancer la balle* to bowl – but 'Howzat' remains the same! Germany played at Lord's in 1992, the game thrives in Hamburg, Bremen and Hanover. Four German universities now have cricket as an official part of their sports programme. In Italy, thanks to Martin Crowe's enthusiastic coaching, performance is starting to equal potential: 1993 was a very happy year. Italy's application to be upgraded from affiliate to associate membership has been deferred for a year, as have those of Nepal and Thailand.

Cricket has been played in Portugal since 1861, and the game has recently been stimulated by visits from Gooch, Stewart, Gower and Lamb. Spain? – there are cricket centres in Madrid, Barcelona, Malaga and Menorca.

In the inaugural European National Cup, France won an exciting final against Germany. France had already defeated Belgium, Italy and Austria; Germany had accounted for Greece, Sweden and Switzerland. Chasing 156, after early disasters France won in the penultimate over of a 50-over match.

Wisden's man in Russia reports that an English touring team, the Explorers, played in July 1993 what was probably the first cricket match in Moscow since the Bolshevik Revolution. Their opponents, the MCC, were the newly formed Moscow Cricket Club. Owing to a misunderstanding, the pitch was originally laid out for a croquet match. Less successful were the Magyar Cricket Club in Hungary. Encouraged by the British Embassy's donation of kit, they arranged to play three matches. Unfortunately the kit was stolen.

The West Indies are helping the game to develop in the USA: Clyde Walcott hopes to get cricket on TV in America. India and Pakistan help with the lesser Asian countries; Australia and New Zealand with Pacific and neighbouring island states.

A last look at county cricket. 'We must grin and bear the four-day diet and coloured clothing,' wrote E. W. Swanton, 'reserving the right of opposition until they have had a fair trial.' He would like to see a programme with a majority of three-day matches, on uncovered pitches, a minority of four-day ones, and the elimination of one of the one-day competitions. Charles Palmer feels that 'the Benson and Hedges competition from a "cricket" point of view could and should go but there are always howls from treasurers if income is diminished.'*

What other bees have we in our helmets?

Ball tampering Jack Bannister dealt effectively with the subject in *Wisden* (1993), when he gave high praise to Wasim Akram and Waqar Younis for some of the most spectacular bowling in the 1992

---

* Letter to the author, 8 November 1993.

test series that spectators in England have ever seen. He suggests a widening of Law 42.5 to what it was before 1980 when bowlers were allowed to rub the ball in the ground. The balance of the game has shifted so much in favour of the batsman, he points out, that treatment of the ball should be permitted as long as umpires can control it. 'If sweat or spit are permissible to shine or dampen one side of the ball,' he asks, 'why should the other side not be rubbed in the ground?' Peebles, thou shouldst be living at this hour! One England cricketer suggested to the present writer that the excitement over ball tampering in 1992 was generated by 'Paki-bashing' in sections of the press, 'the attitude being, if we can't have a go at Princess Di, what about a really good cricket scandal?'*

Bad behaviour Sledging, intimidation of umpires, flagrant dissent, has chiefly taken place in test matches. As stated earlier, this is being dealt with by match referees of high calibre. What bad behaviour there is in county matches usually can be (and is) dealt with by the authorities of the club concerned. In general the courtesies of the game far outnumber the unpleasant incidents. Charles Palmer feels that

> Although it seems in this day and age increasingly difficult to achieve, I believe very great effort should be made by *everyone* to ensure the revival of the decencies, dignities and courtesies which have characterized the first-class game on and off the field for me since I first played in 1938.†

Over-aggressive marketing and commercialism A controversial subject, depending on where you draw the line. Open days in April to encourage those interested to take up membership are reasonable by any standard. In the winter of 1902 my father canvassed six thousand houses to boost membership and got six hundred new members. Was this aggressive marketing? I don't think so. Hospitality tents are used – and abused – at test matches. Advertising?

---

* During the England *v* South Africa test at Lord's in July 1994, Mike Atherton was fined by match referee Peter Burge for being economical with the truth about the dirt in his trouser pocket.
† Letter to the author, 8 November 1993.

'It is right that our test cricketers should be properly paid but wrong that they should become human advertising boards,' wrote Christopher Martin-Jenkins. 'But we are getting logos on cars, playing areas, sightscreens and cricketers themselves.' What about blue jokes in speeches at club functions? Lieutenant General Sir Oliver Leese, Warwickshire president 1959–75, president of MCC 1965–66, would have none of it, though his language in private could be ultramarine.

Sponsorship This has lately tended to be regarded with caution, if not with hostility; but there are sponsors and sponsors. Godparents are sponsors. The Nobel Prize for Peace is sponsored, cancer campaigns are sponsored. The first England tourist team to Australia was sponsored by Spiers and Pond in 1861–62.

A. C. (Alan) Smith, TCCB's chief executive, gave his views on sponsorship and other matters connected with professional cricket in a conversation with me in November 1993. Smith, an Oxford cricket blue – his academic studies did not prevent his winning a soccer blue as well – captained a Warwickshire side that won the Gillette Cup in 1968 and the county championship four years later. Secretary of Warwickshire from 1976 to 1986 he became on 1 October 1986 the first chief executive of the TCCB. Both as wicketkeeper – he played six times for England – and administrator he has had the reputation for a safe pair of hands. Once, captaining Warwickshire against Essex, one of his bowlers leaving the field injured, he took off his wicketkeeping pads, proceeded to bowl with his windmill action and almost immediately did the hat trick, thereby earning himself the sobriquet of A. C. Everything. His versatility will stand him in good stead.

A traditionalist, as anyone who saw him on the cricket field will know, Alan Smith in his present position has to be a realist as well:

'In an ideal cricket world we wouldn't need sponsors, but we've got to infuse money into cricket, so we do need sponsors, and we're very fortunate in the sponsors that we have. We've got to keep the county championship going. And there's youth cricket. In the 1950s, if you didn't play cricket in the summer, there was tennis, and that was the lot. Nowadays, there are plenty of competitive interests to attract the teenager, so we want to make cricket attractive to the young.'*

Uncovered wickets? 'Well, we've got to think of our hospitality chalets. The guests wouldn't find it much fun looking out into the sunshine when there's no cricket because it had rained all the previous day. Besides' – he gestured gleefully towards the Hollies stand – 'just look at the good use we've made of the Brumbrella!'

What about the spinners? 'Some of the greatest spinners in the world have never played on an uncovered pitch. Look at Warne and May – marvellous bowlers. Mushtaq. Qadir.'

Test matches? 'You've seen the gate receipts, haven't you? Test matches bring the crowds in; 22 per cent up on four years ago. As far as three- or four-day matches, coloured clothing, B&H – we'll have to see about all that. We'll know in a year or two, but – this is for sure – the fundamental traditions and ethics of the game must remain unaltered.'

The International Cricket Council became truly administrative in 1993 when David Richards was appointed chief executive and he and his staff moved into new offices in the Clock Tower at Lord's. David Richards, tough and likeable, a more than useful grade cricketer, had previously been chief executive of the Australian Cricket Board. Clyde Walcott, the famous West Indies batsman of the 1950s, became Sir Colin Cowdrey's successor as chairman. David Richards and the genial, shrewd Clyde Walcott should make an excellent combination.

How long will Lord's remain the administrative base of cricket? In the course of time the ICC will presumably have a chief executive from Pakistan, in which case wouldn't Lahore be on the cards? Or Johannesburg? South Africa would have a geographical advantage.

---

* The competitive interests of today include volleyball, baseball, basketball and swimming. Youth interest in golf has increased because of TV coverage. Visiting theme parks, working part time, holidays – all those provide diversions unavailable to generations past.

I enquired of the ICC what the position was. Were they at Lord's permanently or temporarily?

'We've signed a contract for five years,' I was told. 'After that we don't know.'

'So would you say that it's permanent for the time being?'

'Yes, you could put it like that.'

So where are we going? Sir Colin Cowdrey:

> I could not be more bullish about the future of the game of cricket. More and more people than ever before are coming to love the game, more people watching, reading about, viewing on television, listening on radio and playing than ever before. Forty-one countries are playing vigorously. We have just celebrated the third European Cup. Fourteen countries [in Europe alone] are now playing cricket in various degrees of seriousness and skill, from Holland, the best, to Switzerland and Italy. Twenty-one countries compete for the ICC trophy for the associate countries in Kenya in March.
>
> Cricket is beginning to flourish in the United States, and in ten years they will be producing a test team, I think.
>
> Now we have to preserve the old fashioned standards of fair play – the top players known for their integrity.*

There were three historic factors in the cricket world of 1994. First, the explosion of Brian Lara on the scene. The signs and omens were there in 1993 when the West Indies played Australia at Sydney. Scoring at will, with phenomenal backlift and a dazzling array of strokes, he made 277 before being run out. Then came 1994, when he broke all individual test records as a batsman, leaving Sir Donald, Sir Leonard and Sir Garfield behind with his scintillating 375. He then took his pads off and flew to England, where he was given his Warwickshire cap before he had played an innings. Noticing further records to break, he proceeded to do so in the first week of June, when he made 501 not out against Durham. When the match ended, the Warwickshire score a modest 810 for 4,

* Letter to the author, 17 February 1994.

the Durham side formed a guard of honour for Lara. He scored century after century – six in seven innings: his pyrotechnics were inspirational. In the city of a thousand trades, during the heady days of June, in choirs and places where they sing; in schoolrooms, surgeries and supermarkets; in bus queues and beer gardens; in tower blocks and bargain basements; on construction sites and in traffic jams, everyone was asking everyone else – 'Have you seen Lara?'

What was there special about him? The rapier-like elegance of Gower and the rapacity of Macartney. The nearer he got to his centuries the faster he accelerated. A high percentage of his runs were in boundaries. Vic Marks said on *Test Match Special* that Lara has a radar system in his brain that shows him the field placing.

Above all, a marvellous co-ordination of brain, eyes, feet and wrists frames the fearful symmetry of Lara, Lara burning bright.

The second historic factor was Warwickshire's marvellous season, which I have attempted to describe in the Preface to the book, and with which Lara was also connected.

Third was the first visit for twenty-nine years of the South Africans to England. It was seventy years ago that I saw my first test match at Edgbaston and watched Gilligan and Tate bowl the South Africans out for 30. The top scorer was Mr Extras, who made 11. Don't blame G. E. C. Wood, the wicketkeeper; there were 7 leg-byes and 3 no-balls. Herbie Taylor, 7, made the highest score from the bat. Tom Webster, the famous sports cartoonist, complained that none of the batsmen stayed in long enough for him to sketch them. South Africa did better in the second innings, when they made 390.

The arrival of the eleventh South Africans at Lord's was emotive, poignant and joyous. And it is not for us to talk about the return of the prodigal or any of that caper. South African cricket teams, when apartheid was at its strongest, walked off the field to demonstrate their opposition to racist rule. And how superbly Kepler Wessels and his team played – amazing that a South African team could so dominate the game after nearly three decades of isolation. The protea was in joyous bloom, and no wonder Mike Procter waved the new national flag from his team's balcony at Lord's.

The ultimate message comes from Dr Ali Bacher, rejoicing in the African sunrise: 'We see cricket as a positive force for the social unity of our country.'

'Cricket can appeal to the athlete and the aesthete alike; it can veer between lyric poetry, differential calculus and Thai kick-boxing. No game has such range, such depth. But it is all extremely fragile.' Thus wrote Matthew Engel in his editor's notes for *Wisden*, 1993.

There is no game like it. Whatever the political climate, India and Pakistan have no problems in meeting on the cricket field. It now seems a question of when, rather than if, Australia will become a republic. 'What of it?' asks the Prince of Wales. 'It won't affect the Ashes,' says Prime Minister Keating.

What of England's recent conflicts with the wizards of Oz? The first two tests, among other matches, were lost comprehensively: Warne destroyed us. We are playing too much cricket, wrote the pundits of the English press – there are too many one-day competitions; our bowlers aim to contain batsmen, not to get them out. 1995 dawned: the effervescent Darren Gough ensured that, for England, the dawn was a rosy-fingered one. A half-century followed by 6 for 49 won the plaudits of Larwood and Lindwall: Sydney rose to him, as it rose to Larwood sixty years ago. Taylor and Slater put Australia within striking distance, then Fraser, with four wickets in thirteen balls, very nearly pulled it off for England. This was a wonderful test match, and English morale had been restored. As for Adelaide and Perth, much depends on the toss, and on whether Atherton's men retain self belief. The rest of the decade? Of one thing we can be certain, and that is that cricket is an uncertain game.

CHAPTER 16

Last Over

A few months ago I was asked to take an active part in a cricket match. It was at Edgbaston, on the other side of the Pershore Road to the County Ground. I was walking from Hollies Croft on the footpath between Foster Way and Wyatt Close, where there was a strip of mown grass, fifty yards long and thirty yards wide, between the footpath and the trimly kept front gardens.

Half a dozen silver birch trees grew on this strip of grass; one of them stood back eighteen or so yards from the footpath – the perfect place for the kind of cricket that was played long before cricket got its name. And here indeed cricket was being played. The ball was a tennis ball, the birch tree I have referred to was the wicket. The batsman was a cheerful, jacketed English boy of about twelve, his bat a cheap one; the bowler was a Pakistani boy, also about twelve; his jacket, by the footpath, was the bowling crease. The other players, five or six yards from the wicket, alert at silly mid-on and silly mid-off, were girls about ten or eleven years old, clad in gloriously coloured Asian dress: they were possibly sisters of the bowler. As I approached, the bowler, evidently sensing a fifth player, amiably handed me the tennis ball, and said 'Will you bowl?' I said that I would do my best, took a four-foot run up, and bowled a hideous long hop on the leg. The batsman swiped and missed. I apologized for being out of practice and the young Pakistani smiled sympathetically.

Wide though the delivery was, it was great to be taken back to the days when I played similar games on a carless road half a mile away in distance and seventy years away in time. The game which these four youngsters were enjoying meant as much to them as does a test match to the likes of David Gower, Alan Border and Brian Lara – and in heaven's name why not?

For Graeme Wright, cricket 'is a game anyone can play: men and women, boys and girls, plus the family dog as a fielder when appropriate. I enjoy watching a bowler bowl and a batsman bat, whether on a forecourt at a lunch-break, at a public park or at a county ground. The pleasure increases with the standard of play, but at heart the game remains the same.'

For myself, as at eight, so at eighty, I experience the same thrill in hastening to the county ground, bracing myself to face the message of the Delphic oracle on the scoreboard; then to absorb the delights, the excitement, and the glorious uncertainty ahead.